SITDOWNS WITH GANGSTERS

Shaun Attwood is the author of multiple true crime books, activist, speaker, YouTuber and host of the *Shaun Attwood True Crime Podcast* and *Attwood Unleashed*. He is also a former trafficker who ran an international ecstasy ring in Arizona, before he was arrested in May 2002 and served six years in prison.

SITDOWNS WITH GANGSTERS

Up close and personal with the world's
most dangerous men

Shaun Attwood

SEVEN DIALS

First published in Great Britain in 2023 by Seven Dials,
an imprint of The Orion Publishing Group Ltd
Carmelite House, 50 Victoria Embankment
London EC4Y 0DZ

An Hachette UK Company

1 3 5 7 9 10 8 6 4 2

A CIP catalogue record for this book is
available from the British Library.

ISBN (Trade Paperback) 978 1 3996 0712 4
ISBN (eBook) 978 1 3996 0714 8
ISBN (Audio) 978 1 3996 0715 5

Typeset by Born Group
Printed and bound in Great Britain by Clays Ltd, Elcograf S.p.A.

www.orionbooks.co.uk

For Jen and Ziggy

Contents

Foreword by
Christopher Berry-Dee

Straight off the starting blocks, *Sitdowns with Gangsters* should come with a mental health warning because no way should anyone on Planet Earth read this book if they have a delicate disposition, are of the pesky door-knocking Mormon faith, a card-carrying Lib Dem, a blue-rinse member of some local knitting circle or someone who gets very scared watching Robin Hood movies. And here's the thing: was I well pleased when my long-time buddy Shaun Attwood asked me to write the foreword to this book – oh, yes, I was, period, with bells and whistles on!

My own knowledge of gangsters is, may I say, limited *in extremis*, but being an investigative criminologist whose specific field of interest is sadosexual serial homicide, I testify that I truly know unpredictable, terrifying evil when I am one-on-one interviewing these unshackled 'Beasts from Hell'. One can touch these killers, study them up close and personal, smell their hatred – it radiates towards you as hot as a kitchen stove; they do the eyeballing stuff, their twisted mindsets probing your own mind like tentacles, feeling and exploring you – yes, YOU – to see if you react, grimace or even throw up as they relate with blank expressions their godawful crimes.

Shaun's gangsters featured throughout his book are a mixed band of brothers in crime. Therefore, one should not condone or even try to mitigate their previous abhorrent criminal behaviour for in many cases, many innocent law-abiding folk suffered in some way at their hands. That said, I recall former Lord Chief Justice of England, Lord Geoffrey Lane (1918–2005), telling me following the failed appeal of British emerging serial killer, John David Guise Cannan: 'The prospect of a young man spending the rest of his life in prison is appalling. It seems a pity that there seems to be no humane alternative. *Oddly enough, prison sometimes serves to allow that fact to be proved for prison can bring out the better in them* [my italics].'

As you might well agree, it would have been less than tactless for me to have countered with: 'Sir, that motherfucker [Cannan] should have been hanged and his goolies fed to the Tower of London's ravens . . . that seems humane enough to me, m'lud.' Of course I didn't. Why? Because he was footing the bill, that's why! However, where I do concur is that many hardened criminals are not redeemable. They enter what our American cousins call 'The Belly of the Beast', the 'Big Houses', 'The Pens' . . . places I have visited many times in my career, such as: WSP Walla Walla (Kenneth Bianchi); MCF Stillwater ('Harvey the Hammer' Carignan); death rows such as Osborn CF CT (Michael Bruce Ross aka 'The Roadside Strangler'), executed 13 May 2005; Ellis Unit Texas (Henry Lee Lucas and Kenneth Allen McDuff), SQ . . . San Quentin State Prison (Douglas Daniel Clark aka 'The Sunset Slayer'), but these scum stone-cold psychopaths were and are beyond *any* redemption as opposed to the gangsters who sat down with Shaun Attwood and who certainly changed their spots so it goes without saying that we have to admire them for this: they found redemption. Oh my gosh, I'm beginning to sound like some evangelical Bible-thumping preacher man, but I ain't!

Shaun Attwood is certainly no stranger to crime for he previously served 'Big Time' himself, yet used that period in his life to turn over a new leaf. Now, without any question of a doubt, he's one of the most popular, at once controversial podcasters in the world today because he's fearless. If he wants to piss over the 'establishment', he does it big time – and why? He's been there and got many T-shirts too, that's why. So, making no one's bones about it, this book, with its cast of once highly dangerous gangsters, now well and truly reformed villains, will right-hand punch you smack in the face, knock you flat on your back with you getting back up, smiling and begging for more. Hey, bros, there are not many authors who can pull that off these days, so well done you, Shaun.

As is my own literary preference, I always add a few lighter touches to my books, so in preparing for this foreword, I conducted some in-depth research into the aforementioned Robin Hood and I've come to the conclusion that he was a 'fairy'. I've based my professional opinion on the fact that some of the real gangsters in this book wore black balaclavas, were often 'tooled up' and drove fast getaway cars, possibly with more bullet holes in the bodywork than Bonnie and Clyde's Ford V8. Not the alleged Robin of Loxley – no way, Jose! He wore Lincoln green ballerina tights, kinky over-the-knee leather boots, a leather bra and a damned stupid hat with some peacock feathers stuck in it. His numero uno oppo was an obese friar – with whom he was probably having an affair – so no *real* gangster was he.

Anyway, happy days and no nightmares, please.

Christopher
www.christopherberrydee.com

Introduction

Having interviewed over 500 people in the true-crime genre, I have hand-picked some of the most mind-blowing stories for the new *Sitdowns* series of books. My journey towards becoming a trusted listener to prisoners began during my incarceration in Arizona from May 2002 to December 2007 for Ecstasy trafficking. For twenty-six months, I spent the pre-trial section in the infamous Maricopa County jail run by Sheriff Joe Arpaio, aka America's Toughest Sheriff.

Arpaio was the architect of a house of horrors with the highest death rate out of all jails in America.* Guards murdered inmates, including the mentally ill or blind, such as Scott Norberg and Brian Crenshaw, who were arrested for assaulting a police officer and shoplifting respectively. Dead rats were served in the food and cockroaches swarmed our bodies at night. It was fertile ground for extreme stories, which I documented to my family by way of a blog, *Jon's Jail Journal*, the notes for which were smuggled out of maximum-security visitation by my aunt in 2004.

After excerpts were featured in the *Guardian* and the BBC, the blog attracted international media attention and I became a human rights activist. Championing the rights of prisoners,

---

* Prisoners Hang Themselves in Arizona Sheriff Joe Arpaio's Jails at an Alarming Rate | Phoenix New Times

I earned their trust and I began to post their stories online. Hearing about their harrowing upbringings humanised them and made me feel doubly guilty for committing my crimes as I had come from a loving family, had a business studies degree and a successful career in the stock market. Through my writing, I earned the protection of 'Two Tonys', a Mafia multiple homicide murderer serving 144 years, who chose me to write his autobiography, *The Mafia Philosopher*.

In 2007, I was released, deported back to the UK and my YouTube channel and schools talks started. Initially, I focused on publishing my Arizona stories as a trilogy of books: *Party Time*, *Hard Time* and *Prison Time*. Then I moved the stories into video format. Telling my stories was therapeutic. Numerous kind people with big platforms helped get my stories out there and it was my karmic duty to reciprocate as my YouTube subscribers grew into the hundreds of thousands.

In 2018, my *True Crime* podcast was launched with my first guest, Jamie Morgan Kane, who had served thirty-four years in a California prison for a murder he hadn't committed. While incarcerated, he learned he had been born on the Isle of Man, sold as a baby to an American family and subsequently he was deported to the UK, where he knew hardly anyone. The views on his videos reached over 10 million and he ended up with his autobiography getting published in 2019 and we took him to the Isle of Man, where he spoke to school kids and prisoners. The podcast had transformed his life. By 2022, we were inundated with people requesting to come on the podcast. We branched out to interview ex-cops, ex-prison guards, crime victims and journalists and authors at the forefront of true crime.

From the hundreds of interviews, some stories and scenes are unforgettable – and this book includes ten of them: from Chet Sandhu describing a prisoner getting stabbed to death in front of his own parents in Spanish supermax to David McMillan's gripping account of his escape from Thai death row; from Mafia hit man John Alite surviving armed gang warfare in a Brazilian prison to Colombo crime family capo Michael Franzese describing how he navigated being summoned to a meeting by his Mafia boss that could have brought about his death; from Shane Taylor walking away from a fight with a knife handle unaware that he had left a nine-inch kitchen blade in his opponent's skull to Wild Man arriving at Buckeye prison, Arizona, and knocking out the head of the Aryan Brotherhood prison gang in his building. Against incredible odds, these men survived and thrived in life-or-death situations and most importantly, they have emerged to warn young people worldwide about the dangers of the gangster lifestyle. Unless you are completely desensitised, I suspect that some of these stories will remain in your mind long after they have been read.

1

Shane Taylor

Knife Maniac's Redemption

Classified by the Home Office as one of the top six most dangerous inmates in Britain

'You've killed him.'

When Shane hears these words, he knows something bad has happened, but he doesn't know what. Everyone is staring at him with wide terrified eyes, their faces white as ghosts.

'What's up with you?' he asks, his head still swimming in a kind of fog.

'You stabbed him in the head,' one of his friends stammers out.

Bits start coming back to him – the confrontation in the town centre with local hardman, Jon Burns, weapons being drawn, then . . .

'No,' he says, his mind focusing on the weapon still clutched in his grip, 'I've got the knife in my hand.'

Then he looks down and sees it. His hand is still clasping the handle of the nine-inch kitchen knife, but the blade has snapped off. Suddenly it all comes back to him – Burnsy coming at him with a mell hammer, a kind of demolition hammer with a solid chunk of steel for a head, Shane pulling out the nine-inch knife from the set strapped to his waist,

Burnsy swinging the hammer and crashing it down on his head, then Shane plunging the knife down into the top of Burnsy's skull, the blade emerging just above his eyebrow as the handle snaps away in Shane's hand, a fountain of blood spurting upwards, then . . . nothing.

The fight had started quickly. It was the year 2000, Shane was in Hartlepool town centre with a couple of other teenage friends trying to sell some stolen videos on the street. Jon Burns was the local tough nut with a reputation as a psychopath, who had only just got out of prison. This was his territory, so he decided to take one of the videos without paying. Shane's friend, Pete, pulled out a baseball bat to defend the goods from Burnsy and his gang, but Burnsy's reputation as a psycho was warranted.

'That's when he pulled out a hammer,' Shane told me when I interviewed him in July 2020. 'We call them mash hammers, the square ones what you do paving slabs with, and you can get the big long-handled ones or the short-handled ones. He had the short-handled one and he ran up to me and smashed me across the top of my head.'

But Shane also had a growing reputation as a psychopath, one he had gained by targeting hardmen like Burnsy and putting them down, sometimes with his fists, sometimes with a knife. He'd already had his eyes on Burnsy, so when the attack came, he was ready with his own weapon in hand. Incredibly the hammer blow, which should have caved in Shane's skull, just bounced off his head. Now it was his turn.

'I used to walk about with kitchen knives,' Shane told me. 'I used to have the full set all round my waist and I basically pulled out the biggest one, which was the nine-inch kitchen blade, and I stabbed him straight through the top of his head, here, and it came out of his eyebrow, there.'

Blood was fountaining out of Burnsy's head, but, incredibly, he too refused to go down. He stumbled around, waving his hammer wildly with the kitchen blade sticking through the front of his head like some kind of gruesome Halloween accessory. His friends managed to sit him down and fully earning his reputation as a hardman, Burnsy pulled the blade from his own skull, lacerating his hands in the process. Everyone was screaming for the police and Shane and his friends took the cue to escape, sprinting off down a back alley. Shane ran about a mile before his friends stopped him to check he was OK. Whether it was the effect of the hammer blow or the red mist that descended when Shane got into fights, it was only then that he realised everything that had happened. He thought he had killed a man. Incredibly, however, Burnsy would survive, leaving Shane up for an attempted murder charge. It wouldn't be his last.

Shane Taylor's reputation as a hardman and a psychopath was sealed that night in Hartlepool town centre, but the first indications that he would be a tough nut came much earlier. You couldn't get any earlier, in fact.

Shane's mother, Maz Almond, came from a poor estate in the heart of Middlesbrough in the North East of England. When Maz fell pregnant with Shane, her husband, Stephen, became suddenly jealous and paranoid that the baby wasn't his. He started beating Maz, demanding to know who the baby's father was. She says that on the worst occasion, Stephen beat her with a metal dog lead and punched her repeatedly in the stomach, trying to kill the unborn Shane. He then nailed her into a cupboard and left her there with a broken gas pipe spewing out deadly carbon monoxide. Shane was too young to know all the details, but he was born into a refuge for battered women.

Somehow Maz and the baby survived. Maz was moved to secure housing in Peterlee, a nearby town, but on a trip back to Middlesbrough, Stephen found her. Maz was heavily pregnant and not long away from giving birth when her husband beat her almost to death for a second time, purposefully trying to kill the baby. She was rushed to hospital with everyone expecting the worst. The police were already preparing charges for the murder of the unborn baby but those charges would have to be dropped. Just a few days later, on 12 December 1980, Maz's son was born, alive and kicking and screaming his anger at the world.

It was clearly going to take a lot to put down Shane Taylor.

It wasn't just toughness that came early to Shane: he was an early adopter of pretty much any antisocial and criminal activity you could mention. As a four-year-old, he smoked his first cigarette. He was running away from school pretty much as soon as he started. His first robbery came at age six – the money from a payphone at the local leisure centre. The young Shane managed to open the phone casing with the help of his best friend, Dean, and a screwdriver. The two youngsters tried to spend the mountain of change on the centre's vending machines but unfortunately were caught by the assistant manager, who promptly banned them. But Shane had the taste for stealing. On the way home he and Dean popped into the Methodist church and stole the collection box. It was the first day in a long life of crime.

As Shane grew, so too did the sophistication of his crimes. A little later the same year, he was part of his first organised robbery at the local Asda supermarket in Peterlee. His gang of six- and-seven-year-old mates caused a distraction in the sweet aisle while others were waiting by the fire exit. As soon as the security guards were distracted the group opened the fire doors and piled hundreds of pounds worth of audio and video equipment into six waiting trolleys, which they rolled off at speed on to the nearby housing estate. He even burgled his own school, stealing a load of bikes. Maz reported him to the police herself over this crime, but it didn't teach him the lesson she intended. Instead, Shane discovered that, being so young, he couldn't be arrested: he was free, essentially, to do whatever he wanted.

Peterlee, where Shane grew up, is a poor ex-mining town on the north-east coast of Britain. High unemployment and few opportunities meant crime was a natural outlet for boys like Shane and his gang of friends, who were soon making a full-time living out of robbing and causing general mayhem. He stole his first car at age nine and had to stand up while driving because he was too short to sit down and reach the pedals. He joyrode the car around a local football pitch before setting it alight and abandoning it. Meanwhile, burgling houses was the main source of income. As he was still so small, Shane was often used as the one who could squeeze through a small window and let the others in. He received a cut of the proceeds – a small sum but plenty big enough for a nine-year-old. Shane estimates he was robbing four or five houses a day, making between £200 and £3,000. His personal best was ten houses in one day and a £6,000 haul from a single robbery. As a nine-year-old thief, he was earning more money than his mother.

When he left a stolen car wedged upside down between two houses, the authorities had had enough. Shane was still below the age of criminal responsibility of ten, so he was taken into a children's home. He promptly escaped. After almost a year of various children's homes and foster care, during which his crime spree continued pretty much unabated, Shane turned ten. The authorities tried to take a light approach, but with lists of offences sometimes numbering up to twenty at a time, they soon decided to put him in Elemore Hall, a special school in County Durham for children with social, emotional and mental health difficulties.

It didn't work. While at the school Shane caused havoc, at one point escaping to a nearby village, where he robbed a pizza shop of £5,000. He and an older boy then stole a car and tried to drive it to Middlesbrough down the wrong side of a dual carriageway with police cars and helicopters giving chase. He proved too much for the school when he and a bunch of other twelve-year-olds beat an older seventeen-year-old boy almost to death, leaving him lying face down in a lake near the school. Fortunately, the teachers intervened quickly enough to save the boy, but for Shane it was the last chance. He was sent to Aycliffe Secure Centre, the same place where the teenage murderers of two-year-old James Bulger were sent.

Shane was in and out of Aycliffe from his first visit until he was sixteen and could no longer be sent there. He fought the system all the way, refusing to be taught even how to read or write. Believe it or not, despite his reputation for crime, he had been bullied and picked on by older kids for much of his life, mostly because of his ginger hair and short, skinny stature. Shane told me, 'When I was in school, I remember lads saying, "Howay, you can come and play with us," and I would get really excited and run towards them to play with them. They'd turn round and punch me in the face, pop my nose open.'

Now that he was sixteen, he decided enough was enough and started fighting back. He still wasn't big and lacked the psychopathic edge that he would soon acquire, but he was willing, or 'game' in the local slang. He didn't seem to feel pain like normal people and he wouldn't stay down. The turning point came during one of his spells inside a Young Offender Institution. He had his watch 'taxed' – basically taken off him – by another inmate, who thought he could bully the smaller kid. 'I fought for it,' Shane told me. 'I was young in jail. I was soft. I couldn't fight. I was a bit game and a bit mad, but I couldn't fight really. And then I just got fed up afterwards and I was thinking about it, stewing, and then I thought, *Do you know what? This is it from now on, no one's going to mug me off ever again.*'

He won his first real fight not long after and had people queueing up to shake his hand afterwards. After that he went, in his words, 'on a rampage'. He began to bulk up towards his eventual size – nineteen stone of pure ripped muscle. He started carrying around an entire set of kitchen knives strapped to his waist without any sheaths – 'If I'd fallen over, I'd have been in trouble' – and started taking on all comers despite size or reputation – in fact, the bigger the better. On one occasion a friend pointed out someone on the other side of the road who had a reputation as a hardman and a psycho. Shane crossed the road and doubled back, deliberately bumping into the guy as an excuse to start a fight, which he promptly and violently won.

One such hardman who would later play a prominent role in Shane's life was local street fighter, Paul Venis. Paul was due for greatness as a fighter. He would go on to become the world K-1 heavyweight kickboxing champion, winning every one of his fights by knockout in the early rounds. When he first encountered Shane, he knew he could beat him in a fight, but there was something about the young psycho from Peterlee that gave even Venis second thoughts about taking him on. I interviewed Paul for my podcast in 2021 and he revealed the story:

I took a lad to fight Shane's cousin and Shane was there, and my mate was getting beat: he wasn't winning the fight, and I was tempted to join in. I was getting closer and closer, and he just whipped this fucking knife out. And I've had knives pulled out on me before, I've had all that stuff. But this guy, I just looked in his eyes, and I remember like yesterday, he went to me, 'If you join in, I will fucking kill you stone dead.' As he looked at me, he went, 'Listen, I'll stick this right in your neck. I'll kill you.' And I looked at him and I thought, *He definitely will.*

Backing away was perhaps one of the smartest decisions Paul Venis made in his life. By his own admission, Shane was already mentally ill. He was constantly watching gangster films with the most violent murder scenes repeated on never-ending loops. He was still living with Maz but even his own mother feared him and tried to stay away from the house whenever Shane was at home. He fantasised constantly about killing people, especially police and other authority figures, imagining the sound and the feeling of the knife going in. On one night of rare reflection, he realised that something had broken inside of him: that he no longer felt any fear, nor did he feel love for anyone, not even his mum. He also realised he didn't care. He enjoyed the sense of freedom it gave him; he could do literally anything. He had become a psychopath.

True to form, Shane was soon back inside a Young Offender Institution for eight months on remand pending an investigation. It turned out the charges were trumped up after a kid whom Shane's mate had beaten up accused them of kidnapping him and stealing his trainers. When the police investigation concluded the allegations were mostly false, Shane and his friends were released. But the lad who had put him in jail, Smithy, was now on Shane's hit list. He rode a motorbike past Smithy's house to find that Smithy's family were in the garden, having a barbecue. He quickly dismounted and jumped the fence into the garden, brandishing his largest knife and screaming, 'I'm going to kill you all.'

The women and children fled inside while the men escaped as best they could, leaping fences and hedges and scattering across neighbouring gardens. Shane merely laughed, calmly remounted his motorbike and drove off. He says he had no intention of stabbing anyone, but the incident added to his already growing reputation as a psychopath. It was a reputation that was about to be tested to its limits because just a few weeks later Shane had his encounter in Hartlepool with the other local psycho, Burnsy, which left the other hardman with a knife in his head and Shane charged with attempted murder.

Incredibly, Shane was released on bail due to lack of evidence, primarily because no one who had witnessed the horrific scene wanted to speak to the police. He was now a certified knife maniac on the loose and it wasn't too long before his next big run-in with a hardman.

Shane had been dabbling in selling Ecstasy, but no one wanted the batch of one hundred pills he was trying to sell because rumour had got around that they contained heroin. Giving up for the night, he had popped into The Royal Arms, the local pub on his estate, to give the pills to a friend for free. Inside the pub was a local hardcase called Booth, who was connected to Smithy's family – the same family Shane had recently threatened with a knife at their barbecue. The story of Shane running into the garden with a drawn knife had grown in the telling and now included a false detail in which Shane had been about to stab the eighty-year-old grandma before other members of the family had managed to pull him off. Booth now decided he was going to have a word with Shane and question him about his actions. On seeing the upcoming psycho, Booth pointed a finger at him and said threateningly, 'I want a word with you.'

Shane followed him to his seat where two of Booth's other hard mates sized him up while Booth gave him a dressing-down about threatening an old lady. Meanwhile, the pub had gone noticeably quiet as the surrounding punters prepared for trouble. 'Everyone knew I was getting a bit mad now,' Shane told me. 'Everyone was getting a bit fearful and I just had this sense of if I don't do anything to him here, if I walk away it looks like he's pull me up and I've backed down and I'll lose face. So, I made a choice there and then – I'm going to make an example of him so all these people in here know what's going to happen when you pull me up. And then, as I'm thinking this in my head, he said the wrong thing. He came forward a bit on the table and he just said, "You want to mess about with the big boys, do you?" And something snapped in my head and I went into his face, put my head into his face and I said, "No, no, no, no, you've just messed about. Come outside, I'm going to kill you."'

Shane walked out of the pub, drew his nine-inch blade and waited, but no one followed. After a while he went back to open the door and found a group of men trying to stop Booth from going outside. The men were warning him that Shane meant what he said, but the local hardman wouldn't back down. Eventually a voice in the crowd told everyone to let him through and Booth stepped out of the pub to confront Shane.

He should have listened to his friends. As soon as Booth walked out of the door, Shane plunged the nine-inch knife into his chest just below the shoulder.

Shane had often fantasised about how it would feel and sound to stab someone. Now he found out. As he pulled it out, the knife made a sucking sound as it drew the trapped air from the stricken man's lungs. Booth hit the ground immediately and Shane was struck by how quickly the blood came out: 'It was basically just like a tap was on. It went from having nothing to literally like a tap,' he said.

But he didn't have long to wonder over the amount of blood. Booth's two friends had followed him out and were now coming at Shane, both with knives in their hands. Shane was now in a knife fight in which the odds weren't in his favour. The two men approached him from either side, one trying to distract him while the other got through his defences. Shane was barely managing to hold them off, swinging wildly to push one back then turning to meet a lunge from the other. But he had one advantage over his two assailants – he was deadly calm. As the game of cat and mouse continued, he was analysing the repetitive way the two men were lunging and falling back. He soon realised that if he feinted to strike at one, he could quickly turn and catch the second man in the temple as he lunged in. He quickly put the plan into action and it nearly worked: he came within inches of stabbing the man in the side of his head.

It was enough for Booth's mates. They began to back off then, and with a quick glance at each other, turned tail and ran.

The police were on the scene quickly and it was Shane's turn to run. With two attempted murders now under his belt, Shane was the most wanted man in the North East. It would be the beginning of three months of lying low and trying to evade capture. However, Shane didn't quite think of it like that. When I asked him what his main strategy was, he gave the chilling answer, 'To get revenge on everybody before I got caught.'

One impromptu chance for revenge came when Shane was trying to steal a motorbike from outside a house. A man appeared at an upstairs window and shouted, 'Oi, what are you doing?' Nonchalantly, Shane replied, 'Pinching your bike. What does it look like?' But as he looked up at the man, recognition suddenly dawned: it was the guy who had punched his mum while he had been in prison. 'As soon as I saw him, I thought, *I'm on the run anyway, just sack it and get lifed off,*' Shane told me. He took off his helmet and watched with satisfaction as recognition and fear spread across the man's face. Shane ran to the front door and began kicking it in.

By the time he had gained entry the man had managed to barricade himself and his family into the bedroom with furniture while he called the police. Eventually Shane gave up and was forced to leave, an outcome which, today, he is very thankful for: 'I had no morals,' he told me. 'I would have killed anyone in that room if I'd got in it, like I just didn't care. And scumbag or not, who cares? And if I can't get you, I'll come after your mother. if I'd come after your mother, I'll come after your wife. I'll try and get your wife. I'll get you back. This is how I used to think.'

Shane was hiding out at a friend's flat and only going out wearing his motorcycle helmet to avoid detection. Meanwhile, lots of his friends and family were being raided by the police under suspicion of harbouring him. One thing that made escape easier was Shane's classification as armed and dangerous. This meant the police couldn't approach him without back-up, so on the few occasions when officers did spot him, he had time to get away while they called for help. His main problem was money, which he had to continue to earn through crime. One of the easiest ways was 'taxing' his mates, a polite term for stealing. He even stole a wad of rolled-up cash from one of his best friends, Pete, pulling a knife and threatening him and the rest of the group not to tell the police.

Shane was clearly out of control and recognises he was mentally ill at the time. His obsession with knives had become so consuming that he was scaring the people closest to him. He recounted one story of how he killed the atmosphere at a party one night: 'Everyone was wrecked and there were some handy lads in there as well, and they're all wrecked, and I pulled my knife out because it was new. It was one of them Rambo ones. And I'm turning it and I'm looking at it and I forgot where I was . . . and I'm turning the knife round and then I just got this urge – go on and kill someone. So, I looked up and I went, *Howay, let's go and kill someone.* And everyone was all on the end of the settee, all crumpled up to one side, and they were just staring with fear. And one of them just slowly came over and said, "Howay, mate, you're killing the buzz," and took the knife out of my hand.'

Shane thought of himself as some kind of gangster, like the characters in the violent films he continually watched, but he admits now that in reality he was no such thing. He was a lone wolf with a well-earned reputation as a psychopath that made everyone – including the real gangsters – want to stay away from him.

According to him there are three kinds of reputation among local hardmen: 'There's the big boys who are in it for the money and it's all about becoming Mafia kind of figures and Ecstasy kingpins or whatever. And then you've got, under that level, two kinds of reputation – you've got people who can fight and they're hard and there's not many people who can beat them. And then you've got the psychopathic people. And people just think, *avoid him, don't cross him because he'll turn up at your front door and blow your head off* . . . and that was me, like I daydreamed it, literally daydreamed about killing people daily.'

Despite his reputation, Shane's luck was soon to run out. His behaviour towards his friends lost him his place in the flat and he was now sleeping in a car. It was here that he was found by a police officer doing a routine tour of the streets. Seeing someone sleeping in the car through the misted-up windows and checking the registration number with the police station, the officer found it was registered to a friend of Shane's. He called for back-up and more officers and an armed response team soon arrived. In the middle of the night Shane was woken by fists pounding on the car windows and shouts for him to come out with his hands up. He tried to drive away, but found he was wedged in by the cars in front and behind. With no other means of escape, he surrendered.

Shane was charged with two separate accounts of attempted murder in 2001, but both were dropped to lesser charges of Section 18 – going with specific intent to cause harm and threatening to kill – because intent to kill was too difficult to prove. In the end, he got away with just four years and nine months in prison, the first part of which was to be served in North Allerton Youth Offender Institution in North Yorkshire as he was still just twenty. Almost immediately, Shane was involved in several prison fights. In one, he beat a man up in his cell before, naively, turning to leave. As soon as his back was turned, the man hit him over the head with something hard and renewed his attack on the now-staggering Shane. Even so, Shane slowly regained his wits and ended up pulverising the man a second time before the guards arrived. As a later revenge, Shane cornered the man in his cell during free association time and battered him black and blue for a third time.

A riot in a London Youth Offender Institution saw a group of young London criminals rehoused in Northallerton. Shane found himself at the centre of a turf war with the newcomers, who were seeking to establish dominance. His continual fighting meant he was constantly in and out of 'seg' – the segregation unit where problematic inmates were isolated for twenty-three hours a day. The constant isolation did not help Shane's already fragile mental health. His increasing paranoia meant he brutalised most inmates unfortunate enough to have to share a cell with him. When his best friend from home, Dean, landed in the same cell, he almost attacked him, too. Shane thought that Dean was putting glass in his food and Dean had to offer to eat Shane's food instead of his own, then stay up late into the night convincing Shane of their friendship, to avoid any harm.

When he turned twenty-one, Shane was transferred to Holme House, an adult prison in County Durham. One of his first acts was to kidnap another prisoner with a 'shiv', or homemade blade, and hold him hostage in his cell. He had only one demand – a takeaway pizza.

His subsequent visit to the seg saw Shane's mental health deteriorate further. On one visit to his cell, a prison officer saw him staring concernedly at the floor. When the guard asked what the matter was, Shane replied that there were white spiders crawling all over his cell. He began to think his food was being poisoned and one of the few guards he trusted had to eat a spoonful of his meal before Shane would touch it. Meanwhile, Shane was spending most of the twenty-three hours a day of isolation dreaming about violence, replaying scenes of stabbing, murder and revenge over and over in his head. He spent six months in solitary confinement following the kidnapping of the other inmate. By the time he was let out, he was like a ticking time bomb. It wasn't long before he went off.

The catalyst was the gym. Like many prisoners Shane loved working out and, indeed, lived for it. After several years of doing weights, he had transformed himself from a skinny teenager to nineteen stone of solid muscle. As a hardman, his physique was an essential part of his reputation and to allow it to slip would be a critical sign of weakness. In a tough atmosphere like prison, the gym is vitally important.

When gym time came, the prison officer on duty would shout, 'Gym!' and anyone who wanted to go would press their buzzer and be released from their cell. So, when Shane pressed his buzzer one day but wasn't released, he was understandably angry. When he got the chance to speak to the staff, Eric Lawson, the guard told him he must have forgotten and promised it wouldn't happen again. But when next time came around and Shane buzzed for the gym, the guard didn't even appear on his landing. He buzzed until the guard appeared and asked him again why he hadn't let him out. Shane says the officer didn't have an answer except to sarcastically pretend to be thinking. That was enough for Shane: he started making his plans for revenge.

He waited for a few days until the same prison officer was on duty on the wing. It was free association time when all the inmates could leave their cells and mingle. Lawson was standing by the pool table but, little known to him, Shane had concocted a plan with his friend, Rob, to create a distraction. When Rob suddenly picked up a handful of pool balls and began throwing them around the wing, the other officers tried to rush through the gate to subdue him. However, Shane had recruited three other inmates, who were standing by the inside of the gate. As it erupted, the three big men closed the gate to the wing and leaned their weight against it, preventing the guards from entering.

Officer Lawson, although he didn't realise it, was on his own. He moved to restrain Rob, who was still throwing pool balls around. At the same time Shane made his move. He had picked up a giant glass coffee jar and wrapped it in his towel as if he were innocently walking to the shower. As Officer Lawson moved to restrain Rob, Shane brought the coffee jar down hard on the edge of the pool table, smashing it into several sharp, jagged points. Shane now attacked Lawson with the broken jar: 'I was going for his face and his neck,' he told me, 'but he put his hands up, and so I'm catching his hands because he's blocking. And then I'm trying to get him in his stomach. And then he's putting his legs up, and I've tracked him into the corner, and I just started going wild. I'm trying to stab him wherever I could stab him, and I was cutting my own hands as well.'

Another guard made it through the gate and tried to help his colleague. Although he can't remember this part, Shane started stabbing him too, catching him repeatedly in the thigh as the man desperately held his leg up to protect his groin.

Eventually the other guards managed to force their way through the gate and piled in on Shane, bringing him to the ground and raining batons, fists and kicks down on his body and head. If this was revenge, it was instantaneous and brutal. Shane remembered: 'One of the officers picked up my arm, put it on the glass, because the bottom of the glass was still stuck up. There was like one bit sticking up on that round circle at the bottom. But he's got my arm there. He put it on, and he went boom with his knees. He just bounced on my hand. I didn't make a noise, didn't even feel it to be truthful, and that was because my adrenaline was going and I was so full of pride at the time. I didn't want them to hear a noise come out of me.'

The revenge may have been satisfying for the guards in the short term, but it didn't help in the long run. Because of the large gash in Shane's arm the judge at his trial brought the sentence down from eight years to just four. Somehow Shane had got off lightly again.

But he wouldn't get off lightly in prison. He was transferred to HMP Durham, where the prison guards were determined to make him pay for the attack on two of their own. The officers constantly provoked Shane, flicking his light on as they wandered past at night so he couldn't get any sleep, and trying to rouse his violence so they could wade in with truncheons and fists. They took everything from his cell so that he couldn't make a shiv, then teased him about his lack of weapons. It was another mistake.

The light in Shane's cell was encased in a heavy metal housing kept in place by special screws that were supposedly tamper-proof. However, Shane discovered that by burning the end of a plastic toothbrush until it melted, he could mould the end of the handle so that it fitted tightly against the screws, enabling him to remove them.

When the guards next came to take him for exercise, they were confronted with a man wielding a heavy piece of metal at them. Shane swept the weapon in a slow arc across the terrified guards and said in a calm voice, 'Listen very carefully, if I was going to do something I'd have already caved your skull in. This is just a warning – stop winding me up.'

The guards quickly learned not to underestimate Shane again. Within an hour an armoured van had arrived to take him to Frankland maximum-security prison, where the next set of guards took no chances with Shane. He was locked up in seg from day one until he was moved on to another maximum-security prison, Whitemoor. As if to match the ratcheting up of his security status to Category A – reserved only for the most dangerous prisoners – Shane began to up the ante in his war against the guards. He would regularly fight them in his cell even though six or seven guards dressed in full riot gear were required at any one time. After stripping to just his boxer shorts and shoes, he would challenge them until they came at him. Obviously, he came off worst in most of these encounters but he lived for the small wins. One such victory was the boost to his reputation when he managed to last a full fifteen or twenty minutes battling against seven armoured guards inside his small cell.

Taking Shane for exercise was like a small military operation of its own. He described the procedure to me: 'I had to lie on the floor and put my hands up before they'd open the door. Then they slammed the door open. They'd put the shield to the door, then they'd come put the shield on your back, tell you to put your hands on your head. The man on that side would search your body then they'd run back to the door. And then they'd say, "Right, stand up slowly." If you went fast at any time they'd be on you, so you'd slowly get up and then slowly walk back until your back touched the shield, then they stepped back, then you stepped to the shield, then they'd push you up against the wall and you'd be searched again. And that was just to go in the exercise yard. Then you'd have to walk backwards as slow as you possibly could until you got to the exercise yard. Then they'd get in the exercise yard, tell you to lie down. You'd lie down on the floor, put your hands on your head and then they'd shout, "Go, go, go, go!" and everyone would just run. But I would try and get up and run at them as soon as the shield was off me.'

On one occasion Shane got the better of the guards by covering his cell floor and walls with shampoo and butter and coating his own body in baby oil. The guards couldn't keep their footing on the slimy floor and couldn't grab Shane, who was as slippery as a fish. It must have looked like the Keystone Cops as bodies went sliding everywhere. Shane took advantage of the chaos to inflict some damage of his own on his tormentors, even at one point wrestling a riot shield off one of them and using it to hit the man and his colleagues.

Soon somebody was going to get seriously hurt or even killed. It nearly happened one day during a routine search protocol that involved a small army of fully armoured prison officers with riot shields. The guards entered Shane's cell and pushed him against the wall with their shields while two of them held his arms in place. He was then marched slowly backwards to an adjoining cell, where he was strip-searched including the seams of his clothes and every orifice of his body. As he was left standing naked against the wall, Shane felt that the process was taking too long, that some plan was being brewed behind his back. He turned to take a look but immediately his face and hands were smashed hard up against the wall by riot shields.

Two officers were holding Shane's hands against the wall, but he outmanoeuvred them by sliding his hands quickly downwards. One of the guards lost his balance and fell. Shane quickly pushed himself away from the wall, spun and leapt on the downed man. He managed to propel the man across the floor into the opposite corner of the cell, trapping him between the toilet and the wall. The guard's arms were pinned by his shield and the other bodies. Shane, in a haze of fury, managed to free his own arms and was trying to work them under the man's face mask to get at his throat – all this despite half a dozen guards grabbing him, hitting him with batons and even throttling him from behind. Shane picks up the story: 'I had my hands so far up his shield and all I remember doing was looking at him and I just whispered to him, "Do not let me get my hands on your neck today because you are not going home to see your family." Then he started panicking and so did the other officers.'

The guards eventually managed to prise Shane from the stricken guard. What followed was what Shane himself describes as 'torture'. First, he was handcuffed then kicked and beaten to a pulp. Then one of the guards began squeezing his throat until he was turning blue and on the point of passing out before releasing his grip, then starting again. This process went on until one of the other guards stepped in, fearing Shane might actually die.

The beatings went on for days, usually by ten officers at a time, taunting him and calling him a coward. Shane was left cuffed by his hands and feet on the cell floor, unable to move, unable to eat the spit-drenched food that was slung on his floor. Through it all he refused to give in. He made it a matter of pride never to make a sound, no matter how painful the beatings or panic-inducing the strangulation became.

Meanwhile his reputation had reached the highest level. The Home Office had reviewed his case and labelled him one of the top six most dangerous prisoners in England. He was transferred to the segregation unit of another maximum-security prison. This was essentially a prison within a prison where human contact is reduced to practically zero.

Shane was left to rot but the constant isolation also failed to break him. Instead, he used the time to construct meticulous fantasies of his plans for revenge when he was released from prison. He had a hit list of twelve people – guards or other cons who had crossed or betrayed him – and he intended to kill them all in the brief window of freedom he would have between release and recapture. Such an operation would take meticulous planning, but he had the time, the patience and the will. He spent hours on end building up virtual reality-style mental walk-throughs of how he would gain access to his victims' houses, how he would make them suffer, what he would say just before they died. It wasn't just a time-killing exercise, it was a real plan of action.

A side effect of his virtual revenge sessions was that Shane was spending less time enacting real revenge on his guards so, after a while, the governors took the risky decision to release him from the CSC and transfer him to another maximum-security prison on the Isle of Wight. In HMP Parkhurst, he was allowed back on the wing, where he quickly got into dealing heroin.

There is a surprising amount of freedom in England's maximum-security prisons. For example, inmates are allowed to cook their own food on the wings, which means there are knives, as well as boiling-hot water and – much more dangerous – hot oil. Naturally this led to a certain amount of tension. Shane described a typical situation when an inmate was carrying a pan of hot oil through the wing: 'If a lad started walking down the stairs and he had a pan, the whole landing would disappear. Everyone would go behind the doors and you'd look through the gap then just wait for him to go past and think, *it's not me*, and that's the tension.'

But surprisingly, according to Shane, despite an environment where serial killers and terrorists were walking around with knives and hot oil, it rarely exploded. 'Maximum-security prisons are very different,' he told me, 'and so you don't have one hardman who stands out, you don't have one crazy man who stands out, they're all capable. There's a tension. Everybody knows everyone's capable of doing stuff . . . You get on with your jail and if you have to, then you deal with whatever comes your way. But nine times out of ten, people are getting on, cooking together.'

In England's maximum-security prison system inmates are transferred regularly to keep them from forming dangerous contacts and networks within a single establishment. Soon, it was Shane's turn to move again. This time, in 2005, he was transferred to HMP Long Lartin in Worcestershire. It was here that his life would change forever.

Soon after he arrived, Shane was called from his cell to attend an educational class about reintegrating into society. However, when he reported to the guard on the door, he was told his name wasn't on the list for the class so he couldn't be let in. In his usual intimidating way, Shane raged. Rather than risk getting into a fight with this dangerous inmate, the guard wisely directed him to the chaplaincy instead, where a Bible class was taking place. Happy to be let out of his cell for a while, Shane strode off to the new class.

In the chaplaincy, a group of prisoners were watching a video about the basics of Christianity. Shane joined with a mixture of boredom and contempt and rose to leave when the programme finished. However, just as he was about to go another inmate whispered, 'You get strawberry gateau and biscuits.' Shane promptly sat back down and asked to be put on the list for more classes. He attended the Bible course regularly, but only for the food. Most of his time was spent arguing with the converts in the group, pointing out to them what nonsense their beliefs were.

Then one day while he was making a coffee the pastor of the chaplaincy approached him alone and said, 'I've never done this in all the years, but God has just told me to tell you to come here this afternoon by yourself.'

Shane was surprised and dubious but decided to agree. When he returned, the pastor read him two verses from the Bible. The first was about how no one is righteous and everyone is a sinner. The second was about how Jesus died for our sins. The first verse strangely resonated with Shane. He had always believed that religion was only for good people, not bad people like himself. Suddenly, he was confronted with the idea that he could actually be forgiven, he could be loved. It moved him to ask the pastor further questions. The pastor did his best to explain, then invited Shane to pray. Shane didn't know how to pray so the pastor just told him to say what came from his heart.

Shane takes up the story: 'I just remember finding myself saying, "God, if you're real, come into my life. I hate who I am. I hate who I've become. Please, if you're real just do something. Show me you're real." Nothing happened. I said my prayer and we're just in a normal chat now, prayer is over. I started to experience a bubbly feeling in my stomach and I thought, *Okay, what's going on here?* And then it started to get stronger and stronger and it rose up, rose up, rose up, and I just got this feeling shoot up my body and I just burst out, sobbing and sobbing and sobbing.'

Suddenly, all the suffering and pain Shane had caused in his life had come crashing down on his shoulders – all the people he had stabbed, beaten up, bullied or terrified. He poured his tears on to the chaplaincy floor and felt, for the first time, forgiveness flowing into him. Through his tears he thanked God, a God he now believed in. By the time the guard returned to escort him back to his cell, Shane was a changed man.

It wasn't long before the rest of the prison knew about it. Like many converts before, Shane became a sudden and passionate evangelist for his new religion, apologising to guards for his previous bad behaviour, smiling and shaking hands with anyone and everyone, and trying to convert his fellow inmates to a belief in Jesus. Naturally many thought he was acting as part of a diabolical plan. Others took the chance to ridicule a man who, just days before, they wouldn't have dared look in the eye. They called him insulting nicknames and openly made fun of his conversion. But Shane saw it all as a test of his new faith and let it slide off his back.

A bigger test came when one of his enemies, sensing weakness, booked out a kitchen knife to stab him. The man approached him on the landing and struck suddenly with the knife. Shane's fighting instincts activated. He blocked the slash, grabbed the knife-wielding hand by the wrist and wheeled his attacker around, smashing him into a cell wall. After seizing the knife from the inmate's limp hand, he punched him hard in the face. Pumped up on adrenaline and on autopilot, he only just managed to stop himself from using the knife on his attacker, instead throwing him out of the cell and slamming shut the door. It was his first crisis of faith. He knew how close he had come to killing the man. But he hadn't, as the pastor told him when he came to the chaplaincy in distress to recount the story. The pastor said that Shane had merely been defending himself and that it proved just how much he had changed from the old Shane, who would have knifed the man to death without a second thought. Shane saw that it was true and continued trying to live the good life.

It continued for the rest of his sentence, which was just under a year. On his release, several people, who must have been dreading a visit from Shane, got what they had been worrying about for weeks. It can't have been anything like they had expected. Shane made it his mission to visit every single person he had harmed or crossed in his life and make a personal apology. He told me the story of apologising to the prison guard whom he had stabbed with the coffee jar: 'I just remember saying, "Look, I'm sorry for what I've done." I got a bit upset and I said, "Can you forgive me?" And he held up his hand and he said, "I forgive you." And it was crazy because I'm now sat with an officer who I stabbed in a prison who hated me, and I'm sat there and we're having a cup of tea. And do you know when you're very apologetic and you can't help saying, "Really sorry for what I did"? I kept doing this and at one point I took a sip of my coffee and I said, "Look, I am really sorry. I wasn't in the right frame of mind." And he went, "Tell us about it," and we had a laugh for the first time.'

Shane had gone from spreading fear to spreading love. He had an odd knack of converting people, from the lady at the dole office to his wife, Sam, whom he met and married after his release. He was even instrumental in the conversion of Paul Venis, the other local hardman and world heavyweight kickboxing champion, whom he had threatened to stab in the neck all those years ago at the street fight in Middlesbrough.

A decade has passed since Shane's release and he is now happily married with five children. People who knew him before can see that he has changed. They say it's something about his eyes. 'There was something blank there,' Shane explained to me, referring to them, 'even though they're a little dead, they are a bit alive now.' He spends his life working for Christian charities, refusing anything beyond minimum wages, and helps other ex-cons get back into society. He now has a book and film about his life and helps out with the same Alpha course that helped convert him to Christianity. He has given talks to thousands of people, including a TEDx Talk in a maximum-security prison in Uganda.

Rather than create violence, his life now seems to catalyse change in others for the good. He told me about one example of the many coincidences that seem to reveal a guiding hand in his life. In London recently on a speaking tour of the country, he was walking through a packed coffee shop with a copy of his book in his hand. He continues: 'There's a lad there and I just felt God say, "See him over there, that lad there, go to him and give him a book." So I walked over. I said, "Here, mate, I don't know why but I've just got the urge to come over and give you this book, so I'm going to listen to the urge." And I gave him the book. So, he reads the front – the most dangerous prisoner. He jumped up and he went, "Mate, are you being serious?" He said, "I'm on home release from prison." He said, "I'm going back to prison in a couple of days. How on earth did you know to come over to me? How on earth did you know to come and give me that book?" Stuff like that makes me think even more, I know I'm right, and things like that happen all the time. I love helping people. I love just doing the right thing.'

He doesn't deny that every day is still a struggle. People still try to bait him to see if the old Shane will re-emerge. He still battles with the inner voice that can't let things go and that broods over any perceived slight, building it up until he feels the urge for revenge. 'Sometimes, it's tougher and harder for me,' Shane told me, 'because before if I reacted to people and dealt with them then the pressure was gone. I had no pressure. I had dealt with it and I'm happy now. They know not to cross me now. I've got to live with the fact that I'm being mugged off and I've just got to take it. Sometimes it's even more pressure in your own mind, you know, the pride – they think I'm a mug and all that stuff. It's a bigger battle to overcome sometimes.'

It is a battle that, so far, he has won. But he knows he can't let his guard down, and perhaps that is a good thing. It keeps him focused on his mission – to help as many people as he can. In the end it is Shane's own story that is the most powerful weapon in his arsenal, the story of a cold-hearted psychopath who learned how to love. As he says: 'You can change your life. No matter what a life you've had, no matter how much of a scumbag you are, you can change, and I'm proof of that.'

2

John Alite

Mafia Hitman for the Gambino Crime Family

Alite specialised in deadly enforcement work and survived a war zone in a Brazilian prison

Some people are born into a life of crime, others fall into it by chance, but for some the life seems to suck them in, as if they were destined for it.

Such was the case for John Alite, a high-ranking associate of the Gambino crime family, one of America's five most powerful Mafia clans. Alite was the right-hand man, bodyguard and enforcer for John A. Gotti, son of the legendary mob boss, John J. Gotti. By his own testimony, Alite carried out between thirty and forty shootings, over a hundred beatings and at least six killings in the Gottis' name. He was arrested over forty times and spent over a decade in jail, including two years in one of Brazil's most brutal prisons, Bangu. He saw more than a hundred of his friends and associates die, either murdered or from overdoses, all in a career spanning two decades in which he made more than $50 million for the Gambino crime family.

Yet Alite wasn't born into the life of crime. He wasn't even of Italian heritage. He came from a family of Albanian immigrants living in a crime-ridden, poverty-stricken neighbourhood of New York's Queens district, called Woodhaven. His father was a taxi driver who put all his effort into raising his two sons the right way, focusing them obsessively on athletic prowess, especially in boxing and baseball, as a pathway off the streets and away from crime.

But with Alite, it just didn't seem to work. No matter how much he tried to emulate his dad's exacting standards, no matter how hard he tried to escape the life, fate always seemed to intervene, throwing him straight back down to the streets where he had come from. If ever a man were fated to become a gangster, it was John Alite.

It's not as if Alite's upbringing wasn't violent or stressful. In fact, it was characterised by those two things. His father was an inveterate gambler and when he wasn't winning, violence was always only a moment away. 'My father used to throw the kitchen table over all the time,' Alite said during my *True Crime* podcast, published in November 2019, 'through the wall, through the windows . . . When he was on a losing streak, we would stay out of his way because his hands were swinging.'

Alite and his older brother and two sisters grew up in a house they shared with their grandparents, uncles and cousins. Being hit was a normal part of discipline and he learned from an early age how to take a beating. Apart from the physical and emotional violence, he and his brother were subjected to punishing physical routines from an early age. Alite was doing press-ups and pull-ups from the age of four. By the time he was eight, he was doing a hundred press-ups a day and bench-pressing fifty pounds. He was also taught to suppress his reaction to pain or physical suffering – to put up and shut up like a man.

All of this led to anxiety issues as a child. 'I think I was still pissing in my pants in bed until about eleven years old,' Alite told me. 'And, you know, even some of my friends used to tease me. As a kid you're embarrassed, now as an adult you laugh about it. But I guess some of these things are a tribute to it. The way I speak – I always spoke with forced vocal cords. I have a very hoarse voice and I went to therapy for it. Actually, it's better now. I used to sound like a real frog as a kid so some of those things I guess took a toll without me knowing.'

The violence within his family was mirrored on the streets. Woodhaven was a tough neighbourhood to grow up in the seventies and early eighties of Alite's youth. It was a poor neighbourhood riddled with crime and racial tensions, controlled by gangs and rife with drugs. Exposure to violence was common and Alite watched a man baseball batted, possibly to death, certainly into unconsciousness, at an early age. The neighbourhood became so bad, it earned the nickname 'Deathhaven'.

But Woodhaven was just a microcosm of the larger problems overtaking New York in the seventies. An influx of black and Hispanic ethnic minorities was causing racial tensions with the white inhabitants of the boroughs. The end of the Vietnam War saw homeless veterans littering the streets and an economic and industrial downturn meant a lack of jobs and an increase in crime, poverty and homelessness. In the eighties, drugs like heroin and crack reached epidemic proportions and fuelled the crime and violence on the streets. As a child, Alite saw someone knifed on the subway into Manhattan and his own high school had armed police stationed on all the exits to prevent race riots and gang wars encroaching inside the buildings.

Not surprisingly among such an atmosphere of tension and violence, Alite was expected to take care of himself. His father had been a talented boxer in his youth and he would bring other children to the house to fight with his two sons to toughen them up. He taught Alite to block out pain, never to back down from a fight, no matter the odds, and to never give up until he physically couldn't carry on. In his book, *Gotti's Rules*, Alite tells the story of how as an eight-year-old walking home from school, he was roughed up and searched for money by two ten-year-olds. After they let him go, one of the boys flicked his lit cigarette at John, hitting him in the forehead. When he got home and told his father what had happened, his dad told him to go back and punch the bully in the face. Alite dutifully retraced his steps and hit the bully just as his dad had instructed. He of course took a beating from the older kid, but the precedent had been established – John Alite was not to be pushed around.

Alite told me another story about a beating he took as a child: 'I fought a guy – and a big guy – when I was a kid, and I was giving it to him a little bit, and I had the bright idea of throwing him on the floor. Well, I made a mistake and he fell on top of me. And my friends were there, and they wanted to break it up and I wouldn't allow it. Well, that kid pummelled me. He was crying and he just kept begging me, "Can you stop now?" when I was all bloody. And I wouldn't stop and I wouldn't let my friends jump in because my father wouldn't allow something like that.'

The fights weren't just with outsiders. As could be expected from two kids raised this way, John and his brother would go at it like crazy. Jimmy was just a year older than John and every bit as athletic and tough. Although the two generally got on, fights between them could quickly get out of hand. In his book about his childhood, *Darkest Hours*, Alite recounts the story of one fight where his brother knocked him through a first-storey bedroom window. Fortunately for John, the roof of the porch broke his fall and he was able to climb down amid the broken shards of glass. Predictably the thing that most worried the brothers was the beating they'd get from their dad, especially if he'd lost at gambling that night.

Despite all this, it would be wrong to think of John's father, Matthew Alite, as a monster. He cared deeply about his family and he was universally respected and liked among the local community. When Matthew was on a winning streak, he'd treat the family lavishly, taking them out for meals, or accompanying the two boys to the Shea Stadium to watch a New York Mets baseball game. He was John's role model and his hero and as a child, the young Alite strove to do everything his dad told him was right, wanting only to make his father proud.

It was emulating his dad that first brought the young John into contact with the world of gangsters and organised crime. John's dad taught him all the card games, including poker, and when Matthew went hustling, John would be his 'innocent' little helper. 'I'd signal him what hands everybody had,' Alite told me. 'And these guys really didn't figure it out that it was just a little kid that, you know, I have no idea what's going on, and it's not typical for a six- or seven-year-old kid to have the ability to know cards. So I would signal him, creeping around the tables behind the card players.'

Other poker games – ones at which Matthew dared not hustle – were hosted by gangsters. One such game took place regularly in the back room of a parking garage in the Bronx. It was an all-night affair hosted by a cousin of Matthew's and Charlie Luciano, a soldier for the Gambino crime family. Sometimes their father would bring the two boys along and they would be treated to sodas and ice cream from the kitchen, as well as money from the mob associates playing the hands. John was entranced by the atmosphere of easy camaraderie and the casual air of confidence and power exuded by these wise guys with exotic names like Little Al and Old Man Frankie. Alongside his father, he had found new role models for his life.

'I got accustomed to being around gangsters,' Alite told me. 'And I got accustomed to being comfortable about the way they handled themselves. And I started copying them, you know? I started smoking cigars at a young age.'

As Alite grew older, his boxing and baseball careers began to develop. He concentrated first on boxing, following in his father's footsteps. Alite was not a polished fighter but he was fast and could take hit after hit and keep going back for more. This attitude eventually attracted a professional trainer who, at the age of ten, wanted him to fight in the Junior Olympics. Alite's new trainer taught him how to bob and weave and throw counter punches, and soon he was dominating his weight class and preparing for the Olympics. In *Darkest Hours*, Alite tells of how he demolished the previous year's Junior Olympic champion in a training fight over five rounds but by the end of the fifth, he noticed that the other boy's father was haranguing his son so badly for losing that the boy was beginning to cry and was struggling to stop himself from breaking down in the ring. Recognising something of himself in the boy's position, Alite refused to go on: he forfeited the fight and let the other kid win.

But Alite's boxing career was to be cut short in a cruel manner. It began with a beating he took as a younger, less skilled boxer. Alite was training in the gym when one of the coaches asked him to spar with his fighter, who was training for a fight but had no one to spar with. The other kid was much bigger than Alite and in a heavier weight class, not to mention more experienced and skilled. Alite knew all this but agreed to the contest because he had been taught never to back down. He took a pummelling that lasted two rounds before the gym owner interrupted the unfair contest, furious that one of his coaches had used an inexperienced kid as a bigger guy's punchbag. Alite, of course, had taken all the punishment and refused to go down, but the next day, perhaps because of all the blows to his head, he had an epileptic fit. He had another one after the fight with the Junior Olympic champion, falling and passing out in the street.

After that, on a visit to the family doctor, Alite's mother and sister revealed that John's last seizure had occurred right after a boxing match. The doctor, unaware of his burgeoning fighting career, instantly stepped in to get Alite's Junior Olympics preparation matches cancelled. The young boxer's potential career was essentially over before it had begun.

That left baseball as an escape route from the streets. John had been playing the game seriously since the age of seven. His childhood coach was Albert Ruggiano, son of Anthony 'Fat Andy' Ruggiano, a famous gangster from the Gambino family. Alite went on to play for his high school in Brooklyn, on the varsity team all four years, the last two as team captain. After high school and the failure of his boxing career, he won a baseball scholarship to the University of Tampa in Florida, where he quickly moved from the junior varsity to the varsity team. His future looked bright and a move to semi-pro baseball was on the cards, but just as with boxing, his career was cut short before it even began.

John had injured his arm overthrowing in a high school baseball game. Instead of surgery, as recommended by the doctor, his coach persuaded him to carry on playing with cortisone shots in his arm. In his usual way, he trained and played just as hard as ever but by the time he got to university, the injury caught up with him and by the end of the first semester, he was in such excruciating pain he had to undergo ligament replacement surgery in his elbow. Unfortunately, his arm never recovered enough to play top-flight baseball again. He resumed boxing, but the epileptic seizures returned with a vengeance. Once again life had shown him a way out, only to cruelly snatch it away.

For a few years, Alite had held down a part-time job in a local deli. A phone at the back of the building was used by gangsters from a mob clubhouse across the road to take illegal sports bets. It was here that he first got involved in organised crime. It started innocently enough – agreeing to hold packages of money in safekeeping for gangsters, passing on messages, that kind of thing, but his involvement became deeper when a local gangster and stolen antiques dealer, Patty 'Antiques', took offence at Alite, thinking the boy was laughing at him one day in the deli. In *Darkest Hours*, Alite tells how the next day as he was coming out of the gym, Patty Antiques pulled up and shot at him with a shotgun. Alite managed to get away but a couple of hours later, the crazed antique dealer turned up outside his house waving an automatic rifle around and calling for John to 'come out and play'.

Alite decided to call his old baseball coach, Albert Ruggiano, whose father, Anthony 'Fat Andy' Ruggiano, was a Gambino family captain who ran the area. Albert told Alite that the Ruggianos would deal with the situation but soon Patty Antiques was on Alite's case again, trying to shoot him on the street. Now the petty gangster had disobeyed a direct order from a made man. (In the US and Sicilian Mafia, a made man is a fully initiated member. A Mafia associate must be Italian or of Italian descent to become made and be sponsored by a made man. The associate is required to take the oath of *omertà*, the Mafia code of silence.)

Alite was in serious trouble and he knew it because he promptly disappeared. However, Fat Andy made his point. The Ruggianos found Patty's twenty-year-old stepson and threw him off a roof, breaking his back, his arm and both legs and leaving him in a body cast for a year. To Alite it was a mixed feeling – pride that true wise guys had fought his corner but guilt and pity that an innocent young man had had to suffer for the mistakes of his crazy stepfather. It was an early insight into the workings of Mafia justice.

After his brief stint at the University of Tampa, Alite found himself back at the deli again and dabbling half-heartedly in a small-time drug-dealing operation with some old school friends. Things became more serious when his sister's boyfriend, Joe Galliano, asked for help. He and his friend had been dealing a bit of coke in the neighbourhood but had recently been visited by some mob-affiliated gangsters demanding a cut of their money. The boyfriend asked Alite to talk to Albert Ruggiano for help. When Albert found out, he told Alite that the small-time dealers were now under his protection but that Alite should demand $100 a week from them for fixing their problem. When Alite told Galliano what Ruggiano had suggested, his sister's boyfriend went one better: he asked Alite to go into business with him. John quickly agreed. He knew they would be working under the protection of the Ruggianos so it was easy and safe money. Alite began selling cocaine out of the deli – it was well known and already a crime hub of the neighbourhood – and he hid the drugs under his bed at home.

Alite was falling into the life his father had striven so hard to prevent and now Matthew Alite intervened. Finding drugs under John's bed, he flushed them down the toilet and sent him to California to live with an uncle, whom he hoped would set John straight. But in California, fate intervened once again.

John was in a bar in Valencia in Los Angeles County when his friend was accosted by two guys. As was his way, John jumped in to help his friend, hitting one of the men over the head with a bottle and stabbing the other in the side in a follow-up incident. Unfortunately, they were off-duty cops. After a trial, Alite was banned from California for five years. It had been just around a year and he was back on the streets in New York. Something, it seemed, didn't want him to leave.

At home, he resumed drug dealing, but he had one last plan to make a success of his life without resorting to crime – he had been studying to take stockbroking exams. As with anything, he studied fanatically and soon passed his exams, earning his stockbroking licence. Not long after, he secured a job with J.P. Morgan.

Again, it wasn't to be. In his book, *Gotti Enforcer*, Alite tells of how he lost the job with J.P. Morgan before his first day had even arrived. The California sentencing had come back to haunt him – even though his offence fell under a first-time offender programme and should have been expunged from his record, Alite's lawyers had failed to file the necessary paperwork. In their background checks, J.P. Morgan found his criminal record and denied him employment, as would every other Wall Street firm.

It was his last attempt to go straight. From now on, he would embrace his destiny and make his living from the streets. But like everything else he tried, he would do it better, harder and faster than anyone else.

That was when John Gotti Jr got involved. Alite had met Gotti Jr in 1981 when they were hanging around the same bars and clubs in Queens. It was a casual friendship with a mutual sense of respect but nothing more. It wasn't until 1983 when Alite returned from California that the two began to work together. It started with a meeting set up by a boyhood friend of Alite's, Johnny Gebert. The meeting with Gotti Jr had a predictable outcome – Junior wanted a cut of Alite's drug-dealing business. Despite the loss of earnings, it was a good business move for Alite – he was now a step closer to one of the biggest names within the Gambino crime family. Gotti Jr's dad was John Gotti Sr, a captain under Paul Castellano, head of the Gambinos. Although Junior wasn't yet a made man like his father, he worked under his protection and had numerous drug-dealing operations around Queens and Brooklyn that were all kicking up money to him. Drug dealing was officially off limits within the Gambino family under punishment of death, but as Alite would soon find out, this was all just for show and everyone, right up to the top of the organisation, was illicitly making money from narcotics.

Gotti Jr had a reputation as a tough guy and a gangster but how much of this was playing off his father's reputation was hard to establish. Alite had been warned off Gotti Jr by Albert Ruggiano. According to *Gotti's Rules*, Albert had once told Alite, 'Avoid that guy, you hear? He's a punk, a loudmouth. He thinks he's a tough guy. No one respects him. No one ever will.'

Alite didn't know what to make of the warning. Gotti Jr had a reputation around the neighbourhood as a killer, which certainly seemed to be backed up by fact. But rather than take any responsibility for his actions, he made other guys in his crew take the rap for his crimes. He had knifed a guy named Danny Silva to death in a bar fight and although he boasted to friends privately about the killing, it was one of his crew, Mark Caputo, who had to take the rap and go into hiding from the police. Another, even darker, aspect of Gotti Jr's character was illustrated by the killing – according to later witness testimony,

Gotti Jr had returned to the scene of the crime not long after the incident to find Silva bleeding to death on the floor. Staring down at the dying man, Gotti Jr had said in a loud Porky Pig voice, imitating the famous ending of Warner Bros.' *Looney Tunes* cartoon, 'That's all, folks!' None of this put Alite off at the time. He was looking to scale the ladder of the New York organised crime scene and the Gotti name was his ticket on to the first rung. Soon, he was working for Junior, although his first major job should have been a warning of things to come. Alite was asked to assist with a shooting that was a revenge attack on Jamaican drug dealers who had beaten up Johnny Gebert and stolen his money. As Gebert was connected to Gotti Jr, the affront to the Gotti name couldn't go unpunished.

Alite was to drive the car and Gebert was tasked with the shooting. Gotti Jr would follow behind in a blocking car which would stop the traffic and give the lead car a chance to escape if the police arrived. In *Gotti's Rules*, Alite explains how the routine plan unwound. Gotti Jr supplied Alite with a stolen car for the job and Gebert with a .38 calibre pistol. Alite drove past the storefront in the Richmond Hill neighbourhood of Queens where the Jamaicans usually hung out, establishing their presence. He drove round a second time and Gebert let off five or six shots at the Jamaicans, sending them scattering in all directions.

Gebert shouted at Alite to drive but almost immediately police sirens were filling the air. Alite tried to stay calm and drive slowly away, following the plan. However, as he took a left turn, he noticed in the rear-view mirror the discomfiting sight of Gotti's car driving away without doing any blocking. At about the same time, Gebert, who had been smoking angel dust, got out of the car and fled on foot, leaving the incriminating weapon on the passenger seat floor.

Alite had now been left alone with no blocker, an incriminating weapon and the police on his tail. He kept his head together enough to abandon the car down a narrow side street. Throwing the gun into a bin, he bolted to a nearby store. After removing his shirt, he ran back to the rendezvous point, pretending to be a jogger.

Despite being abandoned by his associates, Alite overlooked the incident. Now, he was in with Gotti Jr, which was another step up the ladder. He became an official member of Junior's crew, planning business ventures and money-making schemes and expanding their mutual drug business. It wasn't long before Gotti Sr asked to see him.

John J. Gotti wasn't yet head of the Gambinos, but he had ascended to be a captain within the organisation. He had begun his life of crime as the leader of a gang that hijacked trucks but soon made ties with the powerful Mafia family. In the seventies, he had been part of a hit team that had taken out James McBratney, a member of the notorious Irish gang, the Westies. McBratney had masterminded the murder of a nephew of Carlo Gambino, the family's then boss. Gotti Sr had done time for the hit and on his release had been formally initiated as a made man. He had risen quickly to the rank of captain and was now in charge of the whole Queens area of New York. He was clearly upwardly mobile in the world of organised crime, just as Alite wanted to be, and although neither of them knew it at the time, he would soon rise even higher.

Gotti Sr took an instant liking to Alite and made it clear that he knew his son's character flaws and didn't want to see him in an early grave. From the beginning, Alite understood his role was as much minder and protector to Junior as it was underling and crew member. His differing role in the eyes of father and son led to some complicated circumstances, as Alite told me:

44

'I had to play a little middleman between father and son, and some of the stuff I was doing for the father and the son were a little different. The father didn't want the son to know things, so it's kind of like a tightrope I was always walking.'

It meant among other things that Alite would have to take the rap for some of Junior's many indiscretions, like when he shot a nephew of a Genovese family captain in the leg during a bar fight. It was a serious transgression of the mob code of conduct and Gotti Sr was understandably furious. He demanded Alite tell him who did the shooting, but Alite said he didn't know, even though everyone in the room knew it had been Junior. For protecting his leader, Alite was escorted across the street by two of Gotti Sr's high-ranking associates, Angelo Ruggiero (Junior's godfather) and Willie Boy Johnson, where they had been ordered to give him a beating. However, Ruggiero let Alite go unharmed. He knew exactly what had happened and, according to *Gotti's Rules*, told Alite, 'My fuckin' godson's no good. But what are we gonna do?'

Around this time, Alite had been in a fight that nearly cost him his life. It was 1984 and John had pulled up outside a burger bar in Queens with a friend, Monique, whom he occasionally dated. Alite waited in the car while Monique went to get the burgers. While Alite was chatting with some friends outside he noticed that Monique was getting hassled by a group of guys. As he watched, one of them pulled his trousers down and bared his ass to Monique. Without thinking, Alite strode into the burger bar and confronted the man. He was told 'Fuck you!' and immediately punched the guy in the face. Now alone, he was facing five guys and he paid the price. He had a bottle smashed over his head and an ice pick swung into the side of his face before his friends could arrive and even out the odds.

Most people, no matter how tough, would balk at facing up to five men, but for Alite, it was just what had to be done in the moment. As he told me, 'When I got stabbed up, I went in against five guys, so I knew I was gonna get it, but, you know, I wanted to accomplish what I wanted. I wanted to get one of the guys.'

The burger bar owner called the police and the fight ended, but the night wasn't over for Alite. As he was driving away with his face swelling alarmingly from the ice-pick wound, a monster truck appeared out of nowhere and rammed Alite's car. With its huge wheels it mounted the front of the car, shunting it off the road and into a tree. Three men from the burger bar fight emerged and began smashing the windscreen with baseball bats. Sheltering Monique beneath him, Alite managed to crawl out through the broken windscreen and face his attackers. He got a terrible beating before a passer-by threatened to call the police and the men took off. Still, Alite had it in him to chase down one of his attackers and beat him with his own baseball bat before collapsing on the street. He was rushed to hospital for emergency treatment, suffering from a broken arm and damage to his internal organs, including severe damage to his pancreas. He required more than a hundred stitches to his face and body and spent two weeks in intensive care.

And this wasn't the only threat to Alite's life. Around the same time, he was running around Victory Field, a track at Queens' Forest Park, when four men in heavy coats and wide-brimmed hats entered the track from opposite directions. In *Gotti Enforcer*, Alite tells how his instincts instantly alerted him to the danger. He stopped running and started walking back towards another exit. When the men followed him, he knew his instincts had been correct. While he sprinted away, the men opened fire with 9mm pistols. Alite hit a ten-feet high fence and scaled it in seconds with gunshots flying all around him. On the other side, he dropped fifteen feet and rolled into a ravine filled with underbrush. At the bottom, he found a disused railway track and followed it into the woods before making a circuitous way home.

Having committed so many acts of violence in the recent past, it might have been any number of people behind the hit. But Alite did draw one lesson: he needed to avoid routines and predictable actions. From now on he would have no set schedules and mix up the times and places he did everything. It is telling that this was the main lesson he learned, not that gang life was going to kill him sooner or later. By now Alite was too far in. Fate had taught him that this was his path and nothing was going to stop him from following it to the end. In 1985, something happened which shook the foundations of New York's organised crime scene, leaving it permanently altered.

On a cold night in December, the Gambino boss, Paul Castellano, was gunned down outside Sparks Steak House in Midtown Manhattan. Hits on crime bosses had to be sanctioned by a meeting of the heads of the five major New York crime families, but this assassination was unauthorised and a mystery, at least at first.

In fact, it was John Gotti Sr behind the hit on his own boss. Alite explained to me, 'I wasn't part of the hit, I was a young guy, but I was privy to it at the time, you know? Senior again used his friend Angelo Ruggiero as the scapegoat because they got caught on tape talking about selling coke. He used that as an excuse to go hit Paul.'

Gotti Sr's brother, Gene Gotti, his best friend, Angelo Ruggiero, and another associate, John Carneglia, had been caught on tape discussing their drug-dealing business. The FBI were preparing a case against them and soon everything would be revealed. The Gambinos' rules were that drug selling was punishable by death. Senior must have realised that his close associates and, by extension, himself, would be under threat as soon as Paul Castellano found out. Senior decided to make a pre-emptive strike, taking out Castellano and seizing the reins of power.

As Castellano and his driver, Tommy Bilotti, left their car and headed towards the restaurant in Manhattan they were gunned down by four men wearing trench coats and hats. Gotti Sr and his sidekick, Sammy 'The Bull' Gravano, were watching from a car parked just down the street. The bold and risky move paid off. Two weeks later Gotti Sr was the new head of the Gambino crime family. But Gotti Sr had left himself exposed. By hitting a boss without sanction from the other Mafia families his life was forfeit and sooner or later someone would come after him.

As an initial way of consolidating his position and distancing himself from his drug-dealing associates, Gotti Sr banned Angelo Ruggiero – the most vocal advocate of drug dealing on the FBI tapes – from the organisation, exiling him from all Gambino events and properties and forbidding anyone from seeing or speaking to him. At the time Ruggiero was already dying of cancer. He was Gotti Sr's best friend and Junior's godfather. He had been with him in the early truck-hijacking days and had helped him become a made man. It was clear that under the new Gotti-led Gambino regime personal ties and loyalty would count for little – if you became a liability, you would be sacrificed.

At the time Alite wasn't worried about such things as he was making too much money and Gotti Sr's move up the ladder meant a consequent rise in power and reputation for him. His drug-dealing operation was now expanding into the big time. Before, he had been selling quarter kilos. Now he went into partnership with Gotti Jr and a local big-time dealer, Kevin Bonner, to move cocaine in kilo packages. The new business cornered the coke market in large swathes of Queens and would soon be earning the three partners $100,000 a month each in profits. He also had a profitable heroin business. Besides all this, Junior was always coming up with schemes to make more money, some of which were riskier than others.

One of the riskier plans was to use counterfeit money to buy cocaine from a group of Colombians. Alite and Vinny, another associate of Junior's, were tasked with doing the deal. Both men entered the Colombians' house with concealed weapons. Alite had mixed in some real notes with the counterfeit ones in case anyone decided to check the cash. The four Colombians were all armed and when they began counting the money, Vinny lost his nerve and said he was going to wait outside. Not for the first time, Alite had been left high and dry by one of Junior's crew. He was furious and terrified, but he stuck it out and the deal went through.

Vinny would later pay the price for his cowardice. The next day Alite and Junior picked Vinny up at his house and told him to drive. Junior questioned him about why he had run out on Alite and Vinny gave an unconvincing explanation. He kept glancing nervously at Alite in the rear-view mirror. Junior told Vinny to drive to an isolated marshy spot that was well known for killings. It was too well known perhaps because Vinny got spooked and leapt out of the car just as Junior told him to pull over. Junior pulled out his gun and shot the fleeing Vinny once before letting him escape. Vinny – wisely – was never seen again in the neighbourhood.

Meanwhile the first fallout from the Castellano hit was dropping on Gotti Sr's head. Four months after the murder, Gotti Sr's underboss, Frank DeCicco, was killed when a bomb exploded in his car. The bomb had been meant for Gotti, who was supposed to be attending a meeting with DeCicco. It was a clear sign that the other crime families knew who was responsible for the murder of Castellano and intended to do something about it.

Gotti Sr did not respond with a counter killing but instead concentrated on winning hearts and minds with a media campaign that many politicians would have been proud of. He was always ready to give interviews and sound bites to journalists and TV reporters and to have his photo taken at any opportunity. At the same time he began throwing annual 'block parties' every fourth of July in Queens, complete with firework displays and street barbecues. The media campaign worked so well that six months after the DeCicco killing Gotti Sr had his face on the cover of *Time* magazine.

It was a clever move and Alite understood what he was doing. 'He was very worried about it and it was only a matter of time before they hit him,' Alite told me. 'And because of the way he carried the media around him it was so hard to get near him and I think that's one of the things he purposely did. He understood the media around him is almost like having law enforcement around him.' But at the same time as it was a brilliant strategy, it was breaking another Mafia golden rule – not to speak to the media. While Gotti Sr was busy saving his own life, he was slowly going about killing the very institution he was leading.

It wasn't just a battle for survival against other mobsters that Gotti Sr faced. The federal government was after him too. In the Mafia Commission Trial in 1986, eight Mafia leaders were imprisoned, including Anthony Corallo of the Lucchese organisation, 'Fat' Tony Salerno of the Genovese family, and Carmine Persico of the Colombos. John Gotti Sr wasn't one of them. He also beat the rap on an assault case in 1984, a racketeering trial in 1987 and a murder-for-hire case in 1990. His ability to slip through the hands of justice earned him the nickname the 'Teflon Don'. But it wasn't down to luck. Gotti Sr was putting the screws on defendants, witnesses and even juries. John Alite was part of the Teflon Don's slick apparatus for convincing jurors to 'do the right thing'. In *Gotti's Rules*, Alite describes how he acted as a spotter outside the court-house, who would identify members of the jury as they exited, then radio their description to another guy waiting in the car park, who would follow them home. Once the Gottis had their addresses, the jurors would receive a visit and would be bribed or threatened. One or the other usually worked.

In the meantime, Alite was growing his own criminal empire alongside Junior. He had decided to get into sports betting and loan sharking – offering bookmaking services combined with loans to inveterate gamblers. He and Junior took the burgeoning business to Gotti Sr, who liked the idea and encouraged its expansion. Senior brought in one of his top associates and enforcers, the hulking Willie Boy Johnson. Johnson would provide access to the latest sports betting lines and would stump up the money to cover some of the larger bets. In return, he would take 50 per cent of the earnings. Alite respected Johnson and looked up to him as someone to emulate. But Johnson gave Alite some advice one day that Alite would often reflect on. According to *Gotti's Rules*, Johnson took Alite for a walk and told him to keep his eyes and ears open and mouth shut if he wanted to stay in the life. He told Alite that Gotti Jr was 'pure garbage' and that Gotti Sr was disliked by most of the other crime families even before the Castellano murder. 'You have no real friends,' he told Alite. 'None of us do. Only jealous competitors.'

His advice would prove accurate for both Alite and Johnson himself. In Gotti Sr's 1987 racketeering case, it was revealed that Johnson had been an informant for the FBI for years. The following year, the big man was shot in the head six times by two gunmen as he went to work. Although the murder was never solved, there was little doubt who had ordered the hit.

Another role model of Alite's was the father of his friend, Greg Reiter, the big-time heroin dealer, Mark Reiter. Despite being a gangster, Mark Reiter was a gentleman and, according to Alite, taught him how to act, how to dress and, most importantly, how to live life to the fullest. Reiter encouraged Alite not to hang around clubs playing cards and smoking all day like most made guys did, but to go out and enjoy himself and spend his money. But, like Johnson, drug trafficker Reiter met his end in 1987 when he was convicted and sentenced to eighty years behind bars for racketeering and conspiracy. As if confirming Johnson's point, Gotti Sr immediately turned on the convicted drug felon, calling him a low-life drug dealer, despite the fact that Gotti Sr had made millions of dollars from Reiter.

Through the bookmaking business, Alite started taking large sums of money from a guy called Joe DeLuca, who was placing secret bets for players from the Mets baseball team. The Mets players became regular customers, betting large sums of money on Major League baseball games.

Not all the work was so glamorous, however. Alite and Junior were responsible for making sure debtors paid. That usually involved beatings and Alite had to beat up DeLuca at one point when he began betting wildly with Mets' money.

On another occasion, he had to get creative to force the son of a made guy to pay the $6,000 he owed. Patsy Catalano was using his father's name to avoid paying the debt. 'He thought I gave a shit who his father was,' Alite told me. 'I tied him up and poured lighter fluid all over him, and I beat him up, and I was gonna put him on fire.' It turned out that Patsy's father was also in debt to Gotti Sr's brother, Gene Gotti, over his heroin business. After the beating, both debts were paid.

Getting his hands dirty was something Alite wasn't afraid of, indeed he embraced it as a way to solidify his reputation, so when the opportunity came to make his first hit for the Gottis, he jumped at the chance. The target was George Grosso, a kid that Alite had grown up with. Grosso and his drug-dealing partner, Johnny Gebert – who had left Alite in the lurch during the Jamaican gang shooting – were continually boasting about working for Gotti Sr. Although this was true, they couldn't seem to understand that drug dealing in the Gottis' name was strictly a hush-hush enterprise. Grosso was also using his own product, including cocaine, angel dust and heroin, which made Junior worried that he was unreliable and would soon rat.

When Junior tasked Alite with silencing Grosso permanently, Alite went into action, first establishing Grosso's routine then planning the hit. In *Gotti's Rules*, Alite tells how he turned up one night at one of Grosso's regular haunts with four members of his own crew and started drinking with his old neighbourhood acquaintance. At first Grosso was wary but as Alite bought round after round of shots, his mood began to relax. What Grosso didn't realise was that Alite had already instructed the bartender to only fill his own glass with water. After a while, Alite suggested they go to an after-hours club near LaGuardia Airport. After some convincing, Grosso agreed and Alite told him to jump in the passenger seat while he and an associate, a bent cop called Phil Baroni, sat in the back. The plan was that Alite would ask to stop to urinate in a park near 88th Street and Atlantic Avenue. There, Alite would shoot Grosso and dump his body in the bushes. But Alite didn't like the idea of some children finding the body in the morning, so instead he instructed the driver to continue. They eventually pulled over at an exit off Grand Central Parkway, where Alite put three bullets in the back of Grosso's head and dumped the body in some bushes. Afterwards they went to a late-night diner in Queens, where Alite ate a cheeseburger with extra cheese.

The story sums up the two sides of Alite's character – the concern over the exposure of children to violence alongside the cold-blooded ability to shoot someone in the head at close range and enjoy a meal soon after. He had confirmed that he was truly one of the 'one per cent' of gangsters. As he told me, 'Ninety-nine per cent of these guys are sheep. There's only 1 per cent, I've said it over and over again, of guys like me making money and killing.'

The rest of the criminal underworld must have felt the same way. Alite's reputation had now solidified into someone who could be relied upon by his friends and feared by his enemies. In Junior's case, although he hadn't got his hands dirty, the hit on Grosso earned him a place as a made man in the Gambino crime family. The ceremony was held on Christmas Eve with Gambino underboss, Sammy 'The Bull' Gravano, officiating. Junior was now officially untouchable and with his rise, Alite's own status was even more secure. So was his income. By the late eighties, Altie testified, he and Junior were each earning $100,000 a month from their cocaine operation alone.

But the money was never enough. As well as making their own cash, Junior and Alite were always looking for an opportunity to steal from their competitors and it rarely mattered how dangerous those competitors were. On one occasion, Alite decided to rob a gang of Jamaicans operating out of North Philadelphia who, he estimated, were selling between four and five kilos of drugs a week, which meant they would have around $400,000 in cash on their premises at any one time. Alite knew the Jamaicans were serious gangsters and would kill them in an instant if they showed any weakness so he took three associates who he knew meant business.

When they kicked in the front door of the Jamaicans' house it was like an arsenal, with rows of assault rifles lining the walls and loaded magazines stacked up on the counter. But Alite had caught them by surprise and they had no time to reach for their weapons. The Jamaicans' leader tried to psych Alite out, saying in a slow drawl, 'I'm gonna get you, man.' But Alite wasn't to be intimidated. He immediately cracked the butt of his shotgun into the side of the man's head, splitting it open and knocking him to the floor. The other Jamaicans quickly decided to co-operate and Alite and his pals came away with $100,000 plus a couple of Rolexes. His associate in the robbery, Ronald Turchi Jr, who told the story in *Gotti Enforcer*, said of Alite in these situations, 'John was everything about being a hitman. Alite didn't need drugs, alcohol, or a pep talk to do what he did. He was always ready to go at the drop of a hat, able to go in any direction, and he fought anything coming his way.'

But his reputation for cool-headed violence only seemed to land Alite in more scrapes. People he knew increasingly turned to him to help them out of trouble and Alite, being a loyal friend, always answered the call. When his friend, Joe O'Kane, called him from a nightclub to tell him three guys were hassling him, Alite headed straight over. He found one of the guys on the dance floor and shot him in the hip. The other two guys tried to accost him outside and he shot one of them too for good measure.

Another time, Alite's friend, Joey Mathis, called to say he'd had an altercation with three bikers and they were waiting outside the bar for him with chains and baseball bats. Alite headed down with his own bat and escorted Joey out of the premises. When the bikers intervened, Alite knocked one straight out with a blow of his bat and beat the other two with the help of Joey and another guy from the bar. In *Gotti's Rules*, Alite tells how the bikers came looking for him at the same bar for revenge. He found out where the gang hung out and paid their headquarters a visit. He found one of the bikers' leaders and plunged a knife into his thigh, telling him that if his gang came after Alite again he'd be dead.

Actions like these earned Alite the nickname 'The Sheriff' among his friends. Despite his propensity for violence he had several rules which he considered unbreakable – he would never steal from or commit violence on someone who wasn't already in the life and he always stuck by his friends and his own crew, no matter what the odds. His attitude to his friends was summed up by his actions towards one of his gang members, Johnny Burke. Johnny had been due to do a robbery with Alite but had been run over by a rival gang member's car over drug territory and was in hospital. Alite did the robbery with another guy and made a big haul of cash. He visited Johnny in hospital and gave him $64,000 to buy a house for his family.

But there was a darker side to Alite. He had always had hot blood and a quick temper but as his career in the criminal underworld progressed the violence started to escalate, sometimes beyond control. When a guy who had beef with his brother attacked both of them with an iron bar, the two Alites quickly got the better of the man and started giving him a beating with his own weapon. Jimmy Alite was ready to stop, but John just kept cracking the stricken man around the head, consumed by bloodlust. He left him lying unconscious on the floor, not sure if he was alive or dead. On another occasion, two guys in a bar made some comments about the smart way Alite was dressed and one flicked his tie up in his face. He immediately punched the guy, knocking him out, then beat up his friend too. When a third man, who knew Alite, tried to remonstrate with him, he pulled out a gun and shot him in the chest.

Alite's violence could flare up anywhere any time. In *Gotti Enforcer*, he tells how he was on a bus with his father when he leaned his seat back to relax. The guy behind didn't like this and kicked the back of the seat, shouting, 'Motherfucker!' Alite turned around and gave the man a piece of his mind and the guy threatened to pull a knife on him. At the same time the man sitting in the seat opposite Alite made a similar threatening remark. Alite, as was his habit, went from zero to a hundred instantly. He ordered his dad off the bus, not wanting him to see the violence he was about to commit. But his father, knowing full well what was about to go down, refused. Alite took himself to the bathroom and planned his next move. He took out a gun and decided he was going to shoot both guys in the head then walk to the front of the bus and demand the bus driver let him off. He came out of the bathroom with his gun ready and approached the guy sitting opposite him but in the interim his father must have been doing some hasty explaining of the imminent threat to the man's life because, as soon as he saw Alite approaching, he apologised profusely. As quick as his temper could rise, it could de-escalate just as rapidly. He took his hand off the gun and left the man alone.

Alite puts a lot of his aggression down to his Albanian blood, as he explained to me: 'The problem with Albanians, and myself, and that's got me into trouble, is sometimes we jump without thinking. We use our balls before our brains and that's caused me a lot of, you know, myself getting hurt and stabbed up and beat up, and also me hurting and stabbing, shooting a lot of guys.'

He shot a lot of people, mostly in the legs or shoulders to teach them a lesson. But when he had to make a hit, he was no-nonsense about ensuring the target ended up dead. He told me how he would go about a typical shooting: 'I'd rather hit him to the body if he's moving because that's gonna slow him down, then you put a couple in his head. You have some guys who just shoot him a couple of times in the head. Make sure you finish him. Guys make that mistake and they leave them alive and sometimes those guys that have lived, they're coming back and they're killing those same guys. So, you know, it's when you're gonna do your work, you got to do it precisely and you got to do it like a professional.'

As his violence escalated, his position within the Gambino organisation solidified. He was a trusted go-to guy and this was reflected at weekly meetings at Gambino HQ, the Bergin Hunt and Fish Club, where he sat at Gotti Sr's table. Everyone else on that table was a made man. Alite could never be made because of his non-Italian heritage, but this was Gotti Sr's way of showing him the level of respect he had. It didn't go down well with Junior, however, who was made to sit on another table.

Alite was becoming part of the Gottis' life, spending more time at the family home. It was here that things started getting a little too close for comfort. Junior's sister, Victoria Gotti, was a good-looking but spoilt Mafia princess in her early twenties.

She was in a long-term relationship with her future husband, Carmine Agnello.

Whatever the truth about the relationship, it was doomed from the start. Alite moved on with his own love life, getting married to his long-time girlfriend, Carol Defgard, in 1989. John Gotti Junior was his best man. Alite was settling down and investing his money in properties and semi-legitimate businesses. He had two condos in Queens, two more in Princeton, New Jersey, another in South Brunswick and an apartment in lower Manhattan, as well as a family home in Voorhees Township in South Jersey. This was a fifteen-acre property with three houses, one of which he gave to his parents and one to his grandmother. He later bought another fifteen-acre property in New Jersey called Cherry Hill, where he added a sports complex, baseball cages and an outdoor boxing ring. As with everything else he did, he succeeded as a businessman and ended up owning a parking company and two nightclubs in Tampa, Florida, and a professional gym with Olympic-sized swimming pool in South Jersey. He also moved into the cell-tower business, helping his friend, Ronald Turchi Jr, put up cell towers around Philadelphia. According to Turchi Jr in *Gotti Enforcer*, he and Alite owned pretty much every crane in Philadelphia while their business was expanding.

Another business idea was to 'unionise' the doorman market. Alite and Gotti Jr basically told all the bouncers in Queens that they now had to work through them, with the gangsters taking a cut off the top of the bouncers' wages. It was as simple as that. Anyone who didn't go along with the scheme would face the consequences, Gotti style. Most bouncers and establishments in Queens knew their reputation well enough to comply but one club, called Stringers, refused to accept Alite and Junior's bouncers. They served as a handy example to the rest.

Some of the bouncers working at Stringers also worked at one of Junior's clubs so Alite told them that no one was to work at Stringers on pain of being shot. When he found out that the bouncers were indeed still working at Stringers, Alite turned up at the club and promptly shot one of the bouncers in the leg. Three more bouncers came running for Alite and he shot all three of them. Then he walked calmly into the club and pointed his gun at the manager's head, to further impress his point. Stringers soon joined the bouncers' 'union'.

In 1990, John Gotti Sr was arrested again, this time for the Castellano murder as well as racketeering and four other murder charges. The Teflon Don had survived four other cases but the fifth was to prove one too many. The tipping point came with the testimony of his underboss, Sammy 'The Bull' Gravano, who informed on his boss after hearing FBI tapes of Gotti Sr linking him to several murders. Gotti Sr was convicted in 1992 and sentenced to life in prison.

With its head cut off, the new style Mafia organisation Gotti Sr had created, based on media attention and hypocrisy, began to unravel. Everyone began ratting on everyone else. This was also when things started to go wrong for Alite and Junior. Within months of Gotti Sr's imprisonment, a plot was fomenting to take out the ever-unpopular Junior. John Carneglia, along with Mafia captains Nicky Corozzo and Danny Marino, were in on the scheme, according to Alite. And it wasn't long before he himself was approached.

Johnny Carneglia was in prison at the time, so his brother, a sadistic killer called Charles Carneglia, broached the subject with Alite, who thought about it for a while before agreeing. As he said in *Gotti's Rules*, 'When I first got involved, I would have died for that family. But the longer I was around them and the more I saw, the less I believed in what they were saying or doing.' He hated the hypocrisy with which they made fortunes from drug money, only to turn on anyone who got caught dealing, calling them 'scumbag drug dealers'. Also, he didn't like Junior's casual violence, which he thought was often unnecessary, unprofessional and sometimes sadistic. He saw the way the wind was blowing. With the Gambino family fractured, Junior's was not the faction to be in. Unpopular, inept and bullying, Junior was not a leader who would survive long without the immediate protection of his father.

Charles Carneglia gave Alite the guns with which to hit Junior – ironically the same weapons that Junior had first lent to Carneglia. Alite stashed the weapons at a friend's tattoo parlour and began to follow Junior's routines to set up the hit. But the plans got leaked to Gotti Sr in prison. Alite believes it was one of the plotters, Nicky Corozzo, who warned Senior of the hit, in return for several hundred thousand dollars. Gotti Sr then got to Charles Carneglia, putting him on the payroll of a car salvage yard he owned. With both men paid off, Carneglia informed Alite that the hit had been cancelled.

Alite knew it wouldn't be long before Junior would find out about the plot and his own life would be forfeited. Although he was still making lots of money with his partner, he started to avoid Junior, using other associates as go-betweens. He also began changing his routines so that he couldn't be pinned to any particular place at any known time. He heard rumours that Junior had put a contract out on him. The hearsay was confirmed when the FBI themselves paid him a visit to tell him they had intelligence that his life was in danger. Alite turned down the FBI's offer of protection, instead deciding to put out a false story that the Feds had played him a tape of two of Junior's associates plotting to kill him. He knew this would give him a buffer against an actual hit if Junior believed the FBI had evidence of the plot.

It worked. Soon after, Junior asked to meet him. Alite arranged the meeting at the Queens racetrack – an open and busy venue where no one would try shooting anyone. But the encounter broke down into an argument in which both threatened to kill the other's brother.

The two former best friends gave each other a wide berth for a year or so before their lives of crime began to catch up with them. Alite had been to jail before but never for a prolonged stretch. But in 1996, he was unfortunate enough to be stopped in a random search with a gun in his car. He was already on parole for illegal possession of a firearm so this would hit him hard. Even worse, he was on bail awaiting trial for an assault charge on two police officers after a fight with an enemy at a restaurant. His lawyer advised him to bundle both charges together and plead guilty, which he did. He was sentenced to just over four years in prison.

In 1998, Junior joined him, receiving a sentence of over six years for racketeering. One of his houses had been raided by the FBI and a list of Mafia members from across the city was found – an embarrassing slip on Junior's part that amply illustrated his inability to lead a crime family. The case also sought to identify him as the acting boss of the Gambino family. Junior decided to plead guilty, against his father's wishes, and made a big show of giving up the life while he served his time.

Not long after Junior's incarceration, Alite was released. He was out of jail in 2002 when John Gotti Sr died in prison after battling cancer for several months. Gotti Sr was sixty-one. He had spent five years at the head of New York's biggest crime family and had become the city's most famous gangster, but his reign had left the Mafia in a shambles and contributed to the demise of its power.

For Alite it was a signal that he needed to get out of the life altogether and that meant leaving the country. He had heard rumours that a case was being built against him in Florida for his activities in Tampa and he knew there was also a case in Brooklyn that he had already been subpoenaed for. There was also the problem with Junior and his faction of the Gambinos. It wouldn't be long, Alite knew, before he was either jailed or murdered: 'I was gonna get the death penalty or I was gonna have to kill a lot of guys and eventually I was going to get killed anyway,' Alite told me. There was another reason as well – if he went on the run, he wouldn't have to rat on all the people he still respected within the life. He spent about a year making careful preparations and in 2002 left the US.

Alite booked a holiday to St Lucia with his then girlfriend, Rochine. After six days on the beach, he announced that he wouldn't be returning home with her. He spent the next six months travelling the world, trying to stay one step ahead of Interpol and enjoying himself at the same time. After spending some time in Cuba, he then moved on to Colombia and Venezuela. He later flew to Europe, where he visited France, Spain, the Netherlands, Belgium, Greece, Italy and his home country, Albania. He then flew to the Canary Islands and Senegal, where he obtained six fake passports. Back in South America, he visited Argentina, Uruguay and Paraguay before settling down in Rio de Janeiro in Brazil.

Alite moved into an apartment just a block away from the famous Copacabana beach. He quickly established himself in the local community, becoming known as 'American John', and was regularly seen in the local gyms, bars and clubs around Copacabana. He soon met a local woman, a schoolteacher called Rose, and settled down into a relationship. For a year, he led a tranquil and relaxing life in one of the world's most famous beach resorts. But it wasn't to last. It was 2004 when the police caught up with him. Ironically, he had been planning on leaving Rio that very day. He'd heard rumours from local shopkeepers and bartenders that the police had been asking about him. He bought a bus ticket for São Paulo on 23 November with the idea of heading on to Argentina then back up to Colombia and Venezuela.

Alite was headed for the bus station when he ran into a friend, who suggested they have lunch together before he left. They headed for a local deli and Alite sat outside while his friend called his girlfriend on a payphone. Suddenly something felt wrong and Alite knew instantly what it was – the normally bustling street had gone quiet. A helicopter was circling overhead. Before he knew it, a SWAT team of six men with assault rifles was on him, barking at him to lie on the ground.

Alite was taken out of the city in an armoured car to an abandoned warehouse, where he was interrogated by a police officer, who told him that he would be extradited to the US on murder charges. He spent the night in a cage in the basement of the warehouse. It was his first welcome to Brazilian prison hospitality and it wasn't a good one. He desperately needed the toilet but the armed guard above the cage told him to go where he was, so he was forced to take off his shirt and rip it in half, using one part to shit into and the other to wipe. With his shirt off, he was now an open target for the mosquitoes, which along with the odd rat, bit him all night. On top of the discomfort was the anxiety about his future: 'I'm looking and I'm thinking to myself: *Wow, these guys are gonna clip me*' he told me, 'or they're looking at torturing me, or are they gonna really bring me to a prison?'

The next day he was taken to a press conference, where it became clear that his arrest was big news. He gave as little away as possible and was soon transferred to what would be his home for the next year, the infamous Ary Franco prison, which had a reputation for being one of the worst prisons in Brazil. His reception there set the tone for his stay to come. After being taken to a basement level in chains, he was stripped and soundly beaten. He was then marched to his cell past hundreds of baying prisoners, offering to help the new gringo, who was likely to have money. When the guards delivered him to his cell, one of them hit him again. Knowing that first impressions were important in prison, he retaliated. This sent the watching inmates wild and backed up the reputation they'd already heard of him being a dangerous and tough criminal.

Inside his cell conditions were crowded and uncomfortable, with forty inmates inside a space designed for twelve. Most of the prisoners had to sleep on the floor. Alite knew he had to establish himself quickly in the pecking order: 'I walked in and the first thing I said is, "Somebody's giving up a bunk," he told me. 'And they started arguing. I said, "I'll give you two minutes to figure out which one it's taken from." Alite was smart enough to demand a top bunk, because the rats could get to you on the bottom ones. He also wanted one at the back of the cell. The reason for this was even more chilling. He explained to me, 'If you're in one of those front bunks, they can spit alcohol on you and light you on fire.'

Conditions were indeed hellish at Ary Franco, with inmates regularly beaten, tortured and raped by the guards. The jail was overcrowded and insanitary, with dozens of prisoners having to share a single latrine that was no more than a hole in the ground and with the danger of being bitten on the ass by rats. The sewage system was barely functional and human waste leaked from upper floors on to the levels below. The food was rice and beans served from giant buckets crawling with insects. At first, Alite refused to eat but he soon began to lose weight and forced himself to get used to the vile slop.

As with anywhere, in Ary Franco money talked and Alite had plenty. He quickly formed a relationship with a gang leader called Emerson and they used an illicit phone to arrange deliveries from the outside. All the guards were corrupt and they quickly bribed one called Pedro to bring in food and products. The rule was simple – whatever the guards brought in, it was one for Alite and one for them, plus a fee on top. His first order was two Big Macs, two large fries, one large pizza and six beers. He and Emerson ate the meal on a patio area near the cell and felt like normal people for a brief period.

Death could find anyone at any time in Ary Franco. The only way to survive the harsh regime was to have a group of people you could trust. Alite soon found this with a gang of other foreign inmates, who all watched each other's backs. He explained, 'What we did was we formed a close-knit group of guys. We stayed together, we worked together, we bribed together, we survived together. If we had to hurt somebody, we did it together and we tried to mind our business and get by. There's a bond like somebody going away to war when we're saving each other's lives and looking out for each other.'

It was a good idea to keep your head down and go unnoticed. Unfortunately, Alite was spotted by the wrong people, which led to trouble. His scheme of bribing guards was becoming so successful that it was beginning to rival the warden's own corrupt system, where produce bought from his special 'cantina' lined his pocket. As a warning to Alite and Emerson, the warden had their young gofer, Marcello, beaten so badly he was hospitalised. Alite decided to respond by encouraging other inmates to boycott the warden's canteen. He had now put himself directly in the firing line and it wasn't long before his own time for a beating came. Fortunately, though, the friendly guard, Pedro, warned him and Emerson came up with the uncomfortable idea of stashing a knife – rapped in rags and greased with oil – inside Alite's rectum in preparation for the upcoming fight.

As Pedro had warned, Alite was soon removed and taken to a dark cell in a remote part of the prison. As *Gotti's Rules* tells the story, Alite was stripped and searched but the guards didn't find the knife. He was left alone in the darkness and quickly removed the knife, which had a string attached for 'easy' access. Not long after, the door swung open and two of the warden's trustees entered – hulking inmates serving life sentences who did whatever the warden ordered in return for privileges. Unfortunately for them, they weren't expecting a man with a knife. Alite was on the first man in a split second, knifing him repeatedly until he was a bleeding mess on the floor. The second trustee took one slash to the stomach before he decided to make a hasty retreat.

The plan had worked but the warden now had his sights on Alite. Fortunately for him, the warden was himself the target of someone else. In a riot in another part of the prison, the warden was shot and killed. It turned out that the riot was set up by the deputy warden to get rid of his superior so he could move up the ladder. Such riots were common in Ary Franco, according to Alite, and nearly always involved multiple deaths: 'During riots you're watching twelve and sixteen or forty guys get killed,' Alite told me. 'And you know, it's no joke when lights go off and there's fires all over the prison, and they're coming for you.'

A new warden replaced the murdered one. He wanted to end corruption at Ary Franco, so he too didn't last long. Alite had tried to warn the new man, as he explained: 'One of the new wardens came in to see us. We were downstairs and he's like, "I'm gonna work with you guys and stop corruption." And we told him, "Listen, you're a nice guy, get the fuck out of here. We don't want you to stop corruption and you're gonna get yourself killed."'

Alite was right. Just a few months later, the new warden was gunned down while walking his daughter to school. The deputy warden now got the top job that all his hard work had paid for. The new warden wanted the troublemaking Alite out of his jail and in late 2006, he was transferred to Bangu, a federal prison just outside Rio. At Bangu he was greeted with a customary beating and thrown into solitary confinement. But his connections and cash soon got him out of there and into a minimum-security prison for wealthy inmates on the border with Paraguay. He wasn't there long before he was flown back to the US.

With conditions in Brazilian jails being so harsh, you would think that Alite would have been fighting to get back to his home country but the reverse was true. He had been battling extradition because being tried in the US would likely lead to a life – or possibly even a death sentence. But in December 2006, he lost his extradition battle and was flown to Tampa, where the Florida FBI had prepared a case against him. Back home, he quickly learned that the Florida and New York authorities were squabbling over who would bring the case against him. He also got hold of his case documents and discovered just how many of his former associates had betrayed him while he'd been away. A total of fifty-four guys had ratted on him, Alite told me, while he'd been languishing in a prison cell in Brazil. That knowledge certainly helped him make his next decision.

In 2008, he cut a plea deal and told the prosecutors everything he knew about the Gottis and the Gambino crime family. His testimony led to the arrest of Junior and a dozen other mob guys, including Charles Carneglia, one of the conspirators to kill Junior. Only Junior and Carneglia chose not to plead guilty. That meant Junior would be going up against Alite in court. It was a showdown that had long been coming.

Junior's trial took place in September 2009 in the federal courthouse in lower Manhattan. The reporters had been rubbing their hands in anticipation of the showpiece trial and it didn't disappoint. Dirty laundry was aired in public, such as when Alite admitted that he and Vicky had had 'feelings' for each other. Vicky, who was now a writer and had her own reality TV show, *Growing Up Gotti*, told the press, 'The only feelings I have for John Alite were that I despised him.' Alite was brutally honest, about his own crimes as much as Junior's. When asked how many people he had shot, he answered, 'I shot about thirty-five guys. I was involved in probably forty-five shootings.'

To discredit Alite, Junior's defence attorneys tried to pin on him the murder of a young woman who had been lured to a motel room for sex before being strangled to death. This was a lie, according to Alite, who said that everyone in the Gambino family knew it had been Vincent Gotti, John Gotti Sr's brother. Alite went on to detail the events of the murder as told to him by Junior himself. At this point things got personal. *Gotti's Rules* tells of how, on the way out of the courtroom, Junior mouthed, 'We're gonna kill you,' to Alite, who responded, 'You got something you want to say to me?' Junior then lost it, screaming, 'You're a dog! Did I kill little girls, you fag? You're a punk. You're a dog all your life. You always were. Did I strangle little girls in motels?'

It could have been part natural reaction and part cynical attempt to fix the idea of Alite as the girl's killer in the peoples' minds. Whichever way, it backfired and showed everyone the violent side of Junior's nature that he was trying so hard to hide. Junior's whole defence rested on the claim that he had walked away from the life after being imprisoned in 1998 and that he no longer wanted anything to do with crime or violence.

In November 2008, the jury retired to deliberate their decision. The debates lasted. The jury told the judge they couldn't come to a unanimous decision on any of the three counts. They were encouraged by the presiding official to keep trying. Again, they said they were unable to come to a decision and were pressed to try once more. Finally, after three weeks, the jury said they saw no way of coming to a unanimous decision. The judge was forced to declare a hung jury and a mistrial. Junior's lawyer immediately applied for bail and, after paying a $2 million bond, Junior walked out of the court a free man. He had faced four trials and all had resulted in hung juries. In 2010 the government decided not to attempt a retrial, meaning Junior had succeeded in doing what his father, the 'Teflon Don', had not – he had beaten the Feds for good and would not die in prison.

Alite, on the other hand, faced a possible life sentence for his own charges of racketeering and murder. In 2011 in Tampa, he was sentenced to ten years in prison. He had already served nearly six years and was released the following year, 2012. His punishment had been severely curtailed, thanks to his plea deal and testimony against Junior and the other mobsters.

Despite the threats to his life, he returned to live in New Jersey, doing nothing to hide himself from the many people who wanted him dead. He had decided to live a new life outside of crime, teaching young people to avoid the life that drew him in despite his initial efforts to avoid it. Presently, he has four children with two different wives and does his best to make the family situation work.

Looking back on his time with the Gottis, he doesn't bother to hide his dislike of Junior, whom he sees as a weak personality born into a privileged position that he didn't earn, and who wasn't respected by any of the real gangsters around him. He has a better opinion of John Gotti Sr, whom he regarded as a genuine tough guy, but not a proper crime family boss: 'His guys were bringing in all kinds of money from heroin, construction,' Alite told me. 'He never made a penny from anything. Sammy made the construction money. Guys like Johnny Carneglia made the heroin money, guys like Mark Reiter. But John himself, you know, he wasn't capable. He was capable of running a gang, he wasn't capable of running the mob.'

Ultimately Alite blames Gotti Sr for the demise of the Mafia in New York by breaking all the rules that had kept the organisation running smoothly for decades. First by killing Gambino boss, Paul Castellano, without the agreement of the other families, secondly by courting the media, and thirdly by putting the Gotti name above the rest of the organisation, sacrificing anyone and everyone, no matter how close, if they got in the way of his family's personal ambitions. The result of all these policies was a lack of trust that ultimately had everyone ratting on everyone else and everyone going to jail.

His own experiences with violence led to Alite suffering PTSD, for which he sees a counsellor on a regular basis. His reputation means he has to constantly deal with people trying to goad him into a reaction: 'I got people that test my ego every day,' he told me. 'They say I'm nobody, I was nobody, I'm a punk, I'm not tough, I'm full of shit. I just gotta smile and leave, because I got a second chance in life. Only a fool will go for that bait.'

Alite has the same impulses he always had, it's just that now he has learned to control them. But some days are still difficult: 'There's days when I'm in the house and I'll talk to my girlfriend. I'm like, "I can't let something go." And I just work through it. I'll talk to my therapist and I keep it moving. And I say to myself, "I like myself now. I'm proud of what I do. I like what I do. I like that I'm trying to save kids."'

Alite travels around the world speaking in schools and to other gatherings of children and young people, talking about the dangers of gang life and advising them on ways to stay out of it. He recently helped a young British man who had got involved in gang wars. The young man's best friend had been killed and his father reached out to Alite to try and stop him seeking revenge. Alite spent several FaceTime sessions talking the youngster out of killing the person who had murdered his best friend: 'I could say one thing,' Alite told me, 'if I can't say I saved anybody else, I saved one person's life.'

Alite's biggest advice to anyone finding themselves on the edge of a life of crime is not to react when their buttons get pushed. As he said at one of his talks, 'If you let somebody control your destiny, you're a fool and the important part in life is you control your destiny, nobody else.'

It was a lesson that he himself learned the hard way. After all his failed attempts to escape the streets, it seemed a life of crime was his destiny. But that wasn't the case. After many years of crime, violence and suffering, Alite finally learned that the only true destinies are the ones we make ourselves, as he is now doing.

3

Joey Barnett

Thirty-Five Years in UK Prison

A seriously violent and drug-addicted criminal, who faced a life sentence for armed robbery and possession of firearms

Joey Barnett felt the fear turning to hot panic as he heard the judge at London Crown Court read out the sentences of his co-defendants – ten years, thirteen years, fifteen years. His turn was about to come and he knew it was going to be big – double figures at the very least. He and his notorious gang had carried out over 150 armed robberies in just three years, fuelled by a crack habit that was costing him thousands daily at its height. Barnett was the gang's point man, always first into the bank, blasting his gun into the ceiling to cause maximum shock and fear.

Now the judge was turning to him. 'Right, Mr Barnett . . .'

Suddenly he knew that he couldn't hear that unbearable sentence read aloud. He had to do something, anything. Before he had time to think, Barnett found himself leaping out of the dock and into the courtroom.

Pandemonium ensued. The courtroom was packed with legal teams, friends and family, press and armed police. Everyone started moving, shouts and screams filled the air. The judge disappeared immediately through a door behind him and security guards leapt into action. But the guards were big and burly and Barnett was small, lithe and nimble. He leapt across the tables, on to the judge's bench and headed straight for one of the exits.

The door was blocked by a security guard, double the size of Barnett. But Joey's desperation propelled him with super strength towards the big man. He rugby-tackled him, sending him sprawling to the floor, then trampled over him and through the exit.

Finding himself in a long corridor, Barnett ran for his life. Incredibly, near the end of the corridor, through a revolving door, he could see the street outside. He reached the doors with the police and security guards close behind. Like a scene from a comedy movie, he entered a cubicle of the revolving doors while his pursuers filled up the cubicles behind. He made it through. Then he was out on the street and sprinting.

'I was a dangerous man,' Joey Barnett told me in our interview, 'a very dangerous man.' With a tattoo covering one side of his face, he certainly looks dangerous and his record backs up his appearance. With his fellow gang members, he was one of the UK's most prolific armed robbers in the late 1990s, regularly hitting targets that provided £40,000–50,000 in loot. And the scale of their crack habit meant that regular bank jobs were necessary.

'For about three years or so we was out at least four times a week committing robberies, armed robberies,' Barnett told me. 'I just could not seem to get off the ride. It was too fast.'

But even before he got into his crack and armed robbery habit, he was no stranger to trouble. First arrested at age eleven, Joey had spent most of his life in and out of institutions. Counting up his total sentences in one of our interviews, fifty-three-year-old Barnett estimated that he had spent thirty-five of those years behind bars, with only three prisons in the country that he hadn't visited.

Like so many similar crime stories, Joey's started with coming from a broken home. Born in 1968 in South London, he was raised in the poor area of Tooting. His father was an ex-army mechanic-turned-truck driver. His mother's family was large and came from a traveller background. Her father was a drinker and a hardman, who used to fistfight at the local fairs. Barnett remembers most of his uncles being in and out of institutions for criminal acts while he was growing up. He had two older sisters, Pamela and Angela. 'I'm the only son so I was the apple of my mum's eye,' he told me, 'I was her world and she was my world and I was spoilt absolutely rotten.'

After twenty years in the army, Joey's father was a strict disciplinarian who used his belt to impose a regime of fear on the children. 'I was petrified of him,' Barnett told me. Joey's reaction was to rebel outside of the family home. He started smoking at the age of eight. At school he was uncontrollable and was expelled at nine years old, receiving visits from a state-provided home tutor. This didn't work either and education largely bypassed the young Joey, who would later learn to read and write as an adult in prison.

At around this time, Barnett's father moved out and his stepdad entered his life. John had a fearsome reputation locally for knifing people after pub brawls. On one occasion, he had taken a sword back to a pub where a fight had occurred and 'started chopping everyone up,' in Barnett's words. Whereas Joey's biological father had used violence to discipline his children, his new stepdad took his violence out on the house, especially when he was drunk: 'He used to come home and he used to smash the house to pieces right in front of us,' Barnett told me. 'I'm not talking about smashing the table. I'm talking like the windows, the front windows, the back windows, the TV . . . He used to throw things and I remember once he threw a china plate at my mum's head. I was around nine, and it hit her in the eye and all her eye was hanging out.'

The violence always happened if John went to the pub after work and stayed there all evening. 'I was a nervous wreck,' Barnett told me. 'Four or five o'clock each night if he wasn't home, me and my sister, we'd run up into the bedroom. We'd both be in the same bed. We'd be cuddling each other. We'd be shaking and crying our eyes out.' He added that he has been diagnosed with PTSD from the stress of those occasions.

Sometimes Barnett's dad would come back while John was in the house and then terrible fights would break out. On several occasions, John tried to stab Joey's dad with a kitchen knife, chasing him down the street with the weapon, once slicing him badly on the elbow.

Joey experienced his stepdad's propensity for weapons first-hand after a terrible incident with some local dogs. A Hindu Indian family down the street had three dogs, a whippet, a greyhound and a wolfhound. Joey loved dogs and used to knock on the family's door and ask to take the dogs for a walk. On one occasion nobody answered, so Barnett decided to hop over the back garden wall to get the dogs himself.

The canines attacked him viciously. The greyhound jumped up and latched on to his face, pulling him down, while the whippet went for his eye. Thankfully his screams attracted the neighbours, who quickly jumped in, but his face was cut up badly and he needed a skin graft at the hospital. Several days after his release with his face still covered in stitches, there was a knock on the door: it was the pet owners complaining that someone had killed their dogs. It turned out that John had gone to their house, jumped over the back wall and chopped the three dogs up with a fireman's axe.

The situation with Barnett's stepdad culminated in disaster after one of his usual nights at the pub. Unusually, Joey's mum decided that they wouldn't hang around waiting for the inevitable violence but would spend the night at a friend's house just a few doors down. Barnett takes up the story: 'It's probably around nine, ten o'clock. We went to the front window, was looking out the front window to see if he was out there. And I couldn't believe my eyes, the house was in about a hundred foot of flames, on fire. I heard the sirens. I see the blue lights. My mum said, "No, no, don't go out front." He was still out the front, screaming, "Where are you? Where are you? I'm gonna fucking kill you!"'

John was imprisoned for eighteen months but the damage had already been done. Joey was now stealing cars and motorbikes whenever he could get the chance. He was in and out of the local police station and courts, where everyone, even the judges, were soon on a first name basis with him.

Barnett remembers one occasion when he stole a motorbike, aged thirteen, and was riding it up the pavement just around the corner from Tooting police station. Rounding the bend, Joey crashed straight into a policeman, sending him flying and injuring his face. He managed to get away but the next day the police turned up at his house. The local constabulary knew him so well that the injured policeman had identified him immediately.

On another occasion, the thirteen-year-old Barnett was driving a stolen car, propped up by a cushion so he could see over the steering wheel. As he pulled up at a red light, he turned to see a familiar face in the car waiting next to him: it was his headmaster.

'He was staring at me, staring, and he kept looking at me,' Barnett told me. 'I thought, *Oh no, oh no, oh no*. But yeah, a few miles up the road blue lights came behind me.' Barnett didn't stop and a police chase ensued. Joey drove the car on to Tooting Bec Common, swerving his way through the joggers and dog walkers with the police in hot pursuit. He then drove the vehicle into the woods, where the police in their bigger cars dared not follow. Barnett and friends abandoned the smashed-up car and fled from the scene, still wearing their school uniforms. They were soon spotted by police scouring the common, but somehow got away without being arrested.

'My mate had a good idea,' Barnett told me. 'He said, "We've come over here to look at the trees and the leaves because we're doing a programme on it. We're doing a study on it in school."'

Joey's small size made him ideal for fitting through tiny windows, enabling older teenagers to burgle houses and commercial properties. He remembers him and his friends breaking into a yoghurt factory just to gorge themselves on the produce and a similar excursion to a marzipan factory.

Now he knows he was professionally groomed by the older children, but at the time he loved the attention and the respect that came from hanging out with older kids with big reputations. 'I wouldn't say no to no one,' Barnett told me. 'I just didn't know how to say no. And I thought this is where I'm getting all my attention. This is obviously where I want to go, this is where I want to be. But these older boys have given me so much love and attention, it's like a second family to me.'

With the escalating nature of his crimes it was inevitable that Barnett would soon get his first custodial sentence. It came when he was thirteen. The judge sentenced him to three months in a detention centre for underage offenders in Surrey.

JOEY BARNETT

At HMP Send, he encountered a brutal regime run along the lines of an army camp. New inmates had their hair shaved off and were expected to march everywhere. They were repeatedly punched and slapped by some of the guards and put to menial tasks such as scrubbing corridors with toothbrushes. The guards were so secure in their brutality that one of them hit Barnett in the face just before a visit from his mother, so that he met his mum with blood all over his face. He was instructed to tell her that he had fallen over otherwise he would face worse consequences.

On release, he came back to a changed home. His stepdad was gone and his dad was back. What's more, his mum was in hospital after being diagnosed with breast cancer: 'I remember coming out of the hospital and crying my eyes out,' Barnett told me. His mum had her breast removed but while she was in hospital, Barnett was in for another bad surprise. 'One day in the afternoon I've come home from school, I knocked on the front door and my dad answered the door. I went into the front room and there was two police officers and three doctors in white coats.' The men had come to take him to Long Grove, a mental institution in Surrey. While his mum was in hospital, his father had had Joey committed to a psychiatric hospital in accordance with a section of the UK's Mental Health Act.

'I remember being put on a ward and there was loads of other patients on this ward,' said Barnett, 'but I was the youngest on this ward. I was the only kid on there. Everyone was like in their forties, fifties, sixties, seventies, eighties.' The older patients shuffled around in a daze most of the time, talking to themselves and sometimes playing with themselves sexually. To thirteen-year-old Barnett, it was highly traumatising. At the same time he was receiving daily injections to keep him subdued. The drugs made him feel different, in a kind of permanent haze, and he struggled to talk.

After three weeks, he knew that he had to get out of there. He got up in the early hours of the morning and managed to squeeze himself through a tiny window in the toilets. After escaping the grounds, he managed to find the local train station and jump a train back home, while still wearing his institutional pyjamas. When he got home, he was greeted by his mum, back from hospital: 'We fell into each other's arms. I was hysterical, I was really, really upset, and Angela was crying and we was hugging each other. I was saying, "Mum, Mum, please don't send me back there."'

She promised not to and when the police and doctors turned up, she refused to let him go. The authorities agreed not to take Joey away if he would agree to a psychological test at another hospital. Barnett was seen by a psychologist, who diagnosed him with nothing more than being hyperactive: he would not have to go back to Long Grove.

Despite all this, Barnett was soon back to burgling houses, crawling in through small windows to let his older friends in the front door. He was arrested again and sentenced to three years at Feltham Young Offender Institution, which meant he would get no remission and would have to serve every day of the three years. But after the terrors of Send and Long Grove, Feltham was a breeze to fifteen-year-old Barnett: 'It was nothing like a borstal, nothing like what I'd been through. It was like a holiday camp and it became fun for me. It wasn't a deterrent.'

There were lots of fights at Feltham, which was run like an adult prison. Judgement was usually dispensed in the form of batteries stuffed in socks, smashed over the head of the offending inmate. Despite being skinny, Barnett was game and got in his fair share of altercations. Each wing of the institution was run by a 'daddy', the top dog in that particular section. Barnett was fortunate that the daddy in his wing was a friend from the outside. Another alpha male, a big seventeen-year-old, was a bully who went round taxing the smaller children for their canteens. Barnett was safe from the bully because of his friend, the wing's daddy. But soon his friend was due to leave.

When it happened, the bully targeted Barnett. Joey knew he had to do something so he waited until he saw the bully chatting and laughing with his mates in the association room. He took the square battery from his prison radio, shoved it into a sock and approached the older kid from behind, smashing him over the head with the improvised weapon, splitting his head open and knocking him instantly unconscious.

'I couldn't really have a good fight with my hands because I was small,' Barnett told me, 'but I didn't have no fear because I've seen violence already. I had to compensate for being small so I was a dangerous man because I had to pick things up and hit people. I would hit people with things.'

On his release Barnett was once again embroiled in family troubles. His dad had moved out and his stepdad was back. Then the family received news that his father had died of a heart attack. Not long after, Barnett met his first long-term girlfriend and she quickly fell pregnant. He was seventeen and she was just sixteen.

With a young family of his own, Barnett tried to do the right thing. He got himself a tow truck and started doing breakdown recovery work. It was now the late eighties and the rave scene was taking the UK by storm, the so-called 'Second Summer of Love' with its illegal warehouse parties fuelled by repetitive beats and the new drug, Ecstasy. Joey got into DJing and was soon getting gigs at pubs around London with equipment he'd stolen from his friend's dad.

Life settled down and Barnett had two more children and moved to a council house in Cambridge. But after a couple of years he missed his family and social circles in London and felt himself drawn irresistibly back to the city. He organised a mutual exchange of council houses and the family moved to Stevenage on the outskirts of North London. Soon, Barnett was being pulled back into more than just the city. He met a guy at the local pub who was an armed robber and he soon talked Joey into joining his escapades.

Their first job together was on a scrapyard, where his friend had previously dropped off some copper. He'd seen a glimpse of the safe as the owner had opened it, revealing thousands of pounds of cash inside. The plan was simple – Barnett's friend would go inside armed with his .38 revolver and take the cash while Barnett waited outside in the getaway car. The only sticky feature was that the scrapyard was full of big men who wouldn't be best pleased with handing over their money. But Joey's friend seemed confident, so Barnett went along with it. Barnett tells the story: 'He had wads and wads and wads of money as he got back in the car. And I've put the car in first gear and I've tried to wheel spin off. I've looked around me and I've seen all these blokes running out of the yard. There must have been ten blokes with hands like shovels. I thought, *Oh my God, I'm so lucky I didn't go in there and get caught because if they'd have took the gun off him, we'd have got bashed right up.*'

Barnett began living a double life, towing breakdowns by day and doing armed robberies in his spare time. But the partnership ended when Joey found his friend injecting heroin in his car outside Joey's house. Barnett didn't want things like that going on outside the family home so he told his colleague where to go. He didn't see him again for several weeks so he decided to pop round to his house. Once there he found out from the man's partner that he was much more dangerous than Barnett had assumed. It turned out he had been jailed for life for murder and had been let out on licence. However, he had recently been recalled and was back in prison. Barnett panicked, thinking he would be implicated in the armed robberies, and decided to move house again, this time to Enfield, a borough in North London.

In Enfield, he managed to stay out of trouble while getting his adrenaline kick from banger racing, a sport where old second-hand cars are souped up and raced around tracks, smashing each other up in the process. Barnett had been stealing cars since he was a child so he was an excellent racer, but he didn't bargain for how vindictively violent the sport could become. Joey's team, the 'Suicide Squad', had a fierce rivalry with another team, the 'North London Nuts', who had started painting their cars in the same colours as Barnett's team. The rivalry played out on the track, where the opposing cars began to deliberately target each other with shunts, bumps and crashes, until finally the ill will spilled out into the pits.

'There was a big argument and a massive fight broke out shortly after,' Barnett said. 'We was hitting each other with monkey wrenches, spanners, hammers . . . it was like a fucking spaghetti western in these pits, it was fucking crazy. The fight went on for about twenty minutes, half an hour, and it was all about colours.' The craziness got too much even for Barnett when he saw a friend's car stalled on a bend. He takes up the story: 'I've seen another member from the other team. He stopped at the top of the bend, put it in first, gone through the gears. He's hit him with so much force the roll cage dropped down and you've got a big water tank, which you've got to put in the front of the cars because you're not allowed to run with radiators. So the pipes had split on the water tank. He had twenty gallons of boiling hot water going on to both of his legs.'

The man had to be cut out of the vehicle and flown to hospital in an air ambulance. Barnett gave up banger racing after the incident, but his own life was about to take a disastrous turn. In 1996, his mother was diagnosed with secondary cancer. By the time she was taken into hospital, it had spread all over her body: 'She died in my arms,' he told me. 'I put her in my arms and I was going forward and she died. All my family was in the room. It gave me a breakdown. It broke me in half.'

Joey's mum had always been the centre of his world, his one rock in an emotionally unstable upbringing. Now he was a time bomb. Just a few weeks later he split up with his girlfriend and moved out of the family home. He moved into a house with some former friends and developed a crack habit. Some of them in the ten-person house were into armed robbery and they let Joey into their team, showing him how to load and fire weapons, from revolvers to shotguns. They were robbing banks, building societies and post offices on a regular basis and soon had their routine down to a fine art.

'I was the one going in there first,' Barnett told me. 'I had a .38 revolver. My other [co-defendant] had a side-by-side .410 shotgun. I was letting shots off in the roof before he's going in there to show that we mean business. We was in there for no more than two minutes maximum and we'd be gone, in the car, change cars, out of our clothes, on a bike, in another van, we was home.'

The armed robberies and crack smoking turned into a vicious circle, each one feeding the other. Barnett was already spending £2,000 a day on the drug and together the gang was burning through so much of it that their crack dealer moved in with them. 'It's a very needy type of drug,' Joey explained. 'So basically, you'll put one crack stone on to the pipe. You'll light it, you'll smoke that and the buzz will last you for about two minutes. And two minutes later, you want another one.'

The crack, along with the gang's success and reputation, made Barnett and his friends feel like nothing could stop them. 'I actually thought I was invincible,' he told me. 'I thought I was untouchable. I thought no one can come nowhere near me. If the police come outside and it comes on top, there's gonna be a shoot-out, one of us is going to die. So that's the measures which I was prepared to go to for drugs.'

He and his friends began taxing drug dealers on a street in Brixton, which he described as 'the frontline for drug dealers'. They would pick up dealers in a pretend taxi, asking for crack, with Barnett posing as a taxi driver. As soon as the dealer was in the back of the car, they would pull out their weapons and take all his crack and money: 'We had people all around the place looking for us to kill us,' he told me. 'We just didn't care because everywhere we went, I had a gun on me. As I said, I didn't care if I got shot or got killed.'

According to Barnett, both his sisters were so worried about him that on several occasions they conspired to call the police and have him arrested for his own safety. They had ample opportunity one day when Joey visited his sister Angela's house. On the spur of the moment he decided he wanted to commit an armed robbery but unfortunately his own car had broken down. He asked Angela if he could borrow her car and when she asked him why, he told her he needed to pick up a friend: 'I've took her car and committed an armed robbery in my sister's car. I got away with it, got back, all the police had come around, pulled my sister in and said there's been an armed robbery committed in this car.'

On another occasion, Barnett had a row with his friends and decided to go off and do a bank robbery on his own. He climbed on his Yamaha R1, a 1000cc motorbike that could reach speeds of up to 190mph. After tucking his Browning 9mm revolver into a light jacket and wearing just shorts and flip-flops, he took off on the bike. It was an unplanned spur-of-the-moment job and the bank had cameras outside. As soon as they spotted Barnett coming in, staff hit the panic button and the shutters came down, the alarms went off and the doors locked behind him. Now he was trapped inside the bank with no access to the money and with the police on their way.

'As luck had it, I had a full clip inside my gun,' he told me, 'so I had to blow the doors off. I blew the doors off and it blew a massive hole beside the lock and basically the door just crumbled.' He had left the motorbike running outside so he jumped on and sped off. Heading up the A3 dual carriageway near Cobham to get home, he saw blue flashing lights in his rear-view mirror and knew the police were after him.

'I was just opening this bike up to maximum speed, and I don't know what made me do it, but I looked at the clocks and it said 178mph, and I had sandals on and a pair of flip-flops. Something come over me and suddenly I said, if a pebble comes on the road you're dead, it's going to throw you up like a rag doll, you're going to be in pieces. But because I could see the sirens coming from behind me, there's nothing I could do apart from opening this bike up and try and gain distance on them.'

Within minutes a helicopter had joined the pursuit. Now there would be no pulling away from the hunters. In desperation, Barnett took the next exit from the dual carriageway: 'At this time I was probably doing, coming down to about 130 miles an hour,' he said. 'When I've seen this turn-off, I quickly slammed it down through the gears, went on to my brakes a little bit and ragged the bike over on to this turn-off. How I didn't lose control I will never ever, ever know.' Coming off the main road, Barnett spotted a large supermarket and, on instinct, pulled into the car park, left the bike and helmet outside and dashed inside the shop.

'I can just about hear the sirens coming to the supermarket, so I was running around the aisles all on my own. I don't know what I looked like. I was running up and down the aisles and I thought, *What am I going to do? How am I going to get away?* So I went up to the clothing aisle, I ripped the alarms off a tracksuit, I put the tracksuit on, I put a cap on, a pair of silly glasses, and I walked out of the supermarket. And as I walked out of the supermarket, there must have been thirty armed police. The helicopter was above me and I walked straight out of this car park, I put my head down and I started singing to myself and I was skipping along the road.'

The escapade should have provided a warning about how out of control Joey had become but, as he told me, he was on the ride now and it was too fast to get off. Another warning came when the flat he was sharing was raided by police. He and his friends returned home late one day to find their neighbour warning them not to go inside. When they asked why, the neighbour told them armed police had been waiting outside all day, accompanied by two ambulances and snipers on the roof.

Now the gang knew the police were on to them but it didn't stop them or even slow them down. The inevitable came after another spur-of-the-moment, unplanned robbery on a post office in Croydon, South London. The gang had woken up after a long night's partying with no crack or money left. After facing the gazes of their girlfriends, they tramped outside to find some more cash.

Inside a post office, Joey fired his customary warning shot into the ceiling but on this occasion the staff – a middle-aged Hindu couple – were too quick for them. They pushed the panic button, bringing the shutters down, locking the doors behind them. The only other customer was a Chinese man. Barnett grabbed him and shoved his revolver under the man's chin, threatening to kill him. But the couple behind the counter were unmoved, evidently preferring to see the man shot than relinquish the money. In desperation, the gang shot out the double-glazed window at the front of the shop so that they could escape. But once outside, they heard the sirens rapidly approaching.

They bundled into separate cars and headed off, while hastily changing their clothes. But now a helicopter was in pursuit. Barnett told the driver to stop near a bridge and he and his two friends jumped out. 'Within a few seconds of getting out the car, I just remember really vividly the helicopter came down. There was armed police everywhere. We were surrounded. There are probably around twenty to thirty police. They're all armed up. "Get on the floor! Get on the floor!" Red dots all over us.'

Barnett and the gang were questioned about thirty-five armed robberies and eventually charged with seven. It turned out the newest member of the gang, whom Joey had invited on board out of compassion, was a paid police informant and much of his testimony helped to bring the charges against them. The informant, James, had spun Joey a sob story about a house burglary that had gone wrong. He had claimed that the owners of the house had got wind of who had robbed them and turned up at James's house when only his girlfriend and their baby were at home. Apparently, the men had put the three-month-old baby into the washing machine and threatened to turn it on unless his girlfriend gave them James's whereabouts. Shocked by the story, Barnett had invited James on to the fatal post office job in Croydon to help make him some money. It was a typical spur-of-the-moment, warm-hearted decision from Joey, but one which would cost him years in prison.

By the time the trial came round in 1998 the gang had cut a deal with the Crown Prosecution Service to plead guilty to three armed robberies and have the other four charges dropped. Before that they had been facing life sentences, now they were looking at double figures.

On the day of sentencing at London Crown Court, Barnett listened with mounting dread as his co-defendants' sentences were read out, until he could take it no longer. He jumped from the dock, running around the courtroom and down the corridor, through the revolving doors to freedom outside.

Once on the street, Barnett ran for his life. Slim, fit and fast, he soon left the chasing police and security guards for dust. He ran for nearly two miles until he found himself at Elephant and Castle. Spotting the tube station across a roundabout, he headed across the busy road. As he was crossing he noticed a black cab driving straight towards him but thought nothing of it . . . until the last moment. 'Bang! He's done me,' said Barnett. 'He took both my legs out. I'm on the floor fucking covered in blood and three jailers and security guards got out of the back of the taxi and nicked me and put me in handcuffs in the middle of Elephant and Castle.' Realising they couldn't keep up with the whippet-like Barnett, the guards had hailed down a black cab and caught up with him at Elephant and Castle, where they spotted him crossing the road and ordered the taxi driver to run him over.

Back behind bars, Joey still didn't know what his sentence was. He would now have to be tried at the Old Bailey for attempting to escape custody. In the end he received just six months for the attempted escape but for the armed robberies he received eleven and a half years, meaning a total of twelve years behind bars.

Barnett was classified as a Category A prisoner and his first stay was in London's maximum-security Belmarsh prison. He soon got a reputation as a troublemaker but earned favour with some of the guards by attacking paedophiles. Because of this, and his solid reputation for never snitching, some of the guards grew to trust him enough to slip him details of which new inmates were paedophiles or rapists. Armed with this hit list, he would enact swift and painful retribution. One of his first jobs was a man facing trial on hideous charges: 'I've got the information from a screw that he'd killed his nan,' Barnett told me. 'He held her body in his flat for a week and he put candles around the outside of her, and he was having sex with her when she was dead.'

Barnett entered the man's cell and smashed him over the back of the head with a tin of tuna in a sock. Unfortunately, the man didn't go down and it turned into a fistfight in which the necrophiliac – a bigger man – started to get the better of Joey. Barnett was forced to call in his friend Tony, who had been guarding the door. With Tony now holding the granny killer by the neck, he was finally able to dispense some proper justice: 'I was just bam, bang, bang, bang, bang,' Barnett told me, 'and I was punching him for about five minutes. Every time I was hitting him it felt like I was hitting a calf or a cow, like a bit of frozen meat. I was pile driving him. I must have hit him about ten times all around the kidney – "Oh, oh, oh!" Every time he was doing that as I was hitting him.'

On another occasion, Barnett got a paedophile as he was just emerging from his cell. Joey had filled a jug with boiling water and put a pound of sugar in it. As the man walked through the door, Joey caught him with the water in the face, which it disfigured like napalm. This was a common form of assault in prisons because sugar and water were easy to come by and the dissolved sugar helped the water cling to the skin and melt the flesh.

Next, Barnett was sent to a brand-new Category B prison in Staffordshire called Dovegate in 2001. The prison was so new that Joey was only one of two prisoners in the entire jail when he arrived. After two weeks one of his co-defendants arrived at the prison and the two settled down to enjoy the relative peace of an empty jail. The guards weren't full-time prison officers but relatively untrained security staff from a private security company. Barnett's colleague seduced one of the female guards and began having an affair with her. She started smuggling in supplies from the outside world, everything from drugs to mobile phones, and for six months Joey and his friend lived the high life until they were reported by another inmate and dragged off to the segregation unit.

Barnett was transferred to another Category B prison, Swaleside in Kent. According to him, Swaleside was a dumping ground for all the troublemakers that the other Category B prisons couldn't handle. He described it as the 'naughtiest' prison he has ever been to. There was no work in Swaleside and a lot of addicts – there was so much heroin that inmates called the jail 'Brownside'. The prison was rife with stabbings and the suicide rate was high. Prisoners were slashing their wrists and hanging themselves at an alarming rate – Barnett witnessed three suicides in the twelve months he spent there. Stabbings were so common that during exercise, inmates would stuff hardback books into their belts to protect their torsos from knife thrusts.

Barnett witnessed the violence first-hand when a prisoner was transferred who had testified against another inmate. It was clear that something bad was going to happen to the newbie, but no one could have predicted just how bad. Barnett tells the story: 'The guy had been in the kitchen all day long and he had a big pot like that, massive pot, and it was full up with oil, fucking bubbling . . . This poor guy, he was sitting in the association room watching telly, just like we are now. And this other guy come from behind him with this pot of fat and just sat it on his head, boiling-hot fat that had been in the pan for like hours, boiling. I'll never ever forget the screams. And his face went from like that to like that. It's melted off, his face has melted off.'

On another occasion, the inmates were talking out of their cell windows at night when two of the prisoners got into an argument. Threats were exchanged but Joey thought nothing of it. In the morning, as soon as the cell doors were opened, one of the men ripped a leg from his table with the nail still sticking out of one end. He rushed into the other man's cell and smashed him round the head with it while he was still sleeping, then retired to his own cell to clean himself up. Hearing about the incident, Joey decided to visit the victim's cell to see what had happened.

'I went inside this cell, I pulled the blanket back,' Barnett told me, 'and he wasn't moving. But it was like green and grey stuff coming down the side of his face from his temple, green and grey. He's dead. It's his brains.'

However, even Swaleside wasn't the worst prison Barnett said he'd visited. That was reserved for Parkhurst on the Isle of Wight, another dumping ground for unmanageable prisoners, but many of the guards were violent bullies pepped up on steroids and weights. And because it was an island community all the wardens knew each other so if one took a dislike to you, they all did. They soon took a dislike to Barnett and had him locked up in segregation for twenty-three hours a day, where they would enter his cell and physically abuse him. He eventually resorted to a dirty protest – smothering himself and his cell with his own crap – to prevent the guards laying their hands on him. Barnett needed to get out of Parkhurst as quickly as possible so he settled on a plan: 'I decided I wanted out of that prison and the quickest way out of that prison would be to get a bucket and fill it up with piss and shit and go into the office and put it over the screw's head. I've been brewing piss and shit up in a bucket for a few days running up to it. I see him in the office, I open the door and I park the bucket over his head. There was piss and shit all over him.'

Barnett was kept in the segregation unit for six months for his troubles but after that, thankfully, he was shipped out. His final destination before release was Maidstone, a Category C prison in Kent. Here, the atmosphere was much more pleasant, with the guards taking a hands-off approach and inmates allowed to cook their own food. He got a job in the print shop and was enjoying the relative freedom. Then, in 2006, just three months before his release, Joey's stepdad died, leaving him a £50,000 inheritance. This wasn't good news for a crack smoker in prison and he was soon wasting all the money on drugs while still inside.

With his crack addiction back with a vengeance, he went straight back to his old ways as soon as he was released. He had spent eight years behind bars and yet it was as if nothing had changed. In just eighteen months, he went through the fifty-grand inheritance and was back to armed robberies to feed his addiction. When he was inevitably arrested, fortunately for him, it was for a job that was much less serious than many of the others he had been doing – a burglary of a commercial warehouse. He was sentenced to three years and found himself back behind bars in Wayland, a Category C prison in Norfolk.

This time Barnett decided to use his time more constructively. He enrolled on an education course and at last learned to read and write. He also became a prison tattooist whose skills became so renowned that even a senior warden asked him for a tattoo – on the sly, of course. He also began Bible studies and completed the Alpha course. One evening coming back from his studies he had a conversion experience where he felt a great warmth and light surrounding him and a voice telling him, 'You're with us now.' He was determined to get off crack, which was a struggle but not nearly as hard as the other substance he had become addicted to: 'I went in with an addiction to crack and I come out of that big sentence with an addiction to heroin,' as he put it.

The problem was that crack was too expensive a habit to maintain in prison whereas heroin was cheaper and had the added benefit of numbing you to your surroundings. Even so, the price of heroin in jail is grossly inflated: 'On the street a £50 bit of heroin would be worth in prison let's say £300–400,' he explained. 'So a gram of heroin on the street is £80–100, now in prison you'd be making £500–600.'

Despite the deep grip of the heroin addiction, Joey was determined to come off the drug. His life, while not perfect, took a distinct turn towards a better path. Joey came out determined to go straight. He enrolled in a methadone programme to help wean him off heroin. It helped that he met his future life partner, Sam, not long after his release. Like him, Sam was struggling with addiction. She'd had a succession of partners who had been violent to her and she had turned to alcohol to numb the pain. Barnett helped her get dry and now the two live together with Sam's two children in Littlehampton on the south coast of England. Incredibly, just a few years after learning to read and write, Barnett wrote a book about his life called *A South London Borstal Boys Tales*. After a six-year struggle he has come off methadone and is now clean of all drugs. He has become a peer mentor for young offenders and has set up his own charity along with Sam to feed homeless people in his area.

'I'm trying to really make amends for what I've done,' Barnett said, 'all the damage what I caused people and all the misery what I put people through. I just feel it's time now for me to give back to the community what I've taken out of it.'

Joey still struggles with his mental health. 'Some days I wake up and I can't even look at people, let alone talk to people on the phone,' he told me. But in general, he says he is the happiest he has been in his life. His beloved mum is gone but he still has his sisters and his extended family, whom he is incredibly close to.

As so often with the people I interview, many of Barnett's problems stemmed from his family upbringing – the suffering he underwent at the hands of his dad and stepdad scarred him for life, but at the same time it was family that eventually saw him through to the other side. Without the love of his mother, sisters and cousins, Barnett wouldn't have made it.

As Joey said, 'They never gave up on me, my family. They love me to bits, I love them to bits, and I've got a great family network around me, unbelievable love.'

4

Ian 'Blink' MacDonald

£6 Million Bank Robber

Involved in robberies, gangland warfare, prisons, stabbings and bombs

Blink scanned the front of the Chinese restaurant for perhaps the hundredth time in half an hour, his hand resting uneasily on the .22 revolver hidden in his pocket. For four weeks now he had been on the run and the paranoia was really beginning to kick in. He knew he had been identified as one of the gang in the bungled £6 million armed bank robbery because the police had recently raided his mother's house. It was now just a matter of time before they caught up with him.

That meant they could be following Sheila, his girlfriend and mother to his two-year-old son. It was a risky move to arrange to meet her at the Poa San restaurant on Glasgow's bustling Alexandra Parade, but he couldn't resist it any longer: he had to see her.

'Did you get followed?' he asked as soon as she sat down at the table.

'Stop being paranoid,' was her irritated reply.

He decided to try to follow her advice, to relax and enjoy a rare evening with his partner. They ordered food and he started to tuck in but just five minutes into the meal, the worry

96

returned. A couple dressed head to toe in denim sat down at a table nearby. He had an instant bad feeling about them.

'Undercover cops,' he whispered through his hands.

But his girlfriend balked at his words. She threatened to walk out if he was going to ruin their meal with his constant paranoia. Blink settled back down and tried to think things through rationally. If the police were on to him, he was done for anyway. They'd have all the exits secured, so there would be no way out. That meant whatever would happen tonight, he should enjoy himself as much as possible – either he was going to have a good night out with Sheila, or he was going to eat and drink as much as possible before being incarcerated for a long time.

As he ordered more food and lager, Ian 'Blink' MacDonald, notorious armed robber and Glasgow gangster, thought back on the long run of misfortunes and fuck-ups that had led him to this place.

It had started when Mick Healy had walked into Ian and Sheila's pub, The Talisman. MacDonald's baby boy had just turned two and Blink had been trying to go straight for some time so when Healy – on the run after escaping Scotland's notorious Shotts prison – walked in, MacDonald knew that temptation, and trouble, would follow.

He was right. Healy had spent some time in Torquay on Devon's south coast. There, he had scoped out a bank that was ripe for doing over. A holding bank for the whole of Devon and Cornwall, it would net them a total of £6 million, split six ways between the men Healy had lined up for the job. He cut quickly to the chase – did MacDonald want to be one of them? Despite his new lifestyle, Blink knew instantly what his answer would be: 'I always wanted to be a millionaire before thirty,' he told me, 'and this was my big chance, so there was no hesitation.'

The bad omens started early. MacDonald and Mick Healy's brother, James, took a taxi to Motherwell to avoid the busy Glasgow railway station for their trip down south. But on the way their driver was stopped for speeding. Fortunately, the police didn't recognise the two infamous Glasgow criminals in the back of the cab and the driver was let off with a warning. The rest of the journey was free of incident and MacDonald and Healy were picked up by the rest of the gang and taken to a caravan park in Paignton, where they would be staying for the week.

While they conducted surveillance on the bank, the gang decided to treat their stay in sunny Devon as a holiday. Healy invited two students he had met in France to stay with them and Blink decided to invite Sheila and the baby down. Between shifts monitoring the bank, they took trips to the leisure centre and zoo.

But more ill omens were to follow. While staking out the bank, Blink and two others, Rab Harper and Tam Carrigan, were accosted by a police officer for throwing a crisp packet out of the car window. The policeman asked for their details and the trio gave false names and addresses, which fortunately checked out. But Harper and Carrigan were spooked: they had a bad feeling about the robbery and decided to pull out. Now there were four.

The day of the robbery arrived and just after midnight the gang approached the bank, climbing a wall into the back. They drilled through the rear fire escape and entered the building. It was 1991 and there were no cameras, floor alarms or security beams. Once inside, they cut a hole in a partition wall beneath a staircase. This was where they would hide and watch the vault until all the staff were inside. Once the preparations were complete the team played pool in the staff recreation room until three in the morning when MacDonald left, taking the bag of power tools with him. Blink went back to his caravan and watched TV until eight in the morning when he drove back to the bank and waited down a small back road while the other three carried out the robbery.

'When I saw them come out with no bags, I just put my head down and went, "Something's gone drastically wrong here,"' MacDonald told me. Instead of bags full of cash, the trio of armed robbers were only carrying a holdall big enough to stash the shotguns. Blink drove off and got the story on the way back to the caravans.

The three men had watched the vault as, one by one, fifteen of the bank's staff had entered the building. The robbers had bided their time until they saw a staff member emerge from the vault pushing a trolley laden with bags. They had jumped from their hiding place and quickly subdued the staff only to find that, instead of cash, the bags on the trolley contained only credit cards and paperwork. Worse still, the vault hadn't been opened. The real money was stashed behind a treasury grille gate that was still locked. The robbers demanded the key from the staff, only to be told that the man responsible for the key had not turned up for work. Later at the trial this man, Roy the cashier, was asked how often he was late for work: 'He said in seven or eight years that was the first time he was late,' MacDonald told me.

Beginning to panic, Healy fired his gun into the ceiling, dislodging some plaster which hit a female cashier on the head, drawing blood. Staff now started screaming and crying, thinking one of their number had been shot. At the same time the front doorbell started ringing. Healy knew it was time to leave. The dream of being millionaires was in threads, and the only hope left was escape.

MacDonald drove them as calmly as possible to where the second getaway car was parked. They left the BMW and switched into the new car before heading back to the caravan site. But they didn't notice the vigilant painter and decorator who, thinking the switch looked suspicious, had taken their registration number and was calling the police.

Back at the holiday park, Mick Healy needed to take the French students to the train station before he could make his getaway. He took his brother, James, aside and admitted he had left the tools for the robbery in his caravan. Could James and Blink go back and get them and dump them in one of the ponds situated around the park? MacDonald and James Healy did as they were told, but on the way to the pond Healy said he thought they were being followed. MacDonald tried to reassure his colleague and they continued to the pond. But no sooner had they opened the holdalls than a shout rang out, 'Armed police! Get down!'

The man was a plain-clothes policeman armed with a revolver. He handcuffed the two bank robbers and led them back to a caravan while he waited for his colleagues. 'He made a major blunder,' MacDonald told me. He ushered them into the caravan and pulled the curtains. 'But instead of just sitting there with the gun, he decided to stand outside.'

To compound his error, the policeman hadn't tightened MacDonald's handcuffs properly and Blink was able to free his hands. He noticed that curious passers-by kept approaching the policeman to ask what was going on. Blink waited for the next one to approach and while the policeman was momentarily distracted, he bolted to the back of the caravan and climbed out of the bedroom window. According to MacDonald, 'James told me months later, "When you were going out that window, the whole caravan was shaking." If he'd have turned around for one second, he'd have seen the whole caravan shaking.'

Once safely out of the window, Blink ran as fast as he could and didn't look back. It was the first day of four long weeks on the run.

Back in the Chinese restaurant, Blink was steadily filling his stomach with lager and egg fried rice. He was still watching the denim couple who, he noticed, had a silver pen on their table, pointing in his direction. Was it more paranoia, or was this a directional microphone recording his conversation? He was just telling Sheila how he needed to get out of the country when a crowd of men and women rushed in.

MacDonald's hand went instinctively to the gun in his pocket, loaded with dumdum (expanding) bullets for maximum damage. But he didn't have time to do anything crazy. A bunch of guns were pointed at his head and the denim-clad couple already had him pinned and were choking him out from behind. Someone shouted that they had found his gun but it was all a blur to Blink, who was losing consciousness from the stranglehold.

Suddenly the Chinese restaurant owner appeared, shouting and waving furiously. MacDonald briefly thought someone was sticking up for him: 'I thought he was going to say, "You're going to kill this guy,"' MacDonald told me. But no such luck. Instead the man shouted, '"Who's paying his bill?"'

Blink did have the last laugh though. As he was carried off by Scotland's Serious Crime Squad, all that lager and foo yung came back to help him. He vomited everywhere, managing to splatter three of the arresting officers before being dragged away – 'It was one of the most momentous moments of my criminal career,' he told me with a laugh.

Ian MacDonald had shown early signs of criminality. Born

in 1961 in north Glasgow's impoverished Springburn area, one of Blink's first memories was trying to steal 'pick 'n' mix' sweets from the local Woolworths store. Ian was soon joined by two brothers, Gary and Alan, and later, a baby sister, Tracy. The growing family moved from their overcrowded flat to a two-bedroom house four miles away in the east-end district of Blackhill – one of the most deprived areas in Europe.

The MacDonalds' new house stood in the shadow of the infamous Barlinnie prison and just round the corner from Provanmill, home of the 'Godfather' Arthur Thompson, a gangster who ran Glasgow's underground criminal network and who dealt with gangsters nationwide, including the Krays. Thompson would play an important role in MacDonald's life.

Blink grew up alongside and attended Army Cadets with Thompson's son: Arthur Thompson Junior. MacDonald describes Thompson senior as the scariest man he has ever met. Although the older man was always scrupulously polite, you could tell by the look in his eyes that he was the 'real deal', according to Blink. He described the terrifying ordeal, as a young man, of being summoned to Thompson's house. On one occasion, he was sitting in the lounge when there was a knock at the door. It was Thompson's youngest son Billy with the dreaded words, 'My dad would like to see you.'

MacDonald walked the couple of minutes to the Godfather's house where, after a couple of pleasantries, he was introduced to the subject of the visit. 'He says, "It's about your younger brother, Alan,"' MacDonald told me. 'He says, "He sold my daughter and her friend two chains for two or three hundred pounds and her neck went all green after a few weeks."' Blink tried to absorb the news with feigned surprise while inside releasing a string of invective against his brother. 'This was the Razzle Dazzle scam,' MacDonald told me. 'There was a shop in the centre of Glasgow called Razzle Dazzle that sold all these chains for two or three pounds. But my brother was stealing them and getting nine-carat attachments and putting them on and selling them for £500.' The only problem was, because the cheap chains were made of copper, the victim's neck would turn green after a few weeks – which is what had happened to Thompson's daughter and her friend.

Blink had to promise to get the money back from his brother and return it to the Godfather's daughter. Unfortunately, Alan refused to refund Thompson's daughter and her friend, leaving Blink in an uncomfortable position. Fortunately, the matter seemed to get forgotten and the relationship with the Thompsons stayed on track.

MacDonald got the nickname Blink at a young age. One night he was playing football with the Army Cadets when he stared straight into one of the high-powered floodlights. He was partially blinded and spent the rest of the game blinking furiously to try and get his sight back. Later on, the nickname would be associated with his habit of slashing people with the blade of a Stanley knife – it was said that he would slash anyone faster than they could blink.

MacDonald's father was an avid Glasgow Rangers fan and would drink copious amounts of alcohol around matches at the weekend. He would return from the football drunk and often beat Blink's mother. The three brothers would lie upstairs and listen to the screams coming from the lounge. On one occasion, they couldn't take it any longer and ran downstairs to jump on their father's back. MacDonald longed for the day when he would be big enough to stand up to his dad and give the old man a taste of his own medicine.

Before he got the chance, Blink's mum threw her drunkard husband out for good and he went to live elsewhere. But without the strict hand of his father, MacDonald soon fell for the seductions of crime. Hanging out with the cool older kids on the street corner, he began joining them, racing in stolen cars and breaking into shops for cigarettes and booze. At the age of fourteen, he left the Army Cadets and chucked in his paper round – seduced by the rewards of crime. He was expelled from school around the same time for punching a PE teacher and soon found himself in an Approved School for children with disciplinary and behavioural problems. On weekend release for good behaviour, Blink found himself once more in a stolen car being chased by the police. He ran but got caught in a barbed-wire fence and received a beating from several police with truncheons – it wouldn't be his last.

MacDonald was charged with assaulting the police and sent to borstal, a kind of detention centre for underage criminals. But first he was remanded to Barlinnie, the prison near his house. He was to see the familiar building from the other side for the first time in his life, but not the last. Blink's first experience of Barlinnie was as terrifying as its reputation. The skinny sixteen-year-old was screamed at and threatened with beatings by the beefy wardens. He only spent three days at the prison before being transferred to the borstal at Polmont, but they were enough to put him off crime for life – or so he thought at the time.

MacDonald spent eight weeks at the allocation centre in Polmont before being transferred to an open borstal near Dundee for good behaviour. He got a job in the cookhouse, where he worked diligently. Most of Blink's time in borstal was characterised by good behaviour and he was released a year later. Determined to stay crime-free, he got a job with a lighting firm and started seeing a girl. However, temptation soon reared its ugly head in the form of drunken car theft.

He was soon back in a Young Offender Institution and his job and relationship disappeared. After his release, incredibly, he was offered his old job back. But by now he had made a decision: he would never work a nine-to-five job again. It seemed a life of crime was his fate and he would finally commit to it.

He began his new career shoplifting clothes from big department stores in Glasgow city centre. With a few friends he began making longer trips south of the border. It was on one of these shoplifting expeditions that he was tailed by the police and arrested. He spent a further six months in a Young Offender Institution in Stirlingshire.

True to his commitment to a life of crime, Blink got straight back into it upon his release. This time he graduated to burgling jewellery shops. His technique was simple but effective. He would enter the shop dressed smartly, so as to deflect suspicion, then ask to see a ring from the window display. When the tray was displayed, Blink would grab it and run off, following a carefully planned escape route. Each robbery meant £10,000–30,000 worth of jewellery, which he would clear through a fence for a percentage. He was soon robbing jewellery stores all over Scotland and the north of England.

He even found himself an accomplice. Paul Ferris was three years younger but fit and game, so MacDonald trained him in the art of jewellery theft and soon had him doing his own jobs while Blink waited in the car. Ferris would go on to become one of Glasgow's most infamous gangsters, with several books and a movie about his life called *The Wee Man* (2013). 'Paul at that young age was very, very game,' MacDonald told me. 'He was very, very violent. He'd had a lot of trouble with a family in Blackhill. I think he was getting bullied and he just said, "Enough is enough."'

Along with another friend, Blink and Ferris evolved to smash-and-grab raids, where they would shatter jewellery shop windows with sledgehammers before legging it with as much booty as they could carry. Each raid meant several thousand pounds each and they were soon splashing the cash around the bars and nightclubs of Glasgow, even giving stolen diamond rings to girls they fancied. This was when Blink's nickname took on its more sinister meaning: he and his mates became known as the 'Stanley Gang' for their propensity for wielding Stanley knives. At the first sign of trouble the knives would be produced and their enemies would find themselves slashed in the blink of an eye. Because of their reputation and their young age, they would often be refused entry into clubs. This would come back to haunt the doormen, who would be jumped after work by a gang of young hoodlums wearing balaclavas and carrying baseball bats and Stanley knives.

Around the same time, MacDonald's brother, Gary, was arrested for a more serious slashing: cutting a love rival across the throat. He was charged with attempted murder and sentenced to eight years in prison. Meanwhile Blink had been in and out of jail several more times and his and Ferris's readiness to use knives had attracted the attention of the Godfather.

MacDonald received the call to see Arthur Thompson that he usually dreaded. But this time it was to ask if he and Ferris would work as Thompson's enforcers. It was essentially a full-time job as professional gangsters. Ferris was keen but Blink had other ideas about his future, wanting to move on to bigger robberies. Ferris went to see Thompson and accepted his offer. Blink shook his friend's hand and wished him luck.

MacDonald was already putting his expansionist plans into practice, now graduating to armed robbery with an experienced hand who showed him the ropes. His first job with 'Peter' was on a post office in Glasgow. The pair entered with shotguns and left with £50,000 in cash. Another post office job produced an even bigger haul of £75,000.

Blink was beginning to enjoy the high life, but it all went wrong when he was stopped by an unmarked police car. Two men emerged holding truncheons and Blink decided he didn't want to hang around. He drove straight at them, knocking one detective into the air. After abandoning the car, he ran through some flats. Seeing a door open, he pushed inside and was sheltered by a young woman with a baby while the police searched outside.

Knowing that he had to flee from Glasgow, he got a fake passport and flew to Spain. Unfortunately, while there he got into a fight with another Glaswegian who knew about his fake ID. Once back in Glasgow, the man reported him to the police and Blink was arrested on the tarmac at Glasgow airport. His original charge of attempted murder was reduced to assault because the cop had not been badly hurt. He was sentenced to two years plus another eighteen months for some jewellery thefts he'd been positively identified for. He was packed off to Durham prison, where he was housed opposite a woman's block that held Myra Hindley. MacDonald joined the inmates hurling abuse at the infamous Moors murderer across the space between the two blocks.

Released early on a special scheme, he soon found himself back inside after the drug squad raided the flat he was in and, according to Blink, planted heroin. He was charged with possession and sentenced to twelve months. Back in Barlinnie, Blink would have a run-in with the infamous governor, 'Slasher Gallagher', so called because he had actually slashed one of the prisoners with his own hand.

MacDonald got involved in a dining hall protest over some ham that smelled like it had gone off. The prisoners refused to leave the hall until they were served something fresh. When the warders tried to grab someone on his table, Blink promptly smashed him over the head with a teapot. He thought it would turn into a general riot as all of the inmates had pledged to stick together, but only he and one other man had the courage to take on the guards. He was soon subdued and taken back to his cell to await what he knew was coming.

'The door opened and it was Slasher Gallagher that everybody feared,' MacDonald told me. 'He had this trilby hat on and this long coat and he just went, "Get him!" It was like a gauntlet of prison officers, a sea of black all the way down the stairs. And I'm going through this tunnel, going through E Hall, and every one of them were on me, giving me a kick and a punch. The next morning, I woke up like the Elephant Man.'

MacDonald was due a visit from his mother not long after but the warders told her he had refused it. They knew there would be repercussions if a relative saw the state of his swollen face so they kept him hidden away until the evidence had faded. Then Blink was charged with assault for hitting the warder with the teapot.

On his release, Blink got straight back into armed robbery with his former partner, Peter. Their first job netted £140,000. A security van robbery earned them a further £230,000. And a bank in Liverpool topped the lot with £320,000. Meanwhile he had met his new girlfriend, Sheila, and she had quickly fallen pregnant. Sheila had taken over the stewardship of a pub in Springburn called The Talisman. With a family on the way, Blink decided to try and go straight, helping Sheila out with the business.

MacDonald's son, Daryl, was born in 1989. It was the marker for the start of a new life but another event happened around the same time that would suck him back into his old habits. Incarcerated for armed robbery, Mick Healy had performed a daring escape from Shotts prison, sneaking out in a butcher's van. Healy would soon come calling with an offer that Blink couldn't refuse.

In the meantime, MacDonald's life was catching up to him in less pleasant ways. Leaving a concert on Glasgow Green, he was attacked by three rivals. He managed to get him and Sheila into the car but the men pulled out a spear gun and fired it into the windscreen. As the other windows were smashed, Blink accelerated away. Later, idling at some traffic lights, he noticed a car speeding up behind. It didn't stop but smashed straight into MacDonald's car, sending it spinning. Before he knew it, the three men were surrounding him again, one pointing a handgun into his window. He managed to pull away before the man could shoot, but he and Sheila were badly shaken up and decided to leave Glasgow for a while to stay in a friend's holiday home on the Isle of Bute.

On his return to the city, MacDonald was approached by Healy regarding the bank job in Torquay. He agreed to be part of the team and soon found himself on the run after the job was botched. After running from the caravan where the undercover policeman had left him handcuffed, Blink sprinted back to his own caravan and hastily explained what had happened to Sheila before taking off on foot. He managed to make it to the neighbouring town of Brixham, where he called a friend in London from a payphone and arranged to be picked up. The man arrived after midnight sweating from tension – police were swarming all over the usually peaceful seaside area and helicopters were patrolling the skies.

The friend got him safely away and back to London, where he gave Blink a bed in his Kensington flat. But the next morning, MacDonald had a nasty surprise: 'I was woken up by people shaking me and they were shouting, "Police!"' Luckily, his friend hadn't given away Blink's identity and he was able to give a false name and address. The police let him go, taking his friend with them. It turned out that Blink's friend had been dealing heroin and the raid was completely unrelated to the Torquay robbery.

MacDonald met up with Sheila at a friend's flat in Elephant and Castle and was advised to lie low in London for a while. But he had different plans. His fingerprints were all over the caravan window he had escaped from. It was only a matter of time before he was caught. Instead of staying in London, he took a train back to Glasgow and got hold of a gun.

'At that point, I had a lot of enemies in Glasgow,' MacDonald told me. 'I said, "Fuck it, I'm on the run from the bank. If I see anyone in the street I don't like, I'm just going to shoot them."'

It was four weeks until the fateful meeting with Sheila in the Chinese restaurant and his subsequent arrest, then it was back to his second home: Barlinnie prison. His welcome back present was a beating from the guards, who hadn't forgotten the mini-riot he had instigated in the chow hall. With nothing left to lose, Blink decided he was going to slash one of the guards in retaliation. But when he told Sheila of his plan, she made him promise not to do it – in return she would wait faithfully for him for however long it would take. And so he stayed true to his word, not rising to the taunts of the guards, even when they began peeing on his laundry.

MacDonald received thirty months for possession of a firearm while he waited for the trial for the Torquay bank robbery.

In the meantime, word reached him that Arthur Thompson Jr had been shot dead outside his father's house. Paul Ferris's name was bandied about as the prime suspect. (In 1992, at the end of Scotland's longest gangland trial, Ferris was acquitted of all charges.)

His friendship with Ferris could have made Blink a murder suspect too. For the first time in his life he thanked God he was in prison. As Blink suspected, retaliations weren't long in coming. On the day of Thompson Jr's funeral, two men were found dead in a car outside a bar in the Glasgow district of Shettleston. The timing of the murders was unmistakable – the Godfather had avenged his son's killing.

Meanwhile, MacDonald was transferred to Long Lartin, a maximum-security prison in Worcestershire, to await his trial at Bristol Crown Court. Mick Healy had finally been caught, which meant that all the robbers were now in custody, even the two who had bolted over the crisp packet incident. It turned out that they had travelled to Norfolk, where they had seized shotguns and pistols in a smash-and-grab by ramraiding a gun shop. They had then carried out three armed bank robberies before being caught.

The robbers were reunited at Bristol prison for the trial. This would be a longer process than anyone could have expected due to a number of incidents. The first trial lasted only two weeks before it had to be abandoned after two jurors had to leave. The second trial was even shorter after one of the jurors was spotted having lunch with a barrister. During the third trial, the gang got exasperated with the endless corned beef sandwiches that seemed to be their only fare and began throwing them around the food hall. The next day the troubles escalated and fighting broke out, which resulted in six warders being hospitalised, one with a broken arm.

More was to follow. MacDonald and Mick Healy had been reconnoitring the prison and courthouse for means of escape. They had identified a toilet window at Bristol Crown Court, where they thought someone could smuggle in a gun. They had sneaked out a letter detailing the plan to some friends in Glasgow who were going to come down, climb a fence and leave a gun on the windowsill for MacDonald and Healy to pick up. The wild plan was then to attack as many guards as possible before escaping into Bristol city centre, hijacking a car and making a high-speed getaway.

Unfortunately, the details of the plan were leaked. When the gang turned up in court the next day, armed police were patrolling the corridors and marksmen with rifles were stationed on the rooftops of neighbouring buildings. Trial three was promptly abandoned and the whole case was transferred to the Old Bailey in London – the home of British justice and the most famous criminal court in the world.

MacDonald was transferred to Brixton prison to await the trial. Here, he heard the news that Arthur Thompson, the Godfather of Glasgow, had died. Officially it was from a heart attack, but Blink suspected it was a broken heart after the death of his son.

When it finally did get under way, the trial at the Old Bailey was something of a farce. Mick Healy fired his barrister and decided to represent himself. He called a witness who would only allow himself to be referred to as 'Mr X'. Mr X was a well-known snitch in Glasgow's gangland and therefore not trustworthy. He appeared at the trial clutching his own Bible and testified that Paul Ferris had planned the robbery along with Joe Hanlon and Bobby Glover, the two men killed in retaliation for the shooting of Arthur Thompson's son. The story was preposterous and at one point Mr X even verbally attacked members of the jury. MacDonald recounted, 'He ended up saying to the jury, "Are you looking at me? I'm talking to you!" And he was more or less growling at them.'

The only surprise about the verdict was that it took the jury so long to decide – Blink suspects it was because they were enjoying the amenities of the plush hotel they were staying in. The day of the verdict arrived and the gang was ferried to the Old Bailey by an armed police cavalcade while a helicopter circled overhead.

Inside the court, the jury's verdict was delivered in a damning monotone – guilty on all counts. Then came the sentences – sixteen years for James Healy, sixteen and a half for MacDonald, eighteen years for Mick Carroll, sixteen years for Robert Harper, sixteen for Thomas Carrigan and nineteen years for the organiser, Mick Healy. This was on top of the two and a half years Blink was already serving for possession of a firearm. Thomas Carrigan and Robert Harper were already serving seventeen years each for the three robberies in Norfolk and Mick Healy was serving ten years for a previous bank robbery plus two for escaping prison. His new sentence would be added to the previous to make a total of thirty-one years.

Despite the harsh sentences, the gang took it on the chin, singing the chorus of Monty Python's 'Always Look On The Bright Side Of Life' as they were led down from the dock. But when he was on his own that night, the harsh reality struck MacDonald with full force. The longest he'd served up till then had been eighteen months – he had been expecting no more than ten years. Over thirty years old, he would be behind bars until well into his forties and would miss the entire childhood of his son. In his lonely prison cell in Belmarsh that night, Blink cried himself to sleep.

His first transfer was to Full Sutton, a maximum-security prison in Yorkshire. He was classed as Category A – the most dangerous type of prisoner. However, to his surprise, this didn't mean being locked in a cell on his own for twenty-four hours a day. In fact, the regime at Full Sutton – as with all of England's maximum-security dispersal prisons – was surprisingly relaxed. He was allowed to wear his own clothes, buy and cook his own food and more or less wander around freely so long as he abided by the one unbreakable rule – not to try and escape. This made life bearable, at least in the daytime when there were people to chat to and things to do. But at night, locked alone in his cell, he was overcome by despair.

Moving through England's dispersal prison system brought Blink into contact with many famous criminals. He became good friends with Ronnie O'Sullivan, father of the great snooker player of the same name. O'Sullivan had been jailed for life in 1992 for stabbing to death a gangster called Bruce Ryan, a driver for the Krays. The great snooker player often came to visit his dad and Blink took the opportunity to get a photo. But if he thought that was as close as he would get to the legendary Krays, he was wrong. The eldest Kray brother, Charlie, was moved into the cell next to him in Long Lartin and they quickly became friends. Charlie had been given twelve years for smuggling £39 million worth of cocaine into the country. He talked to MacDonald a lot about Arthur Thompson, whom he knew well and respected.

It was through Charlie that Blink got to meet one of the Kray twins themselves. Reggie was inside for thirty years, alongside his twin brother, Ronnie, for a double murder. But Reggie's time was coming to an end and he was allowed to visit Charlie in Long Lartin. During his visit Charlie introduced Reggie to MacDonald and the two of them chatted about Arthur Thompson. Reggie told Blink his most valuable piece of advice to a young man: a life of crime wasn't worth it. MacDonald should go straight when he got out. He met Reggie Kray a few more times and on one occasion brought up something he thought they shared in common. 'I said, "We're both mammy's boys,"' explained MacDonald, referring to the Krays' relationship with their mother, Violet. Fortunately, the older criminal took the comment in the spirit it was intended and wasn't offended.

One of the Krays' arch-enemies, Eddie Richardson, was on the same wing as MacDonald so he was surprised to watch Charlie, Eddie and Reggie chatting together as they walked around the football pitch on one of Reggie's visits. Someone mentioned how much the newspapers would pay to get a picture of this gangland reconciliation, but no one had a camera.

Blink met several infamous killers such as Peter 'the Weatherman', a keen angler who used the weather forecasts to dictate where he would fish each day. One day, a wrong forecast ruined his plans so he drove to a nearby meteorological centre and shot dead one of the staff. Another was Colin Ireland, aka The Gay Slayer, who had been given five life sentences for killing five gay men after deciding to become a serial killer as his New Year's resolution. Then there was Archie Hall, a butler who had killed five people. He would tell Blink the stories behind his murders, including that of his lover: 'His boyfriend came in this night, steaming, and he pointed a gun at Archie,' MacDonald told me. 'And Archie says to him, "I'll get you back." So the next day he said, "We'll go hunting for rabbits." So he heard him shooting off his six shots, then he just turned around and went bang, bang and shot him dead.'

MacDonald was involved in burning down the cell of one infamous murderer, Paul Bostock, who had killed two young women. Blink spent several weeks in solitary for the attack but told me it was worth it. MacDonald also used to hang out with several IRA inmates despite being a Glasgow Rangers supporter and therefore a Protestant and a loyalist. But Blink described the IRA men as 'chilled'. One of them even borrowed his Rangers football top one day. The Catholic terrorist took a picture of himself wearing the Protestant symbol and sent it to his IRA mates in another prison. Apparently, they all saw it as a great joke.

Probably the most infamous inmate MacDonald met was Britain's most violent prisoner, Charles Bronson. Blink was at Long Lartin when Bronson appeared, drunk and out of control. Someone said, 'Give us a dance, Charlie', and the musclebound villain stripped naked and started dancing on the tables. The guards managed to get him back to his cell but later that night, they heard smashing sounds and roaring noises coming from inside. The next day, Bronson was transferred back to solitary confinement, where he has spent almost the entirety of his sentence.

One of the benefits of dispersal prisons was the variety of cultures among the inmates and the subsequent range of cuisine. 'Some of the meals I tasted in there were cordon bleu,' MacDonald told me. A group of Indians at Long Lartin made the best curries Blink had ever tasted. But his favourite was Jamaican jerk chicken with rice and black-eyed peas, served up by the resident Yardie gangsters.

Cooking wasn't the only recreation. Homemade hooch was brewed using yeast stolen from the kitchen and a couple of bags of sugar, plus any fruit or potatoes going spare. The brew was a heady concoction that was enough to get Blink smashed off a couple of cups.

One Friday every month was 'Ecstasy night'. Blink would load up on pasta at dinner for energy, then pop a pill in his cell at five o'clock. When the door was opened at six for evening recreation, he'd already be high, dancing and whooping along the landing.

'All the other prisoners were looking at us like we were stark raving maniacs,' Blink told me, 'saying, "How the fuck can you take an Ecstasy pill in prison?" But for me it was a release.'

Ecstasy nights had to be carefully organised around drug-testing periods. Drug testing had been introduced to prisons in 1993 by then Home Secretary Michael Howard. This was one of the worst things to happen to British prisons according to MacDonald because, before then, most inmates were content to smoke cannabis. However, weed stayed in the body for twenty-eight days, meaning that it was likely that anyone smoking it would fail a drugs test and thus lose remission and even the chance of parole. When prisoners discovered that heroin only remained in the body for three days, there was a massive switch to the new drug. MacDonald watched the transformation of many tough inmates from hardened gangsters into addicts, begging their families for money, pleading with dealers and willing to play the most sordid tricks to get their next hit.

After five years inside, MacDonald received the news he'd been dreading – Sheila was leaving him. Worse, she had hooked up with a millionaire, who had bought her a luxury pad. Blink struggled with the news, but, strangely, coming to terms with it also enabled him to get his head around serving such a long sentence. With Sheila gone, he was no longer living for the outside. He began to accept his prison routine and to live life as it happened without constantly wondering what Sheila was up to. Ironically, this made the time go quicker.

In 2000, nine years after his imprisonment, MacDonald got his first chance to apply for parole. He was unsuccessful but later that year he was downgraded to Category B and knew that he would get another chance for parole the following year. He asked for a transfer to an open prison but was denied. Instead, he requested a move back to Scotland to be nearer his family. He soon found himself at Shotts in Lanarkshire.

The following year, his parole was granted. He left Shotts in November 2001 in a chauffeur-driven limousine, quaffing champagne alongside his ma. It was a sign of things to come. Blink had decided he was going to enjoy freedom to the maximum and live the most hedonistic lifestyle he could get away with. He spent a year doing little else but going out drinking and clubbing. But it all ended badly when Blink had an argument with his new girlfriend in Victoria's nightclub. The bouncers intervened and he and his brother Gary 'knocked the fuck out of four of them'.

Thanks to the fracas, MacDonald was sentenced to thirty days in jail and because he was still on parole, he was ordered to serve the rest of his original sentence for the bank robbery. He ended up spending a year in prison and was released on 1 April 2004 – April Fool's Day. Blink saw the date as significant – there would be no more fooling around. He had tried to go straight and enjoy himself and he ended up back in prison. Now he was going to dive headfirst back into serious crime and make some real money.

True to his word, within a couple of days of release he was pulling his first robbery. MacDonald was an old hand at this game and with his knowledge and underworld contacts, soon the money was flooding in. He bought himself a sports car, moved into new properties in posh areas and treated his family to holidays and limo rides. MacDonald was doing lots of coke and his West End flat had become a party destination to rival many local clubs, most of which had banned him. 'I used to say to people, "Sit down and have a wine and a line." I was spending five grand a week on cocaine,' MacDonald told me.

For five years, he lived the high life of crime but things started to unravel when a new, younger gang appeared. The 'New Kids on the Block' as Blink dubbed them were muscling in on his territory. One day, a go-between asked him to meet one of the gang at a coffee shop near his flat. The man had promised that only one of the gangsters would turn up for the meeting but instead three arrived. MacDonald stood up and walked outside only to be attacked from behind by one of the New Kids while another assaulted him from the front. Soon they were rolling around, smashing into coffee tables and sending customers running, until the police arrived.

MacDonald started getting Osman warnings from the police – notices of police intelligence that his life was in danger. At the same time the police were hassling him themselves, randomly stopping and searching his car at every opportunity to look for drugs and weapons. When he missed a court appearance over a speeding violation, an unmarked police car suddenly pulled up behind him. Remembering the death-threat warnings, Blink sped off, resulting in a high-speed car chase across Glasgow: 'I was going through bundles of red lights,' he told me. 'I was up to seventy-eight miles an hour.' When they finally caught him, the plain-clothes officers smashed his face into the pavement, almost breaking his nose.

Events culminated in 2009 when British actor, Danny Dyer, was filming an episode of his documentary series, *Danny Dyer's Deadliest Men* that featured Blink. Dyer and his crew got more than they had bargained for. Usually they dealt with men whose gangster stories were in the past, but with MacDonald they walked straight into the middle of a gangland war. While Blink was preparing for a meeting with the production crew, he had a ring on his doorbell. It was a neighbour saying they had seen someone messing around with his car the night before. MacDonald went down to check it out and discovered a bomb under the motor. The bomb squad was called and the whole street was evacuated – except for Blink, who refused. The bomb squad defused the device and said it was powerful enough to have blown up half the block.

As for the team members of *Danny Dyer's Deadliest Men*, the incident proved a tad too deadly for them. 'They said, "Look, we're finishing this film, it's becoming too heavy,"' MacDonald told me. 'They said, "Ian, this is about your past life not your present life," and they fucked off.'

This was the beginning of what MacDonald described as the second worst week of his life, after the week of his sentencing. A few days after the car bomb, Blink was walking to his ma's house. He had just passed Arthur Thompson's old home when he felt a blow to the back of his head. He turned around to see three men squaring up to him. Despite having the chance to run, and being unarmed, Blink stood his ground. As the men circled him, he began fighting and the three of them rolled down a bank, landing against the gates of a church. One of the gang sat on his legs while another tried to cut his throat with a knife. MacDonald managed to fend the knife away from his neck but the attacker slashed his face before the trio ran off.

Blink stumbled back to the road in a daze, his face pouring blood. 'Half my face was hanging off,' he told me. He was taken into hospital and given thirty-six stitches and plastic surgery to repair the wound. The attack left the distinctive scar, which can still be seen running across his left cheek. Three days later, MacDonald was in a bar with his friend, Star Keenan, when the police turned up and arrested him for a breach of the peace offence outside a nightclub. While in custody, he found out that his favourite 'Blinkmobile' – a Mercedes with a personalised 'Blink' number plate – had been firebombed. He eventually made bail, but the week he'd had would rival any in his life for bad luck.

Blink was clearly going to have to make a decision – quit the gangster life or meet a violent end. The final straw came when rumours surfaced that his rivals had paid the UDA, a Northern Irish loyalist paramilitary group, to kill him. MacDonald was nearly fifty and getting too old for a life spent continually looking over his shoulder. He wound down his criminal enterprises and retired the personalised 'Blink' number plate. In 2009, he moved back into his ma's house and dedicated his time to writing a book about his exploits. 'I said, "Right, I've read loads of books in prison." I had A4 paper and I'd be sitting there sometimes till two or three in the morning.'

Blink's son Daryl was at college and would come round and help type up his dad's handwritten notes with his laptop – 'Before I knew it, I had 180,000 words.' MacDonald's book, co-written with David Leslie, was published in 2012 and republished in 2020 as *Scotland's Wildest Bank Robber: Guns, Bombs and Mayhem in Glasgow's Gangland.*

In 2022, Blink now lives in a council house and survives on state benefits. He describes himself as 'a man of peace'. 'I'm not materialistic any more,' he told me, 'and I'm quite happy still to be alive.' Talking to him, now in his sixties, you still get a strong impression of the energy, charm and humour that saw him through so many dark times and life-threatening situations. As with many of my guests, it seems a small miracle that Ian is still alive (he counts seven or eight attempts on his life off the top of his head). But I think in his case, I can figure out one of the reasons – he is an extremely likeable, funny and generous character. People warm quickly to him and you can tell how his popularity among much of Glasgow's gangland community is a strong factor in why he is still around – that and his dogged loyalty to the underworld code of never ratting on an enemy, no matter what they've done or what the consequences.

Having said that, even now Blink's past sometimes catches up with him. He recently met a younger woman in her thirties, who worked at the suntanning studio he frequented. For their first date, MacDonald took her to a number of cocktail bars in Glasgow. As they were coming out of the third bar, he was taken down by armed police, who believed he was carrying a weapon.

The police escorted him back to his flat in order to search it. Blink owned up to a bag of cocaine in his pocket and some cannabis in the bedroom, but the police said they were only interested in weapons. After an hour, finding nothing, they left.

As usually seems to happen, Blink got the last laugh. He promptly got on the phone to his date. Trying his luck, he invited her round to the flat and she agreed to come. MacDonald is still with Ashley today and they have recently had a baby together.

As for crime, that's out of the window too, at least as far as Blink is willing to admit. 'I wouldn't even go into a garage and steal a Mars bar now,' he told me with the customary twinkle in his eye. On his YouTube channel established in 2022, called Blink and You'll Miss It, Ian tells a good story and urges young people to stay away from drugs and gangs.

5

Chet Sandhu

Asian Smuggler in Spanish Supermax

Arrested at gunpoint for smuggling the largest quantity of illicit pharmaceutical drugs in Spanish history

It is New Year's Eve, 1999. People all around the world are partying to celebrate one of the most significant dates in human history. Except for Chet Sandhu. He is languishing in a cell in a maximum-security prison in Spain. Addicted to heroin, he is hardly eating the rat-nibbled food and he has lost four stone in just three months. He is surrounded by some of the most violent men in Europe, many of whom have AIDS or HIV from sharing needles. Death lies around every corner. And to top it all, he recently found out his wife is divorcing him. The biggest party in a thousand years is not a happy occasion for Chet Sandhu.

'I never thought I would be here on this date,' Sandhu told me in the first of five interviews I conducted with him. 'Here I am looking at ten years. I'm twelve stone, full of smack, my wife left me, the coppers have took a hundred grand off me, chances are everybody else in here has got AIDS, I've had fights with them, chances are I've got AIDS, and I thought, *I'm gonna die here.*'

Chet Sandhu is a British Sikh based in the North East of England and at various times a body-builder, model, a high-end fashion shop owner, a bouncer, a gangster, a pimp and an international drug smuggler. Sandhu was arrested in Alicante in 1999 and faced ten years for the largest pharmaceutical drug bust in Spanish history after trying to smuggle a quarter of a million Valium pills into the country. Imprisoned in the notorious Fontcalent prison outside Alicante, he fell into a heroin addiction that led to what he describes as the lowest point of his life on New Year's Eve, 1999.

It all began with a decision to quit being a doorman for some of the North East's roughest clubs and make some real money by smuggling steroids from abroad. Sandhu's initial plan was simple – find the cheapest market and import from there. That meant a trip to one of the most dangerous countries: 'Pakistan is the cheapest place in the world,' he told me, 'because nobody wants to do business with Pakistan – the Taliban, al-Qaeda – everybody stays away. But shit there is so cheap, for anything, for steel, for plastics, for pharmaceuticals, for anything you want, Pakistan's the country. But people are scared to go there because they might get kidnapped and shot or whatever. But I didn't give a fuck.'

Without any contacts or knowledge of the country, Sandhu jumped on a plane to Pakistan with his two cousins and one aim in mind – to find a bulk source of cheap steroids. Getting out of Karachi airport, his first job was to find a decent hotel and one that had prostitutes: 'Prostitutes have a lot of information and they will tell you the truth,' said Sandhu.

He soon found the perfect location. The somewhat ironically named Paradise Hotel was in downtown Karachi. It had eight floors, the top of which was filled with prostitutes from eastern Europe, Turkey and Russia, and was reserved for special clientele including, he would later find out, Karachi's chief of police. Sandhu and his cousins moved into the eighth floor with the working girls and soon started following leads to steroid suppliers around the city. They started by going straight to the source – large-scale pharmaceutical factories. Sandhu, posing as a native Pakistani under the name Jet Khan, visited every major chemist and pharmaceutical factory in and around Karachi. He was surprised to be turned down by every single one of them.

Fortunately, the last chemist they visited gave them the name of a trader in one of the local markets who could help them out. Amid dozens of stalls selling rugs, carpets, pots and pans they found a small pharmaceutical counter manned by an old, white-bearded man surrounded by three younger men, all carrying guns. The old man quickly agreed to Sandhu's massive order of 50,000 ampules of steroids, saying he could have them ready for the next afternoon. Sandhu was shocked but elated. The only catch – the man needed the £30,000 up front. Sandhu's cousins argued against this, saying they should see the product first, but Sandhu decided to trust the man. He handed over the cash, which was promptly passed through a hole in the ceiling to a waiting boy. After that there was nothing left to do except return to the hotel and party with the girls – 'I used to get all the brass fucked up,' Sandhu told me. 'The madam hated me because I used to get them all wasted and then they weren't capable of working.'

Sandhu had formed a friendship with one of the prostitutes, a dark-haired beauty from Latvia called Sasha, who looked like a young Sophia Loren. Sandhu and Sasha would sit up all night after her work had finished, drinking and talking about their lives. Sandhu couldn't believe she was a prostitute because she was so beautiful. Sasha told him that she had to send money back to her family and that she also had a boy-friend in Russia, who guzzled up much of her funds. Sandhu found himself becoming more and more attracted to the girl but he didn't want to feel like he was paying her to be with him, so nothing happened apart from conversation.

His trust in the old chemist was repaid the next day when he turned up at the market to find his order all present and boxed up ready to go. He took the gear back to the hotel but was faced with a problem – the ampules were packed one to each box. Sandhu and his cousins now had to repack them six to a box to compact the stock to carry home on the plane. They began the arduous task in their rooms but it soon became clear that repacking 50,000 ampules was going to take up most of their remaining time in Karachi. Sandhu had a better idea – offer to pay their taxi driver, guide and general factotum, Kabir, to do it.

Sandhu offered Kabir 10,000 rupees – about £250 – to repack the boxes. This was around three weeks' wages for the taxi driver, so it was understandable that he would jump at the offer, but even Sandhu was surprised when he returned the next day with all the boxes neatly packed and the job completed. It turned out the Pakistani had employed the local boys from his village and a clever motivational aid. Sandhu takes up the story: 'I gave him a porn mag, *Men Only*. *Men Only* was a good one and I gave him that because you can't get that in Pakistan. You can't get any sort of porn material there. So what he did, he took it to his village and called all the boys in the street, about twenty-five boys, and he had all the packages there. There's loads of boxes here, about twenty-five boxes. So he goes, "Right, do one box and I'll show you the first page." So he opens the first page and all the boys, they've never seen a naked white woman before in their lives.'

The motivational tool worked perfectly. With one glimpse of porn per box packed, the local boys got all 50,000 ampules repackaged the same night. Sandhu's stash of Western porn mags would come in handy again, but first he had a final night in Karachi with Sasha to look forward to. She came to his room after work at eleven o'clock and they finally had sex before he had to leave for the flight back to the UK.

Sandhu and his cousins had the contraband stuffed in their suitcases. Unfortunately, they were stopped and their luggage was searched by airport security, who quickly found the steroids. Although it wasn't strictly illegal to take the steroids out of the country, the three airport security officers kept shaking their heads and saying they couldn't let it go through. Remembering the motivational power of Western porn, Sandhu had a sudden inspiration. He whipped out another *Men Only* and showed it to the guards, promising them four of the magazines if they would let him and his cousins through. The men quickly agreed and the cousins proceeded. The same drama occurred at the X-ray checkpoint but Sandhu's two remaining porn mags saw him through this final crisis before he and his cousins were safely on board.

They arrived in Amsterdam later that evening and by early morning they were back in Newcastle. There wasn't much security at the airport at this early hour and with the Karachi flight tags hastily removed from their luggage, the three cousins strolled through customs without being stopped.

Encouraged by the relative ease of his first trip, Sandhu and his cousins soon returned to Pakistan. They were picked up by the faithful Kabir and taken to the Paradise Hotel and the welcoming arms of the girls. Sandhu spent his first night with Sasha before visiting his old friend at the market. This time Sandhu had a different contraband in mind with a bigger mark-up back home – Valium. He could get 1000 tablets for £9 from the old man, Bashir, and sell them on for £1 per tablet in England. Sandhu ordered 50,000 tablets repackaged inside vitamin B-12 tubs, which could hold 1000 tablets per tub. Bashir had the whole order packaged and ready for the next day, alongside his usual order of steroids.

Bashir's service was so sharp that Sandhu and the boys had the rest of their week in Karachi free to hang out and enjoy themselves. But they soon received a reminder that hanging out in Karachi wasn't quite the same as hanging out in Newcastle. They were ordering pizza from a local Pizza Hut outlet when three loud bangs rocked the restaurant, followed by the sound of smashing glass. A spray of bullets had been fired through the restaurant window, apparently by a local terrorist organisation that had a habit of shooting up Western businesses. The reality of Karachi quickly sunk in and the three changed their order to a take-out. The rest of their stay would be spent mostly within the walls of the Paradise Hotel.

But even here they weren't safe from outside interference. Back at the hotel, Sandhu got a knock on his bedroom door: it was the hotel manager telling him a senior Karachi police officer was downstairs and wanted to see him. It turned out that this high-ranking official was a regular customer at the Paradise Hotel, where he enjoyed the girls for free in return for allowing the illegal business to operate. Once in the lounge, the chief and his two cronies started questioning Sandhu about his business in Pakistan. Sandhu told them a half-truth – he was a bodybuilder from the UK interested in cheap steroids. The policemen started speaking among themselves in Urdu. From what little he could understand, Sandhu could tell they doubted his story about being a Pakistani. If they discovered he was an Indian by heritage he could be in trouble due to the ill feeling between Indians and Pakistanis.

Turning back to Sandhu, the chief said he and his friends would like to watch him have sex with one of the prostitutes. Sandhu quickly realised that this was a trick so that they could see if he was circumcised, thus proving or disproving his claim to be a Pakistani Muslim. Thinking quickly, Sandhu agreed to the chief's request but selected one of the prostitutes he knew would be averse to having sex in front of other men. He was right: the girl refused. The police chief was appeased. He settled down to have a friendly chat with Sandhu while his two cronies went off to enjoy the girls. They even smoked a joint together and the chief gave Sandhu a massive lump of hash, which the British man spent the rest of the week smoking with the girls.

The connection with the chief came in handy only the next day when the cousins were driving around Karachi with Kabir. Suddenly they were pulled over and asked to leave the vehicle with machine guns pointed at them. It was the military police and they wanted to see their passports. Sandhu handed over the chief of police's card and told one of the men to call it. The officer was sceptical at first but disappeared to call the number and soon reappeared all smiles and apologies and let them go.

For the return flight Sandhu had armed himself with a small stash of porn mags. It was the same three security officers as last time, but this time they wanted more. As well as the magazines they demanded £100 in cash. It was the same story at the X-ray machine – another £100 had to be handed over (plus the inevitable porn mags). He boarded the plane £200 lighter but it was a drop in the ocean compared to the tens of thousands he was due to make back home.

Sandhu started making regular trips to Karachi, often taking friends along to act as 'mules'. He was now bribing Karachi airport's chief narcotics officer directly and so was able to stroll through all the security checks without a hitch. He had also earned the title 'King of Karachi' from the taxi drivers outside the airport after a fight broke out between them to secure his custom.

On one trip, Sandhu decided to take a girl he was seeing called Alma. Without boisterous male company around, he could take it a bit easier, yet things could get weird quickly in Karachi no matter the company. On a trip to the beach, Alma started sunbathing in just a bikini and soon attracted a crowd of unwanted admirers – around forty men all just standing around her, blatantly staring. Sandhu was just trying to chase the men away when a couple of police officers turned up. He told Alma to cover up but, to his surprise, the policemen told her to stay as she was. He shooed the other men away and told Sandhu they were trying to promote tourism in Pakistan so Alma could stay as she was and the police would keep unwanted attention away. Sandhu suspected it was because the policemen wanted an unrestricted view of Alma themselves, but let it pass.

Back at the hotel, the couple attracted attention of another sort. High on drink and drugs, Sandhu and Alma were still up at five in the morning when the Muslim call to prayer started and everyone came out on to their rooftops to pray towards Mecca. Sandhu takes up the story: 'They're all pointing towards me. I'm on the eighth floor and I'm just high as fuck. And then I go by the window. I stood on a chair and they're all looking at me. And I told my bird to come over here and suck my cock in front of all these people. They're praying. I know it's a big insult, but I thought they were praying for me.' Incredibly, there was no fallout, not even a single complaint about Sandhu's antics, and a few days later he was strolling back through Karachi airport with his usual consignment of drugs.

Things didn't go quite so smoothly on the next trip, however. Arriving back at Newcastle airport with Alma and another friend, Sandhu waited for their luggage but it didn't arrive. Their bags had been delayed. Sandhu was told to go home and call the airport later to check they had arrived on the next flight. When he did so he was told that the bags had been searched and the authorities knew what was inside. He was told that if he came to the airport, he would be arrested and charged with trafficking narcotics. Sandhu was gutted: not only had he lost a full shipment, he would now have to change his route.

On his next trip, he took a doorman friend, Tony and Tony's girlfriend. They flew back via Alicante to avoid the usual route through Amsterdam. But as they waited for their luggage at Alicante airport, it soon became clear that something was wrong. Tony, whom I also interviewed, told me, 'We're waiting for bags to come through and we're waiting and waiting and then everyone kind of like disappeared. By that point our suitcases hadn't come and then that's when the shit hit the fan. We just got like surrounded by airport officials, people with guns.'

It turned out Sandhu was being tracked by Interpol. They had intercepted his bags and found a quarter of a million illegal pills, worth half a million pounds in street value. Sandhu was whisked off to a holding cell, where he received more bad news. From a neighbouring prisoner he discovered that the drugs laws were different in Spain. Unlike the UK, there were only two categorisations – Class A and Class B. Only marijuana was categorised as Class B and all other illegal drugs, including illegally trafficked pharmaceuticals like Valium, were Class A.

That meant he would be facing a much harsher jail sentence, possibly as much as ten years, as opposed to the two years he would have faced in the UK.

Sandhu and his co-defendants were taken to Alicante's Fontcalent prison, where Sandhu was locked up in the maximum-security section. It was 1999 and within three months he found himself addicted to heroin and having dropped four stone in weight. It was on New Year's Eve of that year, the eve of a new millennium, that he realised he had to do something about his life or he wasn't going to make it through the long stretch ahead of him. Sitting alone in his cell that night, he thought about his life and what had led him to this terrible low.

Born in 1968 in Hitchin, Hertfordshire, to Sikh parents who had emigrated from India, Gurchetan Sandhu did not have a happy childhood. At school he received racist abuse. He was a small, skinny kid with a stutter and was something of a loner. When his parents moved to Huddersfield, the abuse intensified and Sandhu was soon bunking off school and getting into trouble. 'I was a thief,' he told me, 'fruit machines . . . We used to go midweek, skip school, just go Tuesday afternoon, Wednesday afternoon when it was quiet – crowbar, pop it, steal all the 10p pieces.'

Sandhu started weightlifting at thirteen but soon had to give it up when his parents moved again, this time to Washington, a town within the greater area of Sunderland. His parents bought a shop there and to increase profits they replaced the existing staff with Sandhu and his sister. Between the shop and school, Sandhu had no time to himself. It was the early eighties and his family faced constant racist abuse from the customers, who often blatantly stole from the shop, knowing that the police would do nothing to help the unwanted immigrants.

Sandhu was still young and skinny and could do nothing about the abuse or the stealing, but he remembered the faces of everyone who ever bullied him, knowing that one day he would get his own back. Meanwhile he finished school and got some work modelling, doing the odd catwalk show in Newcastle and Manchester. He was interested in fashion and wanted to set up his own high-end clothes shop. He met a girl called Stacey, who soon fell pregnant. With an impending family on the horizon, Sandhu decided to make a go of his dream. He set up a clothes shop in Newcastle, designed and furnished it himself, and started approaching major fashion labels from London such as Moschino, Vivienne Westwood and Saint George. Nothing like this had been seen in Newcastle before so he was taking a huge risk, but he convinced the London stockists and was soon displaying high-end designer fashion labels. He claims that on his many trips to London he even received personal advice from Vivienne Westwood on how to market and sell his items.

It was through his fashion contacts in London that Sandhu met and even alleges he had romantic moments with famous women, including Kylie Minogue, Naomi Campbell and Kate Moss. Through the shop he also got involved in the rave scene. He was selling tickets to some of the country's biggest dance clubs and would organise bus trips for customers to travel to the largest club nights. Until now, a teatotaller, he began getting into alcohol and party drugs. His first taste of Ecstasy and alcohol came at the same time when a mate convinced him to down a shot of tequila at a club in Glasgow. Unbeknownst to Sandhu, the drink had a crushed-up Ecstasy pill in it. Sandhu danced the rest of the night away and was instantly hooked.

Another less salubrious side effect of the shop was Sandhu's entry into the world of organised crime. Local gangsters started approaching him with stolen credit cards, asking him to run them through his primitive credit card machine in return for a cut. Sandhu would give them a designer item of clothing worth £200 and charge the stolen credit card for £400, pocketing the extra money.

To his parents' displeasure, Sandhu married Stacey, a white English girl. But it was his sister's traditional arranged marriage which would prove far more troublesome and would get him into his first serious trouble. In traditional Indian weddings the bride's family pay for the wedding ceremony and also contribute a dowry. Part of his sister's dowry was £40,000 worth of gold jewellery.

After a few weeks, Sandhu's older brother, sensing something was wrong, questioned his sister about the marriage and she admitted it hadn't been consummated. Sandhu's brother was gay and he suspected that the groom was also gay, having spotted some signs. Sandhu's sister now confronted her husband about why he wasn't interested in her and in the argument that followed he threw her out, accusing her of being a lesbian. She went home to her own family, but the groom's family refused to return the dowry or even her passport. Sandhu's family believed that the man had married her for the dowry, with no intention of consummating the marriage.

Sandhu was only twenty-one and had never been involved in organised violence before but now, to avenge his sister, he organised a gang of friends to travel to the groom's family home in Bolton, where they smashed up all the windows. Unfortunately, the family were all in India at the time so it didn't have the full effect Sandhu intended. He decided to go back and do the job properly. Sandhu continues the story: 'They had a Porsche and a Mercedes outside the house. We set them both alight and started running up the road. But there must have been a lot of petrol in the fucking tanks because the cars just went bang, bang and set fire to the fucking house and the kids were in, the family was in.'

Fortunately, the family all escaped. Even more fortunately, they didn't report the crime to the police. Sandhu's family finally got back his sister's possessions through the courts but not before a mass family brawl for which he was given 180 hours of community service and a £1000 fine.

Sandhu finally had to give up his clothes shop, which was doing less and less business. Newcastle wasn't perhaps ready for the kind of fashion he was stocking, but it also didn't help that well-known gangsters and criminals were hanging out on the premises. The police were watching him too, so Sandhu shut the shop down and went back to work in his parents' store in Washington.

Sandhu had been weightlifting for some time now and was doing a lot of steroids. He had also started working as a doorman at a club in Newcastle. He was a different prospect now to the skinny boy who had taken all the racist abuse in his teens: big, ripped and strong. He was taking twelve injections of steroids a week, he was seventeen and a half stone and he could bench-press 200 kilograms. And, with all the steroid-fuelled testosterone pumping around his body, he was angry. Back at his parents' shop in Washington there were some scores to settle.

The first incident happened when Sandhu caught a young heroin user stealing a can of Lynx deodorant. The lad had been thieving from the shop for years and used to come in with his school friends and intimidate the young Sandhu. Sandhu caught him outside the shop and hauled him out the back. There, he gave the lad two options – either Sandhu called the police or he let his dog, a vicious American Akita called

Cougar, on him. The man must have had a serious need not to be arrested because he chose the dog. Sandhu set Akita on him and the dog went wild, tearing his clothes to shreds but without actually harming him. Badly shaken up, the young man left the shop.

Another incident involved a traveller who had racially abused Sandhu's dad and walked down the aisles knocking all the products off the shelves. Sandhu found out about it and tracked the man down to his camp. He and a few friends went in and dragged the traveller from his caravan. Sandhu gave him a few hard punches to the body, then another man who had beef with the traveller pulled out a metal scaffolding bar and smashed him across the legs with it, breaking his shins.

On another occasion, he smashed a customer's head through the shop door's window for abusing his mum. And on another, he took the four cans of lager that a punter had stolen and threw every single one of them at the man's head at close range. The steroids were making him out of control, but it had the desired effect on the shop – the thieves, racists and bullies stopped coming and his family's life became a little bit easier.

Fuelled by steroid-enhanced testosterone levels, his life started going downhill. He was cheating on his wife Stacey with multiple partners, most of whom he met through his work as a doorman. It came back to bite him though when one of the more regular girlfriends left a series of pictures of them together in his car. Stacey found the pictures and when Sandhu returned home late that night, she had left with their three children and the entire contents of the house, leaving only one bed and a set of cutlery for her cheating husband.

Sandhu also lost his doorman's licence for accidentally breaking a woman's ankle when trying to remove her from a club. Without a licence there weren't many options left to him as a doorman except real dives. He did some work for a strip club-cum-crack den for a while then took a job in Middlesbrough, keeping football hooligans out of a night-club. But he soon realised that the life of a doorman had lost some of its shine. He had already been bringing back modest quantities of steroids whenever he went on holiday. Now he decided to turn it into a regular business doing drug runs to Pakistan.

This was the decision that ultimately led him to that Spanish prison cell on New Year's Eve in 1999, addicted to smack and with an unpleasant, and probably short, future ahead of him.

It was the lowest moment in Sandhu's life but sitting alone in that solitary cell, he decided to turn things around. 'I thought I'm gonna die here,' he told me. 'That's when I packed in the heroin and then that's when I started to smoke weed and that gave me a better mindset. As soon as I packed the fucking smack in, I come around and I started to train again, started to eat again and, boom, all right, let's fucking go, let's fucking do this.'

Sandhu noticed that the halal food was better quality than the usual prison fare. Muslim inmates regularly received whole fresh chicken breasts instead of the usual thin chorizo stew and rat-bitten defrosted meat so he pretended to be a Muslim in order to improve his diet and help him eat more. He also started writing to a female British inmate from another section of the jail, a blonde Liverpudlian in her early twenties who was serving time for smuggling cocaine. But there was more to this relationship than just pen pals, as Sandhu explained: 'If you send letters to each other, correspond for six months, then you can get a window visit and then, after six months of window visits, you can get a closed visit. If you've got a girlfriend, a wife, you get it from day one, but me I had to prove it was my girlfriend. So they want twelve months of proof that you are together.'

He also started using the prison's largely abandoned gym, making his own weights out of industrial bleach bottles filled with water and a punchbag made from an old army bag filled with bedsheets. As his confidence grew, he began to throw his weight around, usually taking on people he considered bullies. One such incident occurred when a newcomer to the wing was found crying in the showers. The man's supply of Valium had been taken by another inmate, a six-foot-two bully by the name of Juan. Sandhu demanded that Juan give the pills back. Juan reacted badly and challenged Sandhu to a fight in the showers.

Sandhu thought it was going to be a fistfight but Juan pulled out a blade, a three-inch penknife strapped to a piece of wood. Luckily, Sandhu's Spanish friend, Miguel, had his own knife, which he handed to Sandhu. 'I don't know what the fuck was going on really,' Sandhu told me. 'I don't know, do I try and hit him, or do I fucking stab him? But anyway, he fucking lunged at me, he caught me, but I moved out the way and instantly I just fucking stuck him. It was only one little stick but he went like that and dropped on his arse.'

Juan was taken to the hospital and Miguel cleaned and hid the knife, so Sandhu didn't get in trouble. However, the incident would come back to haunt him six months later. Sandhu had been training in the gym one day and was bending over the sink to wash his face when he felt something strike his back: 'It didn't feel like a stabbing. I just turned around and he's just stood there with this fucking shank and blood on the end of it. So I just went, bang, give him one, knocked him on his arse, and then I felt the pain. He's stuck me.'

The attacker was Juan's cousin seeking revenge. Sandhu didn't grass him up but pretended he'd fallen on something in the gym. He was taken to the hospital and the wound was stitched up. The man was moved out of Sandhu's section before he could get revenge.

Other knifings weren't so innocuous. One of the major heroin dealers on Sandhu's wing was a man called Hector. Originally imprisoned for burglary, Hector had become addicted to heroin and killed two other inmates over drug debts. He now had a life sentence and to top it off was HIV positive from sharing needles. This made him a dangerous man who had nothing to lose.

One of the odd features of the Spanish system was that inmates could get extra conjugal visits for grassing up other prisoners. This meant snitching on others was rife, at least in other parts of the prison. However, in Sandhu's maximum-security section it wasn't so common – the inmates were too dangerous to risk snitching on. Unfortunately, some newcomers weren't aware of the different guidelines and carried on their snitching habits after their transfer.

One such newcomer decided to grass up Hector for an extra conjugal visit. Hector's cell was raided, his heroin found and he was dragged off to solitary confinement for thirty days. This, unsurprisingly, didn't make him too happy. Once back on the wing everyone was waiting for him to get his revenge on the snitch but, surprisingly, nothing happened for a few days.

Then came Saturday and the family visits. Hector and the snitch were both due to speak to their families at the same time in the special booths that were stationed side by side. They passed through the metal detectors and went to their separate booths to talk to their relatives but Hector had a different plan in mind. Once in his booth, he quickly removed a knife he had hidden up his rectum, before bursting into the snitch's booth. Sandhu takes up the story: 'The snitch, he got a visit from his mum, his sister and niece. So he [Hector] went around, boom, stuck him eleven times, neck and body, bam, bam, bam, in front of his mum, in front of his mother.'

The man died of his wounds. Hector later told Sandhu he could have killed the grass at any time but, for maximum revenge, he had wanted to murder him in front of his mother.

Hector wasn't the only dangerous man on Sandhu's wing. He met an ex-soldier from the Bosnian army called Murat. Disliking army life, Murat had decided to go AWOL. When stopped by military police, he knocked out one of the officers while pretending to reach for his ID card. The other officer shot him twice in the chest, but Murat grabbed the gun off him and shot him back before making his escape. Eventually fleeing to Spain, he had teamed up with some other Bosnians to run a prostitute ring before being caught by Spanish police.

Murat was a fifteen-stone kickboxer who had been transferred to Sandhu's wing after beating up his cellmate. He started training with Sandhu and taught him his unique fighting style, which could take out opponents with great efficiency. However, Murat was a loose cannon who started fights wherever he went: 'He used to cause loads of fucking problems,' Sandhu told me. 'He didn't give a fuck. He just used to fucking knock people out. He'd just go to the library for a book and just fucking knock somebody out in the library.'

Murat's propensity for knocking people out was starting to make him unpopular. Sandhu was approached by another inmate, who told him they were planning on stabbing the Bosnian if he didn't tone down his ways. Sandhu had a word with the ex-soldier, but he said he didn't care, he would fight all of them. Fortunately for Sandhu, who could well have been stabbed too if he was nearby, Murat was transferred out the next day: his lawyer had secured him bail.

There was another dangerous character who, unlike Murat, was not on Sandhu's side. Shev was a tall Russian kickboxer who claimed to be in the Russian Mafia and, according to Sandhu, looked a bit like the Swedish actor Dolph Lundgren. Shev used to train in the gym despite having recently broken his wrist. He was arrogant and one day after training, he threw his gloves on the floor and refused to pick them up, expecting Sandhu to do it. Never one to take an insult lying down, Sandhu challenged the Russian to a fight.

Shev agreed and the fight was organised for the next day in the gym so they could pretend to the guards it was just a sparring session. The two men gloved up, with the Russians and Germans in Shev's corner and the gypsies and Spanish in Sandhu's. The fight started and Sandhu went in hard, following the style of his hero, Mike Tyson.

'He was tall,' Sandhu told me. 'He was a tall kickboxer type but he couldn't take my power. I pushed him up against a wall, bang, body shot him, uppercut.' The Russian had soon had enough and dropped to one knee, throwing his hands above his head, so Sandhu smashed him in the wrist that had recently been broken. 'He starts to scream,' Sandhu added, '"that's an illegal shot!" And I went, "There's nothing illegal in the can baby."'

As the fight illustrated, prison dynamics largely ran along racial lines. The Germans and Russians formed a loose collaboration based on their skin colour. The Spanish formed their own large contingent, as did the gypsies. Then there were the Muslims, mostly from North Africa, who stuck together, and the South Americans. As the only Brit, and an Indian Brit to boot, Sandhu was something of a lone wolf. This could have put him in a dangerous situation, with no one to watch his back, but it didn't seem to bother him. He was happy to go his own way, even protecting some lost causes that made him a target for everyone.

One such was Farid, an inmate recently transferred to Sandhu's section. The other prisoners had found out that Farid was in for a rape charge and now his days were numbered. Farid was an Algerian who had lived in the Netherlands and spoke fluent English. He explained to Sandhu that the rape charge was false and had come about because he had spent the night with a prostitute in Alicante. The woman had asked Farid to score some heroin and he had done so but had no money to pay for it. Instead, he took the fifty euros he had previously paid the woman and gave it to the dealer. In the morning, when she found the fifty euros missing, the woman had accused him of rape.

Sandhu believed the story and stuck up for Farid against the other inmates. This soon made Sandhu himself the object of animosity. All the other groups – the Germans, Russians, gypsies and Spanish – all wanted Farid dead, but Farid was hanging around with Sandhu as much as possible for his own protection, even running to his cell each morning as soon as it was unlocked. Soon Sandhu was being shunned by everyone and even his gym was being boycotted. It was clear that something was going to happen to Farid soon and if Sandhu decided to stick up for him at the time, so much the worse for him. The Germans in particular made it clear that this was the situation.

Sandhu already had beef with the German top dog, a big six-foot, sixteen-stone bully called Marcel, so he decided to kill two birds with one stone. He told Farid he was going to have to sort the situation out himself by taking the fight to the

Germans. If he did this, Sandhu would back him up and give him advice on how to do it. He told Farid to break some tiles off the wall of the outside toilets, smash them up into jagged pieces, then shove them into three layers of socks. With this weapon he was to attack Marcel in the yard.

Sandhu continues the story: 'We've seen the Germans in the yard, Marcel sat on the bench and the other three were just walking around. And I said, "Right, listen, just go up now and just fuck him." I said, "I'll watch from here. This is the only chance you've got. You've got to do this." He went out on four fucking Germans – he was only a little kid – he went out and he just went, bang, on the side of the head. Boom, boom, criss-cross. Blood was all over the shop. Anyway, the screws fucking landed about thirty seconds afterwards and took him to solitary confinement.'

Sandhu's plan worked out perfectly. Marcel had been taught a lesson and was taken off to hospital, and Farid was safe in solitary confinement. His court case was up the next day. The prostitute admitted to lying and Farid walked away with his freedom and his life.

Sandhu had been a victim of bullies growing up so he felt an urge to help those who were undergoing similar treatment, no matter the risk to himself. Another situation that showed his sensitive side was protecting a gay man called Babik, who was being bullied by a Moroccan kickboxer. Babik was a gypsy but because he was gay, the other gypsies shunned him, making him vulnerable. He soon started hanging around with another new inmate who claimed to be the kickboxing champion of Morocco. One day Sandhu found out that the Moroccan was raping Babik and forcing him to give him oral sex.

A few days later, Babik got a delivery of drugs and food from his family but had them instantly taken off him by the

Moroccan. Sandhu found Babik in the showers, naked and crying. The Moroccan had stripped his new clothes off him and even forced his hand into his rectum to grab his marijuana. However, the Moroccan hadn't got hold of Babik's heroin and word soon got round that this was still up for grabs. Babik was now a target for all the addicts in the wing looking for an easy score. He was due to be released in two days' time so Sandhu hung around with him until then, even inviting him on to his table to eat. When he found the kickboxer trying to grab Babik through his cell bars, he challenged the other man, who quickly backed down.

Sandhu still hadn't been sentenced. He believed he needed a new lawyer, one with good connections to judges. He found such a lawyer through a drug-dealer friend of his called Diego, who was one of the top dogs in Sandhu's wing and, along with Hector, supplied most of the heroin to the other inmates. Diego hooked Sandhu up with his own lawyer. The man said he could secure Sandhu a four-and-a-half-year sentence and the same for his two co-defendants. Sandhu agreed and the day of sentencing came around quickly. The lawyer had been true to his word. Sandhu, Terry and Terry's girlfriend would be released after four and a half years, rather than the expected nine. As they had already served two years, this meant freedom no longer seemed such a distant prospect.

But there were still some delicate situations to navigate. Sandhu earned a living in prison by money lending. He would lend out a thousand pesetas and demand one and a half thousand back the following Monday. His rate of interest, despite being extortionate, was much cheaper than anyone else's. He also was something of a soft touch, allowing inmates to pay him back in instalments if they couldn't make their repayment and never hounding them with death threats, unlike the other loan sharks. However, in prison being seen as a soft touch isn't a good thing: people start taking advantage.

There was a young inmate called Santiago who owed Sandhu money. He was half Spanish, half gypsy with a cleft lip, so neither of the groups really accepted him. Sandhu felt sorry for Santiago so he didn't jump on his back over the unpaid debt. Instead he let it go for a week. But another week passed, and then another. Santiago had been locked in his cell and was avoiding Sandhu. Word started to get around that Sandhu was weak because he was letting the little Spanish kid get away with his debt.

The situation was getting out of control, so Sandhu had to act: 'Everybody was saying, "Well, you owe Chet money as well, you haven't paid him." So that makes me look bad. He come in the yard and then he come to shake my hand, and I just got hold of his thumb and I bent it backwards and I broke his thumb. I didn't want to fucking do that, but you have to do that.' It was a calculated show of force and it worked. Santiago paid back his debt the following week and Sandhu's other debtors got the message not to mess with him.

The racial tensions often threatened to overspill, but Sandhu found a way of giving vent to them without violence. He asked if he could stage a weightlifting competition at the gym and the guards agreed. It would be a bit of entertainment for the inmates and might also be a chance for Sandhu to get another one over Marcel, the big German, who was also their best weightlifter. The competition was organised into lightweight, middleweight and heavyweight sections, with Sandhu and Marcel going head to head in the heavyweight division. Sandhu knew it wouldn't be easy. Marcel was on steroids and was the bigger man. Sandhu had been off the drugs since his imprisonment and the maximum weight he could lift was

140 kilos as opposed to the 200 kilos he could lift on steroids. It would be tight, but one thing Sandhu was never afraid of was a confrontation.

They started the competition at just 40 kilos and worked upwards. Soon everyone else had dropped out and it was only Sandhu and Marcel left. Marcel lifted 135kg, but looked to be struggling. Sandhu lifted the same weight with relative ease. Now it came to 140kg, the most Sandhu had ever lifted at the prison. Marcel took on the weight but his arms were wobbling all over the place and he failed to lift it. Now it was Sandhu's turn. The weight felt difficult at first but he pushed himself through the gears and landed it on the bar to the delight of his watching fans, the gypsies and Spanish.

'I've never felt that much sort of ecstasy and happiness here on the out,' Sandhu told me, 'but I felt it in there. You have different emotions inside. Even winning a game of chess is fucking huge. You can kill somebody over a game of chess in jail, or a plate of chips, it's very easy to do.'

Despite the outlet of the weightlifting competition, the racial tensions did overspill one day in the yard. Sandhu was walking with his friend, Diego, when another one of their Spanish friends, Lobo, was approached by Marcel and his Germans. Marcel started to belittle Lobo but the smaller Spanish man didn't back down as Marcel had expected, instead giving back as good as he got. Suddenly Marcel drop-kicked the smaller man with two feet straight into his chest, banging the man's head violently against the wall.

This was enough for the Spanish and gypsy contingents, who had no love for the Germans. They quickly got together and attacked the rival group. 'Boom, and then the Russians got involved,' Sandhu told me, 'and it was like there was a massive fucking fight. The screws come and started bashing every cunt involved, but Marcel was a pure fucking bully. He drop-kicked him, thinking he could get away with it, but he got fucked up. The whole jail just fucking turned on him.' People were looking to Sandhu to get involved in the mass brawl, but he restrained himself. He only had six months left to serve and he didn't want to jeopardise it.

When the day of his release finally came, it was a surprise. He was training in the gym in 2002 when one of the guards told him to go to his cell and pack his things. Sandhu was so ecstatic about his imminent release that he gave away all his possessions except for the clothes he was wearing. Promptly flown back to London, where it was a chilly February, he looked distinctly out of place in just the shorts and vest he had been wearing in Spain.

Sandhu went back to live with his parents near Newcastle, but his life of crime wasn't over. He would go on to run a cocaine smuggling operation and a prostitute ring with some local gangsters, and would eventually be sentenced to another six and a half years in prison in the UK. He now runs his own business selling cannabis oil for the treatment of various ailments. He has written his autobiography: *Self-Made, Dues Paid: An Asian Kid Who Became an International Drug-Smuggling Gangster*. It would be wrong to say he keeps his nose clean. He was recently awaiting trial for money laundering and supplying illicit alcohol.

Sandhu is probably best described as a 'loveable rogue'. Yes, he's definitely got his dark side and clearly a propensity for violence, but it's impossible to spend more than five minutes in his company without laughing. But the tough front also hides a sensitive side. This is the side that stuck up for the underdogs in prison, even when it meant becoming a pariah himself. It's the side that still identifies as that skinny, stuttering Asian boy, suffering racist abuse at the hands of bullies; the side that now fights those bullies and defends the weaker individuals who remind him of that boy.

As Sandhu said, 'It affects me, you know? It affects me if someone's getting hurt. I'm thinking, no, I want to say something, because I *can* say something. Why should I keep my fucking mouth shut? Because he can't, because he's getting bullied, he's not in a position to do that.'

6

John Lawson

The Hit Team Commander

After working for the Maltese Mafia, John was hired by international racketeers to kidnap gangsters

John Lawson checked his phone again before glancing at the two men sprawled handcuffed in the field in front of him. This was turning into the longest ten minutes of his life. Killing the men hadn't been in the agreement but when the high-up gangster known only as 'The German' had changed the orders from kidnap to potential murder, Lawson felt he had to comply – after establishing that he would get double the money, of course. Now he and his three companions were waiting on The German's call to discover the fate of the two men. If the details the men had given about the stolen money checked out, they would survive. If not . . .

Lawson checked his 9mm Browning pistol, dropping the magazine out and back in again nervously while he went over the potential outcome of the call obsessively in his mind. In a life of violence he had never yet killed anyone, though at times he had come close. His mind flashed back to some of those backs-against-the-wall moments – the face-off against a gang of armed Yardies to protect his crime family's business in Soho; the dozens, perhaps hundreds, of fights as a doorman;

the prison confrontations; the high-stakes violence recovering debts for gangsters like The German – all of these situations he had managed to negotiate with a combination of measured violence and cool thinking. But he had never yet been faced with the job of killing another man in cold blood.

As he looked at the prone bodies of the terrified men, the thought repeated itself incessantly in his mind – if he got the call to go ahead, could he kill these men? In answering, he felt a sudden rush of cold exhilaration like he had never experienced before. His fingers twitched on the Browning and suddenly he had to restrain himself from murdering the men right there and then.

As if in answer to his sudden thirst for blood, he heard the low hum of the ringtone: it was The German. Lawson's companions watched him with a mixture of eagerness, dread and anticipation as he raised the phone to his ear and pressed the answer button.

'It's just something that's in you,' Lawson told me about his ability to carry out cold, calculating acts of violence in our interview. 'You detach the emotion from it. And when you detach emotion from something I think it can make you dangerous, because you don't really care. And you're willing to push it to whatever level it takes to get done.'

Lawson's capacity for detached violence was a skill that saw him through a long career in the underworld, as a manager for the Maltese Mafia in Soho, as an elite bouncer working at some of the most dangerous clubs in the north of England, as a prisoner in some of Britain's toughest prisons, and as the leader of a hit team who collected debts for some of the highest-ranking criminals in Europe. Its origins lay in an upbringing that spanned Scotland, Merseyside and South Africa, and involved the hurt and neglect of an absent father.

JOHN LAWSON

Lawson's story began in sixties Glasgow. His father, Lex, was a bus driver who had served in the Merchant Navy. His mother, Josephine, was a bus conductor working for the same company. The two fell in love and were married the same year, 1966. Lex wanted to escape the poverty and violence of Glasgow so, when his best friend emigrated to South Africa, the Lawsons followed suit. They moved to Durban in 1970 when John was just three years old. Lex got a job in the City Police and the couple had another son, Alex, in 1972. The family soon settled down to life in South Africa. Some of Lawson's earliest memories are of climbing trees with monkeys, riding with his dad in his police car and learning to fire his father's pistol at the shooting range.

But the idyllic upbringing changed forever when Lawson was ten years old. Lawson's book, *If a Wicked Man*, tells of how news came through that Josephine's father was critically ill, so she and his younger brother flew back to England, leaving John and his father in Durban. One day at the beginning of the Christmas holidays, Lex told John that he would be working late and John would have to stay at home on his own for the night. He locked his son into the apartment, telling him to be brave. John cried himself to sleep curled up in his parents' bed but the next day saw no sign of his dad. One night turned into two and then three and four. With no food in the cupboards, ten-year-old John got weaker and weaker until he collapsed on the floor, drifting in and out of consciousness.

He was woken by the sound of voices then the front door being broken down. Lawson was rescued by his Aunt Marion and Uncle Les (although not related as it is a common thing to call close family friends 'auntie and uncle' in South Africa). John didn't know it at the time, but his father was having an affair with another woman and had left him locked in the apartment for four days so he could see his girlfriend. Once rescued, he stayed with his aunt and uncle until he was put on a flight back to England. Lex said he would be back to join him soon and the family would be reunited. Confused but hopeful, the young Lawson flew out of Johannesburg in 1977, heading for Birkenhead, just across the River Mersey from Liverpool.

John started school in Birkenhead and waited for his dad's arrival. When Lex finally did return, it was to Glasgow so the family took a trip north to meet him. Back at John's gran's house, the Lawsons reunited and Lex promised Josephine that he had ended his affair and wanted her back. He promised to fly the rest of the family over when the trial had finished – Lex had been involved in policing a riot in which he had shot one of the protesters. Josephine agreed and young John was ecstatic to soon be back with the father he loved and looked up to so much.

Lex flew back to Durban. Days passed but instead of the call they were expecting, a different message arrived – John's father had decided to stay with the other woman. They wouldn't be going back to South Africa.

John spent the rest of his upbringing between Birkenhead, Glasgow and Drumchapel, a housing estate on the outskirts of Glasgow that was renowned for being one of the most deprived areas in Europe. He was intrigued by Bruce Lee films and began to teach himself martial arts from what he could learn in films and books. 'I was really fascinated by seeing Bruce Lee in *Enter the Dragon*,' Lawson told me, 'so I immediately went home and made a pair of nunchakus [training weapons] out of a broomstick – much to my mum's annoyance – and the chain off the bog – and became quite proficient.'

He had his first chance to try out his new skills aged sixteen in Birkenhead when the family next door came banging desperately on the door. It was the mother, Mary, and her four children fleeing from their drunken father, who was threatening to smash the house up again and beat her. John and his brother were able to barricade themselves and the neighbours in their kitchen with the table jammed against the door. The husband, Peter, was soon inside and smashing his fist through the kitchen door. In desperation, Lawson grabbed a screwdriver and stabbed it into the drunken man's hand, drawing a scream and a spurt of blood. The man howled for revenge and called Lawson's mum a 'Scottish tart', thinking it was her who had stabbed him. Peter ran off, screaming with rage but now Lawson felt his own blood boiling because the man had insulted his mother. Running after him, he found his neighbour on the street outside. As the man came at him, he launched a Bruce Lee-style sidekick, sending him stumbling to the ground. The drunken man stood up and aimed a powerful punch at Lawson's head. This time the sixteen-year-old ducked the blow and brought his foot around in a leg sweep, sending the older man sprawling once again. Before Peter had time to react, the police arrived and the fight was over: Lawson had been blooded in battle.

His next confrontation came when he finished school and got his first job as a bartender at a local nightclub. A customer had fallen asleep at the bar and Lawson went to rouse him, but the man sprang up and tried to head-butt him. Lawson parried the blow, knocking the man over a table. The man charged at him again. This time Lawson sidestepped, sending him crashing through another table. Again, the man got up and grabbed his arms. Lawson kneed him in the groin then elbowed him in the temple. Incredibly, the man kept coming. Lawson now roundhouse-kicked the man's head, knocking him down again, before the bouncers arrived and piled on top. It took three bouncers to restrain the man and throw him out. It turned out he was high on speedballs – a mixture of heroin and cocaine that gave the user incredible strength and immunity to pain. It wouldn't be Lawson's last, or worst, experience with the drug.

While he continued working the bar, Lawson met his first long-term girlfriend. He had soon moved from his mother's house and was living with Jackie and her two children in Wigan. He got a job as a bouncer and began to settle down to family life, acting as a father to Jackie's two children. The couple were married in 1987 in Wigan but the honeymoon period didn't last long. Jackie began spending nights out, apparently babysitting for a friend, leaving John home alone with the baby. At first, he thought nothing of it but when he bumped into a friend of Jackie's in town and mentioned the babysitting, the friend told him the truth: Jackie was having an affair.

Lawson left Jackie and serendipitously got an offer at around the same time. He was explaining the situation with Jackie to his Uncle George on the phone when the older man invited him to come down and work with him and his other uncle, Dave, in London. Apparently the two brothers had hooked up with the Maltese Mafia, running sex shows and porn shops in London's sex district, Soho. How two small-time crooks from Glasgow had begun liaising with the Maltese Mafia was a typical story from the crazy lives of Lawson's Glaswegian uncles. Uncle Dave had escaped from Glasgow's Barlinnie prison but had been recaptured and imprisoned in London. In jail, Dave was put in a cell with a man who happened to be the son of a Godfather in the Maltese Mafia, a man Lawson would come to know as Uncle Tony. Lawson takes up the story: 'Uncle Tony, because he had a lot of money, was a bit of a target for other prisoners so a couple of guys came in to bully him and my Uncle Dave stood up, slashed one of the guys and protected Uncle Tony.' Grateful for the protection, Tony offered Dave a job. When Uncle Dave was finally released from prison, eight months after Uncle Tony was released, he went to see Tony and told him he didn't want just a job but a partnership. Tony agreed and the Lawsons were suddenly insiders with the Maltese Mafia.

Wanting a fresh start and a change of scenery, Lawson eagerly took Uncle George up on the offer to come and work for his uncles. Soho in the eighties was a seedy den of street prostitution, drug deals, live sex shows and coin-operated strip-tease acts called peep shows. Almost all of it was owned and run by the Maltese Mafia under Uncle Tony and his partner, Uncle Dave. Lawson's first role was working on the kiosk at one of their live shows while he learned the ropes. He was shown to his new flat and introduced to three of the Maltese enforcers who provided muscle for the operation – Bullets, Fingers and Diamonds: 'Bullets had been shot three or four times,' Lawson explained to me. 'He had bullet wounds in him and on the last one, the guy was gonna shoot him in the head and that bullet didn't go off. He wore it on a chain around his neck, the bullet that was supposed to kill him.' Fingers was a handy card sharp with a propensity for chopping off fingers. And Diamonds – well, he just loved diamonds.

The three Maltese looked like caricature gangsters in pinstripe suits, trilby hats and spats, but they were powerful men, Uncle Tony's lieutenants, and with fearsome reputations behind them. Bullets' father had apparently chopped the head off a rival gang leader and the three of them had even chased the Krays off when the gangland brothers had tried to muscle in on the Soho action. 'They reminded me of The Fonz, [from

Happy Days],' Lawson told me. 'When I first met them I was like, "Where did you get these guys, off of a film set?" But actually, they knew everybody and they were very, very good backup.'

Soon Lawson experienced his first night working the kiosk at one of Uncle Tony's 'live shows', taking the money and issuing tickets for the entertainment. He soon found out that the whole thing was an elaborate scam known as a 'clip joint'. Punters were drawn inside by the promise of live sex. Once inside, the customers were presented with a drinks menu and asked to order a drink. If they refused, they were pointed to the back of their ticket which stated that part of the entrance requirement was to buy a drink. The customer would then – often unwillingly – purchase a drink from the range of phoney alcoholic beverages lining the bar. The clubs didn't have an alcohol licence so all the booze was fake. It was also massively overpriced. A pint of (fake) lager cost £12 when it would have cost 80p in a pub. Still, lured on by the sight of the waiting bed and semi-clad waitresses, the punter would usually endure. One of the hostesses would then ask if he would like her to keep him company. If he said yes, he would have to buy her a drink, which would of course be one of the most expensive cocktails on the menu, costing around £50. Thus, the charges quickly mounted. 'The bill might be around four or five hundred quid,' Lawson told me, 'and all he's ordered is half a coke, because there's the hostess fee for her company, there's her drink, so there's all sorts of charges.'

Eventually the 'show' would start, but not before Martin, the 'Showman', had encouraged the audience to put cash in a jar. The more cash they received, he told the expectant audience, the raunchier the show would get. Finally, after the customers had parted with even more money, a woman would join the Showman on the bed and simulate a sex act. 'It was the weirdest thing,' Lawson told me. 'She would be on the bed kneeling towards the end. The Showman would stand in front of her with his back to the audience so the guys couldn't see and they would simulate oral sex, although there was nothing happening. He just got his belly button out and the guys would be trying to see what's going on. And then, that's it – show's over.'

This was the most dangerous part because there was now a club full of rowdy dissatisfied male customers who had just been fleeced out of a lot of money. But usually various forms of 'persuasion', from gentle blackmail concerning wives and girlfriends to intimidation and the threat of violence prevailed. This combined with the murky lighting, the gangster connotations and the feeling of being out of their comfort zones usually got most of the punters to pay up and be on their way without violence or calls to the police.

Lawson found managing the kiosk easy but boring and was soon promoted to bar manager. In this role he could earn a lot more money, taking a percentage from the proceeds, but he was also in charge of security and therefore had to deal with the difficult customers who refused to pay. He also had to deal with encroaching gangs who wanted to muscle in on Uncle Tony's turf.

The brothers had noticed that a group of Jamaican Yardies were selling drugs at night outside the well-lit entrances to their clubs and shops. This wasn't a problem in itself as the Maltese Mafia weren't into drug dealing, but the presence of the Jamaican gangsters was deterring punters from entering the shows so business was suffering. It became increasingly clear that something had to be done. Uncle George was up for swift and decisive violence but that would mean recriminations and the Yardies had a fearsome reputation for brutality. Rather than start a turf war, Lawson suggested they first try reasoning with them. He laid out a plan to his uncles and they agreed to let him try it.

Lawson spent several days observing the Yardies from a flat across the street. He noticed that although all the drug dealers were Rastafarians with big Afros and lots of gold chains, there was one man who sat in the shadows wearing a simple business suit. Everyone seemed to defer to this man, who was clearly the leader. After a few days, Lawson crossed the street and approached the main man. He was immediately surrounded by a group of intimidating Rastas. Lawson said he wanted to speak to the boss. When he managed to get through, he told the man in the suit that he had a mutually beneficial business arrangement to discuss but they needed to speak in private. When the man asked where, Lawson pointed to one of the flats off the street. The Jamaican agreed and followed him up to the flat.

Lawson takes up the story: 'I invited him to sit down. As he went to sit down, I pulled the Browning 9mm out. He reacted by pulling a big machete out of his coat. It could have gone very, very wrong at that point because one of us would probably die. But I immediately took the magazine out and I pulled back the slide and the bullet ejected. I placed the gun on the table and when he saw that, he put his machete away. And I said to him, "I'm not here for that but I'm here to show you I'm serious. I want to respect you, hence the gun on the table." And immediately the fact that I showed him respect brought the situation right down. And I just explained to him, "Look, we run the sex industry here, you run the drugs. We don't really care about that but you're interfering with our business because you're hanging about outside our premises, and if you're interfering with our business, that's going to cause problems.'

The Yardie leader agreed to Lawson's proposal that his gang move 100 yards down the street, where they would no longer be putting off the punters. When they got outside, the Yardie turned and asked Lawson if he had been serious about the threat of violence. Lawson assured him that he was and, on a pre-arranged signal, his uncles along with Bullets, Fingers, Diamonds and other heavies emerged from an alleyway in a show of force. Convinced that he was serious, the Jamaicans moved down the street. It was a brilliant assessment of how to handle a delicate situation, using the right mixture of intimidation and respect to remove the problem of the Yardies while avoiding a bloodbath.

But just as he was capable of this kind of cool analytical approach, sometimes Lawson's impulsiveness got the better of him and it was this that ended his career with the Maltese Mafia. It was one of the live show's difficult customers that proved the catalyst. An American punter reacted badly when he saw the bill and made a run for the door, knocking a hostess over in the process. Lawson moved to block the man's exit but instead of simply restraining him, angered by the man's handling of the waitress, Lawson side-kicked him in the chest, knocking him through some tables. He then dragged the American to the bar and smashed his head on the counter. The man soon paid his debts and fled the club.

Unfortunately, he ran straight into Inspector Atwell, a policeman who had long had it in for Lawson due to previous acts of violence on difficult customers. Now the inspector had a witness who was willing to testify. Lawson was arrested and taken to the station for questioning. He was released on bail but Uncle George said he had to get out of Soho for a while:

he had brought too much heat down on the live shows and had become a liability.

All the time Lawson had been in London, he had been visiting his son, Danny, back in Wigan. Determined not to be like his own father, he would drive up north and have custody of the boy for the weekend every fortnight. Now, when he returned to the north to lie low, he determined to gain custody of his son full-time. He won the case and, together with the help of his mum, was able to start raising Danny on his own. But almost immediately disaster struck – he was sentenced to nine months in prison for his attack on the American customer. No sooner had he won back his son than he had to leave him again, this time without regular visits. Despite his good intentions, he seemed doomed to repeat the sins of his father.

Prison was a rude awakening: 'I'll never forget walking into Brixton prison the first time,' Lawson told me, 'and just seeing the brown stains coming down the windows, of faeces, and the smell. And I'm watching these guys going around with shovels, picking up these newspapers full of poo, and socks, because guys are crapping in socks and throwing them out the window, because you don't want that smell in your cell all night. So they'd crap on newspaper or an old pair of socks and they'd fling it out.'

Fortunately, he had an old hand as a cellmate, who quickly showed him the ropes. Rule number one: don't get put on the bomb squad. These were the unfortunate inmates who had to go around picking up the shit-filled socks and newspapers. John kept his head down for four weeks, but when he was transferred to Wandsworth in 1988, his impetuosity got the better of him again. He was waiting in line at the food hall but the guy whose job it was to place the butter on his plate was more interested in talking to his mate and left Lawson waiting. Losing his patience, Lawson grabbed a pat of butter for himself and slammed it on to the plate before moving on. Feeling disrespected, the man behind the counter shouted at Lawson, who retaliated, telling the man to shut his mouth. The other inmate didn't react well to this and shouted back that he was going to kill him.

Lawson was a naïve first-time prisoner who didn't realise that he had committed a cardinal mistake: angering someone into making a threat in public. Now the man would have to carry it through or he would lose face and become a target for everyone else. Worse still, Lawson soon found out the man was a lifer, so he had nothing to lose. Lawson's life was now in danger. To compound the threat, during exercise, he saw the man pointing him out to his friends: he had clearly been targeted.

But fate smiled on Lawson in the form of a toilet break. He had buzzed the guard to be let out of his cell to use the bathroom. When he got downstairs to the toilets, he saw the man who had threatened him leaning over a toilet bowl, cleaning it.

'I thought, *I have to do something here*,' Lawson told me. 'I have to do something because the guy's going to kill me. So I walked in and I just kicked him on the back of the head. His face smashed into the toilet and some of his teeth came out and there was a lot of blood and he was knocked unconscious. And I quickly went back to my cell and shut the door.'

The man was taken to the prison hospital and no one pinned the blame on Lawson, who was shipped out just a week later.

Back on the outside, Lawson rejoined his mum and Danny back in Birkenhead. He soon found himself work as a doorman at a nightclub in Oldham with his brother, Alex. On his first night a disgruntled punter tried to stab him with a knife.

Lawson used his martial arts training and disarmed the man with a double open-handed blow to the wrist. The nightclub manager happened to be watching and immediately promoted him to head doorman.

His first test as the team leader came quickly and again involved speedballs. A couple had seemingly passed out at a table so Lawson ordered two of the bouncers to wake them and escort them outside. But just as they bent over the pair, the couple sprang to life. The woman lashed out with a glass, smashing it into one of the doorman's faces, almost severing his top lip. Lawson and the other bouncers piled in, but the couple were so high on speedballs that the woman alone took three men to restrain her. Once outside, Alex had the male half of the couple pinned up against the wall, but then it all went wrong. 'The guy snap-kicked my brother in the shin,' Lawson told me. 'All I heard was the scream that you don't really want to hear from your brother. It completely snapped his shin.' The man managed to break free but Lawson ran after him and eventually brought him down with a rugby tackle then laid into him on the ground before the police turned up and arrested him.

But the drama wasn't to end there. The man turned out to be a drug baron who had murdered a rival by throwing him off the top of a block of flats. Lawson and the other doormen managed to get the customers out early and closed up the club half an hour earlier than usual. He and the others were sitting in a car across the road about to leave when four Range Rovers pulled up outside the club. Twelve men jumped out carrying shotguns and stormed the club doors. 'Fortunately, they're looking at the club,' Lawson told me. 'They aren't looking at us because we're over here. So we just slid down in our seats in the car and tried to hide, and they didn't see us. A few minutes later there was blues and twos and these guys jumped in the cars and were gone, but it was a close call.'

Lawson and his team were doing such a good job at the club in Oldham, they were recruited by a security firm led by Mike Ahearne, the former 'Warrior' from the TV show *Gladiators*. Lawson and the team were given special police training in handling violent situations. They were to form an elite group of doormen who could be parachuted into the most dangerous nightspots in the North West where the current bouncers had lost control. Among the team were Jay, a former paratrooper, and Rico, an ex-South African special forces operative.

One of their first jobs was at a nightclub in Blackburn. A previous bouncer had been badly beaten up when he had refused to let in a gang of local drug dealers. The gang had broken the doorman's arm. Lawson and his team moved in to take on the door and waited for the gang to return. When they did, the bouncers let them in and waited until the gang had settled in with some drinks. When they were comfortable, Lawson and the other bouncers moved in. They drove the gang out of the emergency exit and into the backyard, where they beat them up with truncheons and knuckledusters. Lawson found the man who had broken the previous doorman's arm: 'I broke his leg over two beer crates,' he told me. 'I dropped something heavy on it and it broke, and that resolved that situation. And again, I didn't care about that, it was nothing to me.'

Lawson justified his violence by telling himself he always stayed in control. 'I was a very controlled person,' he told me, 'so I would never exert more violence than was necessary. The guys I worked with on the door used to think that I was a bit of a nutcase because they never saw me really get very angry. I was very controlled. I was measured, so I would measure my blows. I don't profess to be the hardest man on the block or whatever but I would be very calculated. So if I'm gonna punch you, if you're a threat to me, I'm thinking I'm just going to punch the throat and take you out. Or I'm gonna stick my thumbs in the eyes. So I want to inflict maximum damage in the shortest time, instead of fighting you for ages and risk killing you.'

Another job was at a club in Preston, where drug dealers from Manchester had encroached. On his second night there, one of the bouncers found two men dealing drugs on the dance floor and Lawson kicked them out. Not too long later there was an emergency call from the same area. Lawson and the other bouncers rushed in to find fifteen men all challenging them to fight. All the memories of those martial arts films must have kicked in, because Lawson pulled out a hidden pair of nunchakus and, swinging them around his head Bruce Lee-style, launched straight into the gang, knocking down two and chasing out the rest.

On another night a gang infiltrated the club and started making trouble. They were soon kicked out but decided to smash up the Italian restaurant across the street. Lawson and the team stepped in and the situation turned into a mass street fight. He continues: 'It was very, very brutal and by the end of it, I think there was about eight or nine of them unconscious on the floor. It got really violent and every single one of them was knocked out and I had overstepped the mark. I had to pull some of the guys off because they didn't quite have the self-control that I had. But it was very proficient. One guy had a bottle and I worked well with Jay, the paratrooper, so as I gave the guy a leg sweep, he went up in the air, Jay elbowed him. By the time he came down, he was unconscious.'

Soon the police arrived, asking awkward questions. But Lawson's team was prepared for just such eventualities. They all had spare uniforms, so when the police searched them for evidence of the fight, their clothes were all spotless and free of bloodstains. Still the officer threatened to come back and arrest them as soon as the gang had regained consciousness and could testify against them: 'Fortunately for us they were all on temazepam and they couldn't remember a single thing,' Lawson told me.

But things proved to be more serious in Manchester. At their first night at an American-themed nightclub called JFK's they saw bullet holes spattered across the front doors. They were informed that someone had recently attempted to shoot one of the previous doormen with a sub-machine gun. At another club, Lawson stopped a local gang member from entering. The gangster soon returned with backup, who were clearly carrying weapons. Lawson decided to try and front it out, reaching inside his jacket for a pretend pistol. Incredibly his ruse worked and the men quickly faded away. At the same moment another gang of men turned up. Lawson was introduced to Brian Phillips, a Mancunian gangster whom the security team had got onside and whose reputation trumped any of those trying to get into the club. Belatedly, Lawson realised it was Phillips's presence, not his pathetic ruse, that had scared the gangsters away: 'Brian was a very, very dangerous man,' Lawson told me. 'There was rival drug dealers and they petrol bombed his house. His wife and kids were burned to death in the house and so he didn't care after that.'

Lawson grew fed up with trying to raise children in violent and impoverished Birkenhead. He had remarried and he and his wife Jenny were raising a baby son together, as well as her daughter from a previous relationship and Lawson's oldest son, Danny. He determined to move the family back to Scotland and in 1999 they did so, just before the birth of their second son, Lewis. The family found a nice house in a respectable seaside town called Port Seton just outside of Edinburgh on the east coast. Lawson soon found work as a doorman and was offered work for a security team protecting the Rolling Stones, who were performing in Edinburgh. He did such a good job protecting Keith Richards during a false fire alarm set off by the press, that he was offered a permanent role with the band's security team. Sadly, he had to decline the offer. With a growing family he couldn't start jetting around the globe. And anyway, he had his eyes on an offer that could prove more lucrative.

Through a prison contact Lawson was introduced to a man known only as 'The German'. The German had made his money on a VAT tax fraud scheme that involved importing goods from Europe, selling them on to other front companies, then exporting and re-importing the same goods in an endless loop, claiming VAT refunds each time. The same number of goods could be recycled up to thirty-five times, claiming VAT back each time, so big money was involved. 'That's going to attract gangsters on a much higher level,' Lawson told me, 'The real gangsters, the gangsters behind the gangsters, come out of the woodwork at that point, the businessmen gangsters who don't like to get their hands dirty.' Such a gangster was The German, a multi-millionaire who owned several mansions, a fleet of cars and even his own helicopter.

The problem was The German worked with other gangsters and gangsters who were untrustworthy. Several of the people working with him had siphoned money off his operation to the tune of millions of pounds. One in particular, a gangster from the North East called 'Spider', had set up companies in The German's name, netting himself several million pounds, before disappearing to Spain. Having heard of Lawson and his friends' reputation for professional violence, The German wondered if they would be interested in reclaiming the stolen money from Spider and several other debtors.

Lawson was up for it and assembled a team that included Jay, the ex-paratrooper, a former South African special forces soldier called Antony and John Rhodes, a doorman, to carry out the work. (Names have been changed.) The first job was on a man known only as Luke, who owed The German £13 million. Lawson and his team would receive 20 per cent of the money plus anything valuable they found in the man's house if they returned the £13 million to The German. Lawson's plan was to stake out the man's vast mansion and grounds to find the best time to approach, then pose as police officers and make their entry. Once inside it should be easy enough to 'persuade' the man to return the money. Everything went to plan, with Lawson, Jay and Antony gaining entry through an unlocked back door. But something was immediately wrong – Lawson heard the sounds of children's laughter coming from one of the downstairs rooms. Unwilling to have kids involved in the potential violence to come, he pulled the plug and quickly backed out of the house.

Two weeks later though he was back. This time there were no kids and the operation proceeded. Posing as police, they quickly rounded up and subdued everyone in the mansion, including the man's girlfriend and two friends. With guns held to their heads, the man soon agreed to transfer the money from his South African bank accounts to the Swiss account details Lawson provided him. But the operation didn't go as smoothly as it had started. A painter and decorator turned up at the front gate and Lawson had to turn him away, posing as a policeman. Then a kitchen fitter turned up. Meanwhile, the two cleaning ladies had arrived and not being let in, had jumped over the back wall and got in through the open back door. They too had to be subdued. Eventually the money was transferred and Lawson forced the man to empty the safe, which contained £28,000 in cash. He gave the cleaning ladies £10,000 each to keep them quiet and the gang left.

The next job was on three men from Newcastle who owed The German £7 million. Lawson and the gang were to kidnap them from their homes in Newcastle then drive them to The German's factory premises in Cornwall, where they would extract the information to regain the money. By monitoring the men, Lawson found out that two of them met regularly at a factory on the outskirts of Newcastle – the perfect place for a kidnapping. Posing as police, Lawson and the team swooped on the factory and soon had the two men handcuffed and bundled in a van heading for Cornwall. During the six-hour journey it became apparent that Lawson and his team weren't in fact cops. The men became rowdy and started threatening him with repercussions, so he hit them a few times, mentioned The German's name and put pillowcases over their heads. Thinking they were about to be killed, one of the men lost control of his bowels, causing an indescribable stink that Lawson and the crew had to endure for several hours – 'It's a smell that I'd never want to smell again,' he told me, 'the smell of fear and urine and faeces together.'

At the factory, The German interrogated the men about the whereabouts of his money. When answers weren't forthcoming, Lawson boiled a kettle and threatened to pour the contents over one of the men's groins. The man quickly changed his mind and coughed up the answer, but now the mission changed. The German told Lawson to take the men to the woods and wait for his word while he checked the veracity of the information. If it was false then Lawson was to kill both men. Kidnap had suddenly turned into potential murder and Antony and John weren't happy about it. But Lawson kept his men under control, taking responsibility for the job himself. If the call came through to do the job, he determined, he would shoot both men in the head with his 9mm pistol. He had always been known for his cool, calm acts of violence. Now, he felt sure, he could use the same detachment to kill in cold blood.

The ten minutes spent waiting for The German's call were the longest ten minutes of Lawson's life. When his phone eventually rang, everyone's eyes turned to him as he hit the answer button. Several pairs of eyes scanned his face as he listened carefully to The German's instructions, looking for any sign of the fate awaiting the prisoners. After several seconds of terrible waiting, feelings of worry and sheer terror turned to blessed relief as a smile broke across Lawson's face: 'The information they'd given was correct,' he told me, 'and we let them go.'

But Lawson and the team never got their money. The German was arrested not long after the kidnapping and all his assets were frozen. However, Lawson and the team didn't let this stop them. Still determined to go after the cash, they decided to target The German's biggest debtor, Spider, who was holed up somewhere in Benidorm. They had heard from an inside contact that Spider had millions in cash stashed in his Spanish villa. With The German off the scene, this could now be all theirs. They flew to Spain and obtained weapons and Spanish police uniforms from a local contact then monitored Spider's villa for the best way to approach. The plan was much the same as with the previous victims – to gain entry posing as police then get to work. But this time they intended to kill Spider and bury his body in a nearby building site that would soon be covered with cement – an idea Lawson got from a gangster movie. When the time came to decide who would pull the trigger that ended Spider's life, again Lawson volunteered.

But again, luck was against them. On the day they were about to go in, a minibus full of Spider's family turned up and entered the villa. There was no choice but to cancel the mission and come back another time. The problem was that when Lawson and Jay returned for another recce, they both came down with a mystery illness that left them incapacitated. Barely able to walk, they spent the whole time in their beds until they had just enough strength to get back on a flight. As soon as they were flying home, the illness disappeared. Clearly the mission was not meant to be.

Still undeterred, back in the UK the team were keen on another trip to Spain, but first, they needed funds. The opportunity presented itself when John told them his new girlfriend's ex-husband had ripped her off to the tune of £90,000. If Lawson and the team could get it back, they would receive a share. Lawson first tried breaking into the man's house and waiting for him to return, but instead it was his girlfriend who turned up and so the team had to beat a hasty retreat. Next, he tried calling the man and extorting the money. But here his luck ended: he was called to the local police station for questioning.

After Lawson's team had broken into his house and confronted his girlfriend, the man had contacted the police, who were now recording his phone calls. A voice analysis expert had identified Lawson's accent by its unique mixture of South African, Scouse and Scottish. The police searched his house and car and found a stun gun and truncheon in the Range Rover and a tray of shotgun cartridges in the garage. Lawson was arrested for kidnapping and attempted extortion. He was found guilty of attempted extortion and sentenced to five years in prison. All his assets were seized and his bank accounts frozen. To compound the punishment, he received an extra fifteen months for contempt of court because he refused to give evidence against his colleagues, John, Jay and Antony.

He was transferred to Glenochil prison near Stirling, where he quickly got his head down and tried to behave himself, getting work as a cleaner in the prison library. But soon the news came that he had been dreading – his wife Jenny wanted a divorce. She had always turned a blind eye to his criminal activities but having her house searched by armed police in front of their well-to-do neighbours had left her with a permanent sense of shame. She couldn't access any of their bank accounts and she was probably going to lose the house. She had finally had enough. Lawson accepted her decision as philosophically as he could but spent hours crying in his cell later that night. He knew he had ruined everything for the family he had sworn to take care of. He had always striven not to be like his own father yet here he was separated from his children for several years. He seemed doomed to repeat the mistakes of his family's past.

A Nigerian inmate had been pestering him to attend Bible classes so Lawson decided to give them a try if only for the free cakes, which he intended to pilfer while everyone had their eyes closed in prayer. 'But before I could steal anything, this pastor guy moved us to the other side of the room,' he told me. 'And then these guys, they start singing these Christian songs. And I'm thinking, *I just don't want to be here*. And they handed me this song sheet with these Christian lyrics on it. And I'm not ashamed to tell you that in that moment, when I look at these hardened criminals and I was reading the lyrics,

I knew I was going to cry, but I didn't want them to see me crying so I hid my face behind the song sheet.'

Troubled by the experience, Lawson went to see the pastor a week later. The man laid out the Christian faith in terms that made sense to him. He said that just as Lawson had been judged in court, one day he too would be judged by God, but the way to escape this judgement was by repenting of his sins and surrendering his life to Christ. 'It made me think,' Lawson told me. 'And I spent the next week really thinking about this whole God thing and whether it's real and whether it's not. About a week later, I prayed for the first time in my life. I became a Christian in that prison and my life really did change. Thoughts of crime began to go. I began to have more empathy for people.'

Released in 2007, Lawson has since devoted his life to spreading the Christian message throughout some of the toughest and most run-down prisons in the world. Spreading the word is a full-time job for him now, but one for which he does not receive payment, relying on voluntary contributions to cover the expenses for his travels. Money, the motivating force for most of his life, now has no hold over him. He has had no income for twelve years but has done more in those twelve years than the rest of his life put together.

My impressions of Lawson are definitely of a gentle man who spoke of his offences and violence without any trace of pride or boasting but with the cool detachment of someone who has transcended that part of his life. But more than that I detected, through his stories, that there was always a good side in him just waiting to emerge. Yes, he could be capable of cold calculating acts of violence and yes, he was emotionally detached from his crimes and the suffering he caused, but he was never a psychopath. There was always an element of the hurt little boy striking out at the world because of the pain of his abandonment by a father he looked up to and loved so much. Throughout his life of crime, he always strove to be a better dad than his own father and stuck by his family through thick and thin. Eventually, his circumstances, and a powerful encounter with religion, brought that goodness to the forefront, dissolving the anger and hurt that had characterised most of his life up until that point.

Lawson's story, ultimately, is an example of how circumstances and upbringing can turn intrinsically good people into violent offenders but it also illustrates how that same innate goodness can be rediscovered and redeemed. As he said to me when recalling some of these incidents, 'I don't like remembering these things because it's disgusting really, it's horrible. My life is very different today so the things I'm telling you, I'm not telling you in a boastful way. I'm really disgusted with myself.'

7

David McMillan

International Smuggler's Thai Death Row Prison Escape

A criminal mastermind who faced the death penalty multiple times and co-ordinated breathtaking escapes

As the death-row inmate slithered along a plank sixty feet in the air, he felt the cut edge of the cell bar digging into his back.

'More,' he called to his companion. The big Swede heaved with all his might to twist the steel bar back further. It was just enough. David McMillan slid his oiled body through the gap and out into the night air of Bangkok. His first breath of freedom for two years. But he had only escaped his cell: it would take much more to get through the compound of Bangkok's maximum-security Klong Prem prison, aka the Bangkok Hilton, a jail from which no Westerner had ever escaped.

He said a quick farewell to his Swedish friend through the cell window. Sten and his other cellmates would face harsh reprisals for allowing a cellmate to escape but there was nothing he could do about that now. Facing death by firing squad for smuggling heroin into Thailand, there was only one option left. He crawled out along the eight-foot-long plank of wood, most of which was now hanging out of his cell window, and looked down into the compound several storeys below. All was quiet.

174

Balancing on the end of the plank that once served as a bookshelf, he extracted from his pack a hundred-metre length of army-boot webbing that would serve as a rope. He looped one end around the end of the plank and dropped the rest to the ground sixty feet below. The plank was necessary to clear a sloped awning that jutted out from the wall of the building.

Climbing down on to the rope, he relaxed his grip slightly and let it slide through his hands. Too fast. The thick nylon burned his palms as he tried to slow his descent. He just managed to break his fall by lodging a foot into one of the safety loops he had tied every two metres in the rope. He came to a juddering halt. His hands were torn and he was now swinging in a wide circle just below the level of the awning's roof, coming perilously close to the wall. Below, he could see the cell full of trustees on the ground floor – prisoners who would sound the alert at the first sign of anyone trying to escape. Some of them were awake.

With his heartbeat pounding in his ears, he was forced to wait for his uncontrolled swaying to stop before he could continue the descent. Once the rope was still, he saw there was no other option than a semi-controlled drop to the ground, thirty-five feet below. Easing his grip, he slid the rest of the way down, burning and cutting his hands even more and landing with a painful thud.

He had made it and without any major injuries that would foil his escape. If he were caught, like all the previous escape attempts he had witnessed, he would almost certainly be beaten to death by the guards. But there was no time to think about such things. With seven internal walls still to climb and a three-times higher outer wall topped with electrified barbed wire and dotted with machine-gun towers, the hard part was still very much to come.

I have interviewed David McMillan twelve times – in a series titled *International Smuggler Thai Prison Escape* – and his story could fill several more podcasts. An Australian citizen born in the UK, McMillan has been many things in his life, among them a children's TV host, a technological whizz-kid, an escapologist, a multi-million-dollar drug trafficker so successful he retired at the age of twenty-four and a criminal mastermind who led the US Drug Enforcement Administration (DEA) a merry dance for over four decades.

Just talking to the witty and urbane McMillan you can tell he has a capable mind. Oddly, it may have been his own brilliance that was the cause of his demise. He was so good at what he did, it seems sometimes he couldn't stop himself from taking that extra risk. More than that, his brazen success so embarrassed several crime agencies in Australia and abroad that they took it as a personal challenge to bring him down at whatever cost. This would be true of one US intelligence officer in particular, a man called Bill Shenkmann, who would become McMillan's lifelong shadow and nemesis.

'He kept appearing over the years,' McMillan said of Shenkmann, 'nearly at all my international arrests. He certainly appeared in Bangkok just to have a gloat.'

It was the indomitable pursuit by Shenkmann and the DEA that led to McMillan's arrest in Thailand. Already imprisoned for eleven years in Australia for heroin smuggling, he had been hassled and surveilled by police ever since his release. Fed up with the heat and having lost his wife Clelia to a prison fire (she had been held on the charge of importing drugs), he had decided to retire from the game (for the second time around – his first retirement was just before his first imprisonment at age twenty-four) and was flying to the UK to start a new life. But over the years McMillan had invested a lot in Thailand

and he couldn't help making a short stopover in Bangkok to see what, if any, of his business affairs remained intact. Little did he know his two-day stopover would turn into two years.

It was December 1993 when thirty-eight-year-old McMillan landed in Bangkok using a fake passport and a false trail of clues leading Australian police astray. The deception was sealed by his friend Michael Sullivan calling his mobile phone number – which was tapped by Australian police – and playing a recorded conversation saying that he was staying in the hills outside Melbourne.

Confident that his presence in Thailand was unknown, McMillan went about his business. He called then met up with two old smuggling contacts – Tommy, the nephew of one of Thailand's biggest drug barons, and Lee, an old employee in McMillan's Bangkok smuggling operation. What McMillan didn't know was that year the Thais had installed a new telephone operating system supplied by US companies which contained a back door allowing US intelligence agencies to listen to virtually any phone call in the country. Worse still, Bill Shenkmann was in the country at the time and on the hunt for drug traffickers.

His brief business over, McMillan headed for Bangkok's airport. In the check-in queue, he began to notice signs that triggered his hypersensitive smuggling instincts. He spotted several men who, by their body language and demeanour instantly gave away – to McMillan at least – that they were undercover police. McMillan told me 'watching policemen everywhere betray themselves with one trait. Despite nervy glances in all directions yet focusing on nothing, and artificial gestures of chin rubbing and arm stretching, they can't move their feet. As though anchored to the floor like a kitten pinned by the tail to a flagpole.' Two were standing on an overhead walkway and one by the immigration desk. The men were clearly waiting for someone, but who could it be? Confident in his own invisibility it didn't even enter McMillan's head that it might be him.

That changed when he got to the check-in desk. Something about the way the woman reacted when she looked at his passport told him instantly – it was him. She made a poor excuse about checking something and asked him to wait for a moment. But McMillan was too experienced to wait even a second. As she left the desk, he backed away and headed for a drinks machine then suddenly shot left and down some stairs to the arrivals hall. He squirmed through the busy hall and out to the taxi rank, grabbing a cab from the middle of the queue and directing it quickly away from the airport.

McMillan now headed to a friend's travel agency in Bangkok's Chinatown, where he had a second fake passport stored which he could use to escape the country. He rightly guessed that the heat must have been triggered by Tommy's phone being tapped. Kindly, but foolishly, he stopped to call his friend to warn him that the police were on to his communications. Even more stupidly, he told Tommy – in code – where he was headed. Unbeknownst to him, Tommy then called their mutual friend at the travel agency to tell him that McMillan was on his way. This call was intercepted by Shenkmann and the DEA, who were waiting to arrest McMillan the moment he walked into the travel agency: 'My grey hair almost happened overnight,' McMillan told me about the shocking suddenness of his arrest.

McMillan was kept in a holding cell for seven days, where he witnessed another foreign inmate unsuccessfully attempt suicide with sleeping pills. 'Chinatown police station is probably one of the more miserable places to be locked up in the world,' he told me. 'It's bars within bars within mesh. The cell was small, people in there very despairing.' The Thai police had relatively little to charge him with, only the use of a false passport. So, probably at the encouragement of the DEA, they fitted him up with an ounce of heroin – just enough to leave him facing the death penalty – and shipped him off to Klong Prem prison, the infamous Bangkok Hilton.

He was first placed in the so-called 'Cure', the remand section of the prison for drug offenders. Floored by his unexpected arrest and death sentence, McMillan was suicidal and in a kind of coma of hopelessness for his first few weeks but a visit from an Australian police officer who gloated over his fate catalysed an anger in him that reinvigorated his fighting spirit. He bribed his way into the less harsh main prison and started to think about escape.

His first night in the main prison was spent in a hot, overcrowded cell with twenty-one inmates and thousands of bedbugs. This, it turned out, was a way of weeding out the rich from the poor prisoners. Given the terrible cramped conditions, the prisoners with money soon offered to bribe their way to a better cell and the guards then knew whom to deal with to line their pockets. The poor, of course, received nothing but the lion's share of the brutality. During his time in the prison, Klong Prem had a death rate of two inmates per day, according to McMillan.

He paid his way into a new cell with some foreign inmates, enjoying the relative luxury of half a dozen to a cell, not to mention an attached bathroom and toilet. While McMillan's trial crawled on, he managed to get some ATM cards smuggled in, which the main guard of his block used to supply him cash – minus a 10 per cent commission, of course. He also rented some office space in one of the factory huts where inmates were put to work painting portraits of Thai royalty. He even employed a handful of servants, including a personal cook, two cleaners and a butler to run the whole show. Money talked in Klong Prem, but one thing McMillan soon discovered was that no amount of riches, influence or power could buy your way out: escape seemed the only option.

His few enquiries into escape methods didn't provide optimistic responses. Almost no one ever tried it and no one in living memory had succeeded. This was not so much because of the multiple internal walls, the massive outer wall, the electrified barbed wire, machine-gun towers or moat, but mostly because all the inmates helped the guards. Reprisals were so terrifying following escape bids that nearly anyone who witnessed an attempt would immediately raise the alarm. Of the few foolish enough to have taken on these odds and attempted an escape, all had been unsuccessful and nearly all had died. As an example, there was the salutary tale of the four Thais and a Singaporean who had most recently tried to flee.

The five men had somehow managed to escape their 100-man dormitory without anyone squealing, by dint of bribes and threats of violence. They cut their way through the cell bars and made their way over the internal walls with the use of a rope. But the rope proved too short for the massive external wall and they had no other means of scaling it. They tried forming a human pyramid before it became obvious that the attempt had failed. On their return to their building, they handed themselves in. They were placed in individual punishment boxes – pitch-dark, stiflingly hot metal lockers with only room to crouch. The four Thais were taken out and beaten every day with heavy sticks – 'They didn't survive it,' McMillan told me. 'Within three months all except for the Singaporean were dead. And when he got out, he never spoke again and he was a colour I've never seen on a human being.'

Still undeterred, McMillan thought constantly about escape. He was facing the death penalty after all, which in Thailand at the time involved being shot to death by machine guns after receiving thirty lashes with barbed wire. Most death sentences were commuted to life, but even so, life in a Bangkok prison was not something he was prepared to contemplate. He first tried bribing a trial judge to grant him bail based on a fake medical report, but the $50,000 disappeared with no results. Another idea was to escape from the prison's car repair shop in a specially fitted cavity in the back of a VW van. But the plan was foiled because he could find no inmate mechanics who could be trusted to keep the secret. Another idea was to use help from back home – flying out some of his armed bank robber friends to bust him out of court during the trial. Some of the friends flew over to scope out the potential: they counted 135 armed police in and around the courts in just one hour. The plan was cancelled.

McMillan eventually settled on the traditional method of sawing through the bars of his cell. He smuggled a message out to his old friend and business partner, Michael Sullivan, who sent him four hacksaw blades concealed inside the frame of a poster. One of his cellmates, a big Swede called Sten, was in on the plan but he changed his mind after two Israeli prisoners were moved into their building.

The Israelis had been arrested smuggling drugs in the northern city of Chiang Mai. They escaped through the roof of their prison and scaled the wall but had nowhere to hide except a hostel, where they could lie low until the heat died down. Unfortunately, the hostel owner shopped them to the police, who caught them again. This time the police took no chances. They smashed the two men's legs with steel bars then dropped rocks on them to prevent the breaks healing properly. 'Their legs looked like a kid at McDonald's who grabbed all the drinking straws and crushed them in a tiny fist,' McMillan said. It was enough to put his Swedish friend off the escape attempt but not him.

When the fateful day came, McMillan waited until his cellmates were ready for sleep before making his attempt. He turned off the cell light switch and went straight to work. He was lucky the preparations were complete because he'd just heard from his lawyer that his trial would be ended within two weeks and it looked bad – probably the death sentence. When he asked the lawyer why his case was being rushed through to such a harsh conclusion, he was told foreign agencies were leaning on the Thai authorities – Bill Shenkmann and his friends at the DEA again.

At around midnight, McMillan moved to the shower screen in the cell's bathroom and removed the four tungsten-tipped hacksaw blades which he'd hidden there earlier that day. He then took a small wooden table and unfolded it into steps which allowed him to reach the cell window. He took the webbed matting that made up the underside of his mattress and unravelled it to reveal 100 metres of army-boot webbing that would form his escape rope. He had hired skilled carpenters from among the Thai inmates and unbeknownst to most of his cellmates, almost every item of furniture in the small room concealed an object to aid his escape.

McMillan climbed up to the cell window and began sawing, but the sound of a full stroke was terrifyingly loud. He had to hold the bar with a wet towel, oil the blade and work much more slowly. This turned the work of perhaps ten minutes into a slow, laborious and tiring effort of several hours. It wasn't until 2.45 in the morning that the bar had been cut through at one end and halfway through at the other. He didn't feel he had enough time to continue cutting, so asked Sten if he could bend the bar back far enough for him to squeeze his body through the gap.

Sten managed to pull it back just far enough that McMillan thought he could, with the aid of an oiled torso, slip through the gap. He quickly removed some more escape aids from a hidden cavity behind a cupboard and then, with Sten's help, began to move the eight-foot bookshelf from the wall and slid it through the gap in the cell bars. This would be required to clear the protruding six-foot awning that prevented a straight descent down the wall. The trouble was most of its eight-foot length would need to be outside the window, with just a couple of inches inside the cell to provide a counterbalance. McMillan had solved this problem by constructing a footstool which cleverly unfolded to form an angled object that would lock the plank firmly in place and hold his weight.

Once the plank was fixed in place, McMillan was ready. He signalled to Sten and the big man started to pull on the bar: 'He grabbed a hold of that thing and bent it like he was strangling every guard that had ever given him a hard time in his entire life,' McMillan recalled. It near enough worked and he managed to haul himself through the tiny gap with only minor scratches.

Once outside it was like he had entered a different reality. 'Suddenly everything was still and different,' he told me. 'The sound was different. I was like a visiting creature who'd landed on the side of the prison, some winged griffin that had been clutching the thing. And I looked in at them – my life in there meant nothing any more. That's the end of that. Whatever's to come, that's the end of that.'

With a few more heart-stopping manoeuvres, he was soon on the ground. It was gone 3.30 a.m. and he had until 6 a.m., when the prison awoke, to reach and scale the outer wall. It would definitely be tight.

McMillan had always been resourceful and, it seems, influenced by money. In his book *Escape*, he tells about early film footage showing him as a one-year-old learning to walk in London's Hyde Park. As encouragement, his father waves a £5 note at him from the corner of the screen. The young McMillan tries and fails to walk but grabs precociously at the money. The short film ends with the baby sitting on the grass waving the note triumphantly. He didn't learn to walk, but he did get the money.

Born in London in 1956, McMillan was the son of a British ex-army major-turned-television executive and an Australian radio copywriter who'd emigrated to London looking to be dazzled by those in the new world of TV. The marriage didn't survive its first decade due to his father's infidelity, so in 1958, two-year-old David, his older sister, Debbie, and his yet unborn brother, Simon, moved back to Australia, where they settled down in Melbourne with his grandmother and aunt.

McMillan travelled a lot as a child, by air and ship, and was often left alone for long periods of time, taken care of by his older sister while his mother was away overseas and their new stepdad, a French businessman, was away at work. He was first arrested at the age of nine, having broken into a matchbox factory to get his young hands on the collectible labels. He was found by a security man and handed over to the police. At the police station the officers tried to find the name and contact details of his parents but nine-year-old McMillan refused, holding out until nightfall when he realised he was going to be in trouble with his mum. Co-operating with police, it seems, was never in his nature.

Always precocious, at age twelve he got a job reading the news on children's TV. At the time he was attending a rough inner-city school, where the bullies didn't take well to TV stars. After school, the young McMillan would keep a knife hidden in his jacket while looking for a taxi to take him to the television studios. He was later moved to a more civilised private boys' school but he was expelled before graduating for attempting to cook LSD in the school lab.

McMillan finished school and began drifting. He found a job as an usher at a sex cinema and filled his spare time working on a magazine for legalising marijuana, while dreaming up a number of illegal get-rich schemes. None of them worked and the most ambitious – a plan to use private-hire Learjets to smuggle $3 million worth of marijuana from Thailand to Australia – brought a warning from his family lawyer to back off. Apparently, the DEA was taking an interest in the Learjet movements and their enquiries had led them to McMillan. He was now on Shenkmann's radar.

Rather than let these setbacks stop him, McMillan decided to quit all attempts at a normal life and throw himself full-time into being a criminal. In 1975, he flew to Beirut, ostensibly to help an old friend of the family with some filming work. There was also the possibility of some large-scale marijuana trafficking with the friend's rich and well-connected family. But McMillan's visit coincided with the outbreak of the civil war in Lebanon and he soon left again in fear of his life. However, one incident in Lebanon illustrated his genius for technological solutions and out-of-the-box thinking.

At a dinner party, some of his host's friends were complaining of the tenant laws in Lebanon, which meant they couldn't kick out underpaying tenants. McMillan came up with a scheme to make the tenants leave of their own accord, making money from grateful landlords in the process. Aware of the deeply superstitious character of the Lebanese, he ordered a high-powered laser to be shipped in from the UK. Hiding in buildings opposite his targets, he would train the laser through the tenants' windows, burning an image of a devil's face on to their sitting room walls while the family sat around. Not only did this method clear the tenants out of the house, it did so in record time.

It was Thailand where things would finally fall into place and heroin was the missing piece that completed the puzzle. In Australia, in the early eighties, a kilo of heroin was worth over $3 million in today's money – around sixty times more than its current value. At first, McMillan smuggled it from Thailand on his own but he was soon able to afford well-paid highly professional couriers willing to take part in hugely complex multi-flight operations involving several switches and the use of fake passports.

One of his first couriers, who later became a lifelong friend and business partner, was Michael Sullivan. Sullivan was an ex-Olympic pole vaulter-turned-art-teacher-turned-marijuana farmer and drug dealer. They had originally met when Sullivan supplied illegal morphine to a doctor who performed abortions in the sixties when the procedure was still illegal. They met again and became friends under even stranger circumstances. McMillan's girlfriend, Clelia Vigano, wanted him to meet a friend of hers who had fallen on hard times. When they arrived at Sullivan's house they found Sullivan and his wife, a Colombian called Marie, being held hostage by armed robbers. McMillan recognised one of the gunmen as a small-time criminal he knew. He crept back to his car and fetched his 9mm pistol with attached silencer before entering the house.

'I waited to pick my moment until the shotgun had been lowered,' he told me, 'because I knew if he wanted to swing it around, he'd hit the coffee table. So, I had it pointing at him but I went straight into a normal conversation: "Don't mind the gun, Lou; what the hell are you doing here? Take that sock off your face too." He had to gather his composure and almost immediately started making excuses.'

Unlike Sullivan, McMillan had powerful friends whom he made lots of money for, so Lou and his friend weren't long in making their apologies and vacating the premises. The visit went well from there on and McMillan and Sullivan became friends. Michael Sullivan had fallen on hard times after a business partner cheated him, stealing most of his money, and he soon became a courier for McMillan. Sullivan joined a small gang of highly professional, Western, middle-class drug traffickers smuggling heroin from Thailand to Australia via a complex series of routes that might make an airline pilot's itinerary look simple in comparison.

In his book, *Unforgiving Destiny*, McMillan describes a typically intricate operation which involved three weeks and four couriers to smuggle several kilos of heroin from Bangkok to Australia. His best courier, Peter Dale, left Bangkok for London carrying four kilos of heroin smuggled inside the casing of a stereo. A courier based in London then took two of the kilos back to Australia. This was because someone arriving from London was far less suspicious to Australian customs officials than someone coming from Thailand. Meanwhile, another courier took the other two kilos to Colombia, where McMillan and Sullivan were waiting to do a deal with a Colombian cartel to swap it for twice the weight in cocaine. Dale and Sullivan then split the cocaine and smuggled it back to Europe, where Sullivan picked up a reserve two kilos of heroin and smuggled the lot back to Australia. Meanwhile, McMillan diverted to Belgium to convert some of his ill-gotten gains into diamonds before returning home.

Each of McMillan's couriers had at least two fake passports, which he created from the real identities of dead people, usually children who had died too young to get their own passports. He would then create a fake life for these people by entering them into the electoral roll, obtaining fake addresses, then providing them with library cards, bank accounts and other proof of an existence that had long ago ended.

The profits for an average operation would amount to just under a million dollars, according to McMillan. At the height of his career he estimated he was earning around $5 million a year. He had several houses and apartments dotted around Melbourne and a getaway car disguised as a Ford Cortina. The vehicle had a sports car engine hidden under the bonnet and a tank of water at the rear that could be dumped on to the road to lose any chasing cars. But such a lavish lifestyle attracted attention. McMillan soon realised his phones were being tapped and his movements monitored by police. His fake passports all had to be dumped and new ones painstakingly acquired, all under the watchful eye of the Australian Feds. This was the beginning of Operation Aries, a $3 million, three-year police operation to take down McMillan's trafficking enterprise.

The combination of the heat and the large amount of money he'd already made gave McMillan the impetus to retire from the game. He was just twenty-four years old when he began making his preparations to exit the smuggling world and leave Australia to start a new life in the UK.

It was about this time that Tommy entered the scene. Just two months before McMillan and Clelia were due to fly to London, McMillan got a call from Sullivan, saying he had a problem. Sullivan had recently been connected to a Thai businessman called Tommy, who smuggled heroin from Bangkok for him, hidden inside the lining of ornate cutlery sets. Tommy had recently arrived from Bangkok with another load of heroin but Sullivan was unable to collect the drugs because, for some reason, Australian police were all over the travelling Thai. It turned out that a drug-smuggling contact of McMillan's – Peter Howard – had been raided and caught with half a kilo of Thai heroin freshly delivered by Tommy. Looking to save his skin, Howard had offered to help set up the man they were really after – McMillan – using Tommy as an unwitting dupe. As McMillan was no longer smuggling, they'd gone for his old business partner Sullivan instead, hoping McMillan would get drawn in. This was exactly what happened.

McMillan agreed to help Sullivan out of his sticky situation by assisting him to pick up Tommy's heroin while somehow avoiding Tommy's police tail. He arranged to make the switch at a local hospital handily located inside a natural bowl of encircling hills: 'I had to find a place where the police radios wouldn't function,' McMillan told me, 'so I planted a couple of cars around the area and gave instructions for the meeting time.'

McMillan waited with Tommy at the hospital surrounded by easily identifiable undercover police. When he heard Sullivan approaching, he ushered Tommy to Sullivan's car and dumped the cutlery box full of heroin through the window. Sullivan sped away with the drugs while everywhere, the undercover cops leapt into action. Meanwhile, McMillan and Tommy ran to a nearby car park to pick up McMillan's souped-up Ford Cortina. They sped after Sullivan and rendezvoused at a nearby residential road which had two metal poles that could be raised to stop commercial vehicles cutting through it during peak traffic. The night before, McMillan had swapped the padlocks on the poles for his own. He now raised these poles, locked them in place with his own padlocks and raced away in his car, just in time to see the pursuing police get helplessly blocked by the trap.

Tommy got safely out of the country and McMillan patted himself on the back for a job well done. However, having embarrassed the Australian police so thoroughly, it was even more essential to get out of the country. The problem was McMillan and Clelia had to wait until January for their fake passports to arrive – there was just time to enjoy one last Christmas in Oz.

That was when tragedy struck. Unbeknownst to McMillan, Tommy had flown back to Australia to visit Sullivan and had attracted his usual swarm of tailing police. They finally arrested him on a bus travelling from Perth to Melbourne. It was their cue to move in on everyone. Despite having no evidence to arrest him on smuggling charges, the police obviously felt they had to do something before McMillan slipped from their grasp.

The following morning, McMillan heard the sound of a key being slipped into his front door. The door was stopped from opening fully by the chain. The brief moment of silence was shattered by the sudden sound of a sledgehammer smashing the door down. 'The sledgehammers were not the panicky banging away of robbers or intruders,' he told me, 'because I was reaching for a gun and I thought, *Wait a minute, slowly.*'

McMillan, Clelia, Sullivan and his wife Marie, who'd recently had a baby, were all arrested, as well as dozens of others – couriers, friends, even family. 'My mother was dragged in,' McMillan told me. 'She wasn't locked up but whatever jewellery she had, they said, "Oh, that's all stolen."' Despite the intimidation no one talked.

With no evidence, the charges were limited to conspiracy. McMillan and the others were kept behind bars while the police did their best to pin evidence on them by fair means or foul. Clelia and Marie were held in a women's prison in Melbourne. The police planted a female informer into the dormitory which Clelia and Marie shared with half a dozen other women. The informer had been promised her freedom if she could obtain confessions from Clelia and Marie. When neither of the women was forthcoming, the unhinged inmate came up with a plan that quickly turned disastrous – setting fire to their cell.

'The fire was, as I understood it, to get them moved somewhere else, to bring them closer together, to have something in common, a little protest,' McMillan told me.

The wooden-furnished cell was locked securely within another part of the prison. The fire spread quickly through the room, burning it to the ground and killing the informer with it, as well as Clelia and Marie.

'When something's taken away from you, something so eviscerating and emptying, it's as if there's nothing there,' McMillan said about his reaction to Clelia's death. 'And guilt, let's not forget guilt. Something about my life had brought this upon her, something about my life did this.'

McMillan and Sullivan were shattered but the police showed no sympathy. Instead, according to McMillan, they pinned the deaths on him as an attempt to get rid of witnesses. A coroner's inquest backed this up, saying that Clelia had caused the fire on McMillan's orders. The authorities then used this as ammunition to have McMillan and his co-defendants moved to a super-maximum security prison and to force his couriers to finally agree to testify against him. The police persuaded his ex-employees that McMillan was operating a policy of killing all witnesses, as evidenced by the fire.

The police kept up their dirty tricks campaign, working hand in hand with the press to throw as bad a light as possible on McMillan and his co-defendants. Headlines like, 'Heroin Gang Imported $96M Using Dead Babies' were a loose reflection of how McMillan had used dead children's identities for his fake passports.

Even more dramatic headlines followed when it transpired that the conspirators had organised an armed prison escape using a helicopter and an ex-SAS commando based in the Philippines. This turned out to be more foul play. The whole thing had been set up by the Australian police to try and entrap McMillan into an escape attempt. He didn't fall for it, but his initial willingness to listen was enough. Stories about the foiled 'escape' were leaked to the press, who dutifully headlined them: 'The newspapers all had it everywhere,' McMillan told me. 'In fact, a copy of the equivalent of *The Sun* was put on every juror's table with "$96 Million Heroin Syndicate Helicopter Their Way out of Prison".'

The prosecution was clearly worried about the strength of their case because of the lack of evidence. Bill Shenkmann and the DEA dutifully stepped in to help, providing two kilos of heroin which were placed in front of the jurors each day as 'evidence' of the kind of drug the traffickers were importing. It didn't seem to matter that the heroin on display had nothing to do with McMillan or his friends. Shenkmann as ever, it seemed, was taking a personal interest in McMillan's demise. At last McMillan found out why. It turned out that Tommy's uncle, one of the largest drug barons in Thailand, had been involved in the killing of a DEA officer. The DEA had killed Tommy's uncle in revenge but this, it seemed, wasn't enough for them: they wanted to take down anyone and everyone connected to him.

With the odds thus stacked against them, despite the lack of evidence, the trial began. McMillan was charged with eleven counts of conspiracy to traffic heroin, most of which were based on couriers' testimony. The hearing dragged on for a full six months. Despite the police manipulation, the jury were clearly not as convinced as the authorities wanted them to be. Also, McMillan turned on his considerable charm, wit and intelligence, which must have helped. At one point, he used a legal technicality, called an unsworn statement, to speak to the jury for three whole days, putting his case to them personally. On another occasion, he and his co-defendants sang to the jury: 'It was a big hit by The Nylons back then,' McMillan told me, 'called "That Kind of Man".' Another time, McMillan waved his notepad pencil back and forth like a pendulum, saying to the jurors, 'Watch the stick. You are relaxed. We are innocent.'

The jury took a week of deliberating to finally come to a verdict. McMillan, Sullivan and Tommy were found not guilty of all charges except one. Despite this, the judge dished out minimum fifteen-year sentences to all, with McMillan receiving seventeen years in jail. Worse was to come. McMillan was one of the first to fall foul of Australia's new Proceeds of Crime Bill, which meant all his money and assets could be seized by the government. And a year later, incredibly, he was found guilty of the fake helicopter plot and received an extra year on his sentence.

McMillan and his co-defendants were imprisoned in Jika Jika prison in Melbourne. Originally built for terrorists, the supermax facility housed mostly home-grown psychopaths, who were kept under twenty-four-hour surveillance. The forty-eight inmates were held in six-man blocks. Of the five inmates in McMillan's block, four were murderers and one an attempted murderer: 'The death toll every year was about twenty,' McMillan told me. 'People would kill each other the first chance they got.'

McMillan witnessed this first-hand early on in his stay. One day, he was having a polite conversation with a fellow inmate about gardening when he noticed the prisoner was calmly cutting his palms with a knife. The man returned to his cell and minutes later, the alarm sounded. It turned out that McMillan's conversation partner had just minutes ago murdered another inmate and had been cutting his own hands to make it look like self-defence from a knife attack.

On another occasion, he was in the day room making pan-cakes while two other inmates sat at a table, listening to music. One of the prisoners was using strong adhesive to glue together teddy bears for a charity scheme. Suddenly the man gluing the teddy bears stood up and walked behind the other inmate, dumping the large tin of glue over his head and smothering it into his hair and uniform. Just as the victim stood up to react, the attacker produced a thick wad of matches held together by elastic bands. As McMillan watched dumbstruck, the attacker lit the matches and threw them at the man soaked in adhesive, turning him instantly into a human torch.

The man was still alive by the time the guards arrived to put out the flames, but in a terrible state. 'He was black and charred,' McMillan told me, 'and his testicles swollen to the size of apples.' He died three hours later in hospital.

McMillan spent much of his time thinking about escape but surprisingly never attempted it. He was young and felt that he could last out the ten years minimum sentence without too much trouble. In the end he was released from the supermax by disaster rather than escape. Five inmates sharing a block decided to stage a protest by burning their mattresses. As the whole building was linked by air conditioning, the idea was that smoke would spill into the guards' room, providing them with a timely warning of how vulnerable they were. Each of the inmates had scooped the water out of their toilet bowls and once the fires had been lit, were supposed to stick their heads inside their toilets and seal them with wet towels. In this way they could breathe clean air while the toxic smoke proliferated. Unfortunately, one of the protesters got worried about the proximity of the fire to his foot and lifted the edge of his towel to look. This broke the seal and toxic green smoke was instantly sucked through the pipe system into the faces of all five inmates, who immediately began choking. 'The protest was very effective,' said McMillan, 'and the place was closed because those six guys were charred remains by the end of the day.'

Because of the fire, the supermax was closed in 1987 and McMillan was transferred to a less traumatising institution. After several other prisons, he spent his final stretch in an open prison on a farm, where he worked at the café and could regularly visit the outside world. He spent a total of eleven years behind bars before being finally released. But if he thought he'd be free to live in peace, he was very much mistaken. Almost immediately upon being freed, he was followed, bugged and monitored by a surveillance team that seemed to have forgotten the passing of time. He even spotted people tailing him when he tried to visit Clelia's grave. 'There were two policemen following me,' McMillan said, 'and I thought, *Well maybe they'll give me a bit of peace*. But they didn't. They got closer to me behind as I got to the grave markers. And I backed away like a robber who backs away from a job turned bad. And to this day I've never been there.'

With the heat approaching intolerable levels, McMillan decided to leave the country again. He obtained a fake passport and laid his plans secretly before flying out of Melbourne for the last time, heading for a new life in the UK. Unfortunately, he couldn't resist that one little stopover in Bangkok. He was arrested and imprisoned in the notorious Bangkok Hilton while the Thai authorities – spurred on by Shenkmann and the DEA – worked hard to secure him the death penalty.

We left him having escaped his sixty-foot-high cell by rope and having just touched the ground. From there he still had seven inner walls to scale, followed by a massive outer wall topped by electrified barbed wire and studded with machine-gun posts. Worse, he only had two and a half hours to do it.

Retrieving his rope and with one last wave to Sten, McMillan slipped on a T-shirt and headed for the office space he rented at the painting factory. He clambered through a prepared hole in the fence and through the factory to his office. Once inside he unlocked his cupboard and opened a hidden panel to retrieve a set of street clothes, four rolls of black gaffer tape, some thick cable ties and a collapsible umbrella. He collected eight heavy picture frames which he had assembled in the run-up to the escape and lashed them tightly together. He then moved to a nearby box-making factory, where rows of bamboo canes were stored. Laying out his picture frames on the floor, he used bamboo canes from the factory, along with gaffer tape, to bind the frames together to form two sets of ladders.

Racing against time but forced to be deathly silent, he dragged the assembled ladders out of the factory, through the car repair shop and out the other side, sliding the ladders under the gate while he climbed over the obstacle. He was now facing the first of the inner walls, but a noise alerted him to the presence of a guard. The man was taking a drink from the water trough in the open air. McMillan had planned for such contingencies and reached inside his pack for a fake automatic pistol and silencer created from aeroplane model balsa wood and painted black. The only part of the weapon that was real was the laser sight, which would place a red dot on his victim's chest that looked real enough to ensure their quick silence and co-operation. He could then bind and gag them with the cable ties and gaffer tape. Fortunately, he didn't need to use the weapon: the guard finished drinking and stumbled, half-asleep, back to his bed.

McMillan climbed the first wall, using a crude hook to pull down the barbed wire that topped it, and pulled the ladders over after him. He climbed the next five obstacles by lashing the two ladders together, climbing them, then seesawing down to reach the other side. The last obstacle before the outer wall provided an unwelcome surprise – rows of barbed wire at the foot of the wall. McMillan was forced to remove one of the picture frames from his ladder to wedge a gap in the barbed wire through which he could squeeze. At the foot of the outer wall was a two-and-a-half-metre wide canal running with sewage water. He tied one end of his rope to the ladder then angled it across to make a bridge before clambering across. On the narrow patch of ground on the other side under the wall, he used the rope to pull up the other end of the ladder, clearing the moat and propping it vertically against the wall. Despite its missing rungs the makeshift ladder was still long enough for him to reach the top of the wall. He took a deep breath before climbing this final obstacle.

At the top of the wall, he witnessed for the first time in two years the long-imagined horizon and freedom. Unfortunately, that horizon was tinged with orange. 'Not a lot of time to enjoy it,' McMillan said, 'because that glow was fast turning into the tip of a shining sun and my watch was telling me I'd got sixteen minutes before the official time of the guards arriving for work.' He climbed back to the bottom of the ladder and changed quickly into his street clothes, donning a pair of heavy rubber gloves to tackle the electric wire. Back at the top of the wall, he tied his rope to a steel post and used his rubber gloves to manhandle a path through the electric wire. Once across, he slid down the rope to the outside earth nine metres below.

Once on the ground, he opened the collapsible umbrella that would serve to conceal his face from onlooking guards. Holding the umbrella low over his face, he headed round the outside of the wall to a bridge that crossed the surrounding moat and led to the prison's main entrance. One of the guards in the machine-gun towers spotted him but didn't react. With his civilian clothes and umbrella, the man must have thought he was just another guard taking a shortcut home after a night shift.

At the entrance gate hundreds of staff and visitors were already crowding into the prison. McMillan walked calmly against the tide of bodies, keeping his umbrella low, and made his way through the gate and across the main road outside the prison.

Standing on a raised walkway to look for a taxi, he took one last look at the prison that would probably have seen the end of his life. 'It was my first view from height of this huge prison after over two years,' McMillan recalled. 'I looked back at all the buildings. I'm looking back at perhaps 8000 people in there. I've left them but that's all still going on – the struggle for food, the battles who to bribe and who to pay. But that's behind me.' Turning away, he hailed a taxi and jumped inside before disappearing into the blessed anonymity of Bangkok.

McMillan escaped Thailand and finally made it to London to start his new life but it wasn't the end of his adventures, or his experience of foreign jails. He spent a year and a half in a Pakistani prison and a further six months in a Danish jail – both thanks to the continued attentions of Bill Shenkmann and the DEA. It would take another seventeen years – and the death of Shenkmann, who died from apoplexy – before McMillan's life would finally settle into some vestige of normality. In 2014 he was arrested in the UK and held in Wandsworth prison while he fought a drawn-out legal battle to avoid being extradited to Thailand to face the death penalty again. The extradition order was cancelled just two weeks before he was due to be flown back to Thailand. He was finally released in 2016.

However, he did get the last laugh over Shenkmann and the DEA. Going to visit a friend in the US, he smuggled in half a kilo of coke using the innovative method of concealing it inside the advertising panel attached to his luggage trolley. Despite a thorough search of his luggage by US customs officials, he successfully got the drugs into the country. After all he'd been through, why risk it? Because he could and because he wanted to get one over the agency that had dogged him all his life.

While in America, McMillan took a trip to Shenkmann's burial place at Arlington National Cemetery. The 600-acre site is divided into courts. Standing over the monument to the dead intelligence officer, he took some of the cocaine he'd saved from his imported package and sprinkled the white powder over Shenkmann's tombstone. There is no way of knowing what the strait-laced DEA man would have said if he was looking on, but McMillan doubts it would have been interesting.

'He never said anything quotable,' McMillan told me, reflecting back on all the times Shenkmann had turned up to gloat after his arrests. 'I almost felt like making up some lines for him because he's supposed to be the towering villain in the thing. He was such a flat character. Even when I'm finally at his graveside, it was only by coincidence I found some parting words for him.'

What were those parting words? Two strangers walking by asked McMillan politely if the buried man was family. 'No,' he replied, moving away from the gravestone. 'I think I've ended up in the wrong place. I should be in court number nine.'

8

John Abbott

San Quentin Prison, Shoot-Outs and Escape

During two shoot-outs with the cops, John lost his brother and crime partners

The young men's blood turns cold as they hear the sound every criminal fears above all others – police sirens. The oldest, just twenty-one, thinks furiously about their next move: there have been no alarms at the jewellery store they are robbing so they have either been victims of incredibly bad luck or – more likely – they have triggered a silent alarm. He curses their stupidity and prepares to make a quick escape but his eighteen-year-old companion has other ideas.

As the police arrive outside, the younger man draws down with a .22 rifle and starts firing shots at the squad car, hoping to stun the rural California police with surprise fire, allowing the two thieves to escape, but he has underestimated the experience of the cops. One of the officers is a Vietnam veteran who is used to gunfights. As they escape out the back, he is waiting in ambush and fires his shotgun, hitting the younger man in the face and dropping him to the ground. The older thief just manages to avoid a shot intended for him and scrambles away with gunfire ringing all around him. It is the start of a long night on the run.

The man who got away was John Abbott, whom I started to interview in 2019 for a series of podcasts. The other thief was his younger brother, shot and killed in a gunfight with the police in 1976, aged just eighteen. Abbott would go on to serve a five-to-life sentence in some of the US's toughest prisons.

No surprise there, you might think, except that Abbott and his brother weren't hardened armed robbers. They weren't even criminals. Abbott was a university student, the son of middle-class academic parents who taught at the University of California. His upbringing was idyllic; his life was on an easy road to money and success. So how had he ended up robbing a jewellery store and getting into a shoot-out with the cops? And, more importantly, how would this skinny middle-class white kid survive the jungle of maximum-security prisons like San Quentin during the peak of the seventies race wars?

'It was stupid shit that young guys do,' Abbott said in our first interview. 'My brother and I were walking along and he told me that he was an excellent car thief. And I said, "What do you mean?" He said, "Well, I can steal any car you can point out in ten seconds." And I said, "You're full of shit, show me." So, we went to this parking lot and sure enough he stole the car. And then that turned into, it was my turn to do something. So, I had my eye on this jewellery store. So, I thought, *we'll try and be super cool and burglarise the place*. And unfortunately, of course, not being professional criminals, we set off the alarm.'

Abbott's father was English and his mother Canadian. Born in Carlisle in England, he had been raised in Canada. He and his brother had moved to California when their parents got teaching positions at the university. Now Abbott found himself in a California county jail. His time on the run hadn't lasted long. He had made the mistake of phoning the hospital the morning after the shoot-out to check on his brother's condition. The call was traced and Abbott was arrested by plain-clothes police.

In the quiet Yolo County jail, Abbott's crime made him something of a star, but this would soon change. It was 1976 and the protocol at the time was to send all new inmates in northern California to the California Medical Facility in Vacaville for psychological and behavioural profiling before sentencing. This meant Abbott was soon rubbing shoulders with hardened criminals, gangsters and murderers.

Not just this, as a medical facility, Vacaville housed some of the most notorious serial killers in US history, such as Charles Manson and Edmund Kemper. Abbott says he saw Manson from afar, sitting cross-legged in a monkey cage with long, dirty, unkempt hair, looking like a 'hobo' or a 'deadbeat'. But what surprised him most was the amount of fan mail Manson received: 'He got more mail in one week than every other prisoner in the prison did. It was just endless pictures, and people volunteering to marry him, and people wanting to come visit him, people sending him money . . .'

As for Kemper, Abbott was told a story about how the other prisoners had decided to test his strength: 'He was a huge guy and so somebody talked him into going to the weight pit to see how much he could push. And he didn't push weights, but he lay down on the bench press, and they piled on all the iron they could find and he bench-pressed it. And of course after that, nobody wanted to be near him, right, because he could put one hand around someone's throat and just choke them out.'

But these were just stories and things seen from afar. Abbott's first direct experience of violence came quickly. As a 'middle-class college white geek' with no experience on the street or gang affiliations to protect him, he soon realised he was out of his depth, so he headed to the weight pit to begin the long process of bulking up. He takes up the story: 'Almost the first day I was there I saw this guy. He was huge, great physique, lying there doing bench presses, and you thought, *well, this guy would have no problem at all.* And I'm sort of admiring him there and the second I'm doing that a gang of Nesters has come from behind the handball court, knocked his spotter out of the way and then they're jumping on him. One of them hit him on the head with a ten-kilo weight. He's unconscious and they're [makes stabbing motion] in the chest. I don't know what to do and so I'm standing there, and everybody's running like deer for the gate and then the guns go off, bang bang . . .'

It was a cold, hard shock. If this monster of a man could be taken out so easily, it could happen to anyone. Being buff clearly wasn't the only solution to surviving in prison, but if Abbott had one advantage on his side it was his ability to learn fast. Prior to his arrest, he had been studying Japanese as an undergraduate and had an IQ of 180. He soon realised that prisoners were experts in sniffing out weakness and that weakness could come in many forms. It might be as simple as handing out a cigarette to someone who asked for it or, conversely, trying to hide your cigarettes as if frightened of someone taking them. Intelligence itself, he soon realised, could be a weakness. As he told me, 'The more intelligent you are, the more you see things from both sides. There is no other side, there's just the survival side and you'd better see things that way and not be worried about what's motivating the other guy.'

Abbott realised that he had to toughen up in more ways than just physically. Behaviour and attitude were every bit as important as muscles in the fight for survival. His priority now became not just to make himself look tough, but to develop the mental attitude to back it up.

After ninety days in Vacaville, his sentence came through – five to life for assault with a deadly weapon and five to life for armed robbery, to run concurrently. Five to life was a psychologically brutal punishment which meant a minimum of five years behind bars with a possible maximum of life, but with no indication of when release might be. This deprived prisoners of that crucial element of hope which a release date provides.

Abbott was sent to a medium-security prison called the Sierra Conservation Center. It sounded like an agricultural college, but if he thought it would be a breeze, he would soon be proved wrong. During his first meal there, he noticed something strange happening in the line-up for the food. 'These young guys,' he recalled, 'these convicts were cycling along the wall with their trays held up over their chests. I mean, they were expecting to get attacked any minute.'

Abbott asked a seasoned old-timer what was going on and found out that these men were gang members who had just transitioned from Tracy, a maximum-security facility where there were so many stabbings that they literally had to queue for dinner with their backs against the wall and their trays held up as shields. And if he thought this behaviour was overly paranoid for their new medium-security setting, it was another mistake. Also watching the parade of paranoid gangsters was a white giant: 'He was like one of these six-foot-four, two-hundred-pound Viking gods,' Abbott told me. 'He was just huge and he had the SS runes on the neck and the whole thing. And he's standing there and suddenly this young Chicano runs up and just stabs him right in the back, just a perfect shot right between the shoulder blades.'

It was a second lesson in how survival of the fittest didn't necessarily mean survival of the biggest. 'Have you ever heard this saying, the tough guys are all dead?' Abbott asked. 'Well, that was a saying and as far as I could see, it was true. The dangerous guy in prison, the guy who is really dangerous, is small. He's small and quick and he's afraid, and he's the guy who'll put the knife, like that Chicano did, right in your back. The big guys, they don't have the experience. They're always confident and they've been big so they don't have to fight. People are afraid of them, naturally, and so that makes you overconfident.'

The stabbing was Abbott's introduction to the race wars sweeping US jails. The reason for the hit, it turned out, was because the Aryan giant had leaned on the little Chicano, demanding the smaller man iron his clothes. By doing this the Viking had crossed a racial line and the Chicano's friends from the Nuestra Familia gang ordered the young man to put a hit on the giant. The young man was only in for a short sentence but he had carried out the hit right in front of the guards because, evidently, not obeying a direct order from the gang involved a far worse fate than extra years on his sentence. It was another salutary lesson: don't get involved in a race war.

But this was easier said than done. In the late seventies, the US was gripped by interracial violence on the streets, which of course spilled over into the prison system. In California prisons at the time, according to Abbott, there was a roughly equal split between white, black and Hispanic prisoners. There was an ongoing war between the whites and blacks. The blacks were mostly represented by the Black Guerrilla Family, a street and prison gang founded in the sixties, and the whites were represented by the neo-Nazi, Aryan Brotherhood. But there was also an ongoing race war between La eMe, the Mexican

Mafia based in Los Angeles and Nuestra Familia from northern California. These ongoing wars were causing hundreds
of stabbings a year in California prisons. The violence was
often confined to gang members but it could spill over at any
time, especially during a riot when everyone was expected to
'represent' their own race.

But even if you didn't cross the race line, you could still
get in serious trouble with those of your own skin colour, as
Abbott found out one sunny day while queueing for ice creams
for himself and his friend. He takes up the story: 'I go over to
the canteen to get some ice creams and as I'm standing in line
this AB [Aryan Brotherhood] member is behind me. And he
says, "Buy me an ice cream, bro." That's all he says. Now that's
the moment of truth in the jail system. It might not sound
like much. You know, maybe you could just buy him an ice
cream, that'd be fine. I buy the two ice creams and I turn and
look at him, and he's just covered with muscles and tattoos,
and the guy looks like a caveman. I mean, he's straight out of
the fifth century, a berserker.'

As Abbott said, this was the moment of truth. Did he acqui-
esce, buy the ice cream and forever be treated as a punk? Or
did he refuse, stand up to the giant and probably get his head
kicked in? Abbott chose the latter. He turned to the berserker
and said, 'I ain't your bro.'

True to his appearance the man went berserk, challenging
Abbott to a fight in the dorm. Abbott walked off with his
two ice creams, ignoring the man, but he knew the situation
couldn't be left as it was. He had walked away from a challenge
and that was as bad as buying the guy an ice cream.

Abbott checked with his friend, who told him the man was
called 'Stormer' and as well as looking the part, was also the
prison middleweight boxing champion. Nevertheless, Abbott

would have to do something. He decided to wait a couple of hours to let the bigger man cool off before confronting him. 'He's over playing cards with all his hangers-on,' Abbott told me, 'and we walk up and I look him in the eyes, and I tell him, "Stormer, I'm ready for the dorm now. Let's go." And he just looks at me and he says, "Ain't no thing. Ain't no thing."' Abbott had made the right move, but it could easily have ended in blood.

The uncertainty about his future with the five-to-life sentence was beginning to get to Abbott. He had a grandfather who had served in the First World War and had escaped from the Germans seven times, so an escape attempt had always been on his mind. His first chance came at the Yolo County Jail when another inmate told him about a fencing weld that had come loose in the yard. Abbott found a blind spot behind which the guard couldn't see him and went to work on freeing more of the fence. He couldn't work enough of it free the first day so he had to leave it. In the meantime, someone ratted on him and he was seized by the guards.

Abbott's second attempt was less dramatic but more successful. In California, convicts were used to fight forest fires as they were seen as expendable. Abbott was assigned to one of these firefighting teams as a clerk. His escape was as simple as arranging for a friend – a tourist visiting from Canada – to park a few miles down the road from the forest camp. Abbott waited until the early hours of the morning when the guards would be snoozing and simply walked out of the dormitory and down the road to the waiting car.

The most difficult thing turned out to be not escaping but managing to survive in the outside world. Abbott headed to the Tenderloin, San Francisco's version of Skid Row, where he rented a cheap room with the prison money he'd saved

208

and began a hand-to-mouth existence, shoplifting food and possessions from the local stores.

A man Abbott describes as his crime partner was soon released on parole and came to join him. This was the catalyst to propel Abbott from a life of petty crime to far more serious transgressions. With his partner, Abbott soon started robbing the many drug dealers around the Bay Area, a process which, he said, 'warmed my heart'. One of his first taxations was a couple of dealers who worked for the Hells Angels, who had stiffed the wife of a friend on a drug deal. Abbott and his partner reconnoitred the dealers' house before swooping in for the strike with weapons drawn. Unfortunately, one of the Hells Angels turned up as the robbery was going down.

Abbott continues: 'It was really exciting because there were three doors. I could hear his Chopper sort of pulling into the garage and there were three doors he could be coming out of and we didn't know which one it was, right? So, we're standing waiting for him and suddenly the door opens and there he is. And he's the quintessential biker, you know, with the bandanna and the beard and the sunglasses and all the accoutrements. And he looks at me as I say, "Freeze!" But he didn't really believe me. I guess I was sweating too much. But my partner put the gun under his jawbone. He believed that, right? So, we tied him up. And, there were drugs, there was money, there were leather coats, racks of champagne – you know, whatever you wanted, Bose speakers, the latest of everything. So, I had died and gone to heaven. We spent about three hours there packing up everything, took his Chopper, took everything.'

Ballsy operations like this one got the pair a reputation and soon they were being used as guns for hire. One of their jobs was working for the Italian Mafia in a gang war against the Hells Angels in the San Francisco Bay Area. The Hells Angels had decided to go into competition against the mob in the sandwich-truck business. In typical Hells Angels fashion, the gang had done this by burning down the competition's trucks by placing hand grenades under the gas tanks. Sandwich trucks were burning fast in the so-called 'Sandwich Truck Wars' so they hired Abbott and his partner to cruise their truck sites, looking out for Hells Angels armed with hand grenades.

But Abbott's crime spree couldn't last forever. He soon got sloppy and started recruiting others, which helped the word spread back to the FBI. The fateful day came when he was in his apartment in San Francisco. A fireman came to the door and told him there was a gas leak. Abbott's sixth sense immediately knew something was up. He had two choices – to start firing and try to blast his way out, or try to sneak away. He opted for the latter, climbing down the back stairwell. But he met more firefighters on the way up. He tried to bluff his way past them but they recognised him instantly and arrested him – 'It turned out the FBI had taken over the Nob Hill fire station,' Abbott told me, 'taken the uniforms of the firemen, told the firemen to stand down, to not inform the San Francisco police because they didn't trust them.'

As a notorious armed robber, Abbott was now destined for a maximum-security prison but he did have one amazing stroke of luck – somehow he got no time added to his sentence, either for the escape or the numerous crimes he had committed while outside. He explained: 'In California at that time there were literally tens of thousands of criminal cases coming up every week, so every jurisdiction was just avalanched, inundated with cases, just endless cases. And so how do you manage this? Each one costs money and the county has to pay. But if I say, well, I just plead guilty, I'm making it easier for them and the quid pro quo is they don't add any extra time.'

On the less fortunate side, Abbott was now destined for San Quentin, one of California's maximum-security prisons, with a brutal reputation enforced by its intimidating appearance. 'Parts of it look like the gates of hell,' he said. 'I mean, you've got great big iron doors, massive. And you just look about this big. And you're walking around looking like you're on the way to hell and there's no getting out of it.'

Abbott describes the atmosphere of San Quentin as like the 'Colosseum' or the 'savannah'. The guards were happy to have an easy life so long as no overt violence took place in front of them, so the prison was basically run by the inmates. The law of the jungle – or the gladiatorial arena – prevailed. Anyone fighting in front of the guards was basically shot, so violence was confined to areas where security was scarce, such as the library or gym. Knives were everywhere. Abbott described how some prisoners were running a knife-making business from the metal workshop. Any inmate could nab a stainless-steel dinner knife from the food hall and give it to the guys at the metal shop, who would grind it down to a lethal blade.

Stabbing was so commonplace in San Quentin that Marin County's stab unit at the time was considered the best in the US, according to Abbott, from the sheer number of cases coming out of the prison: 'Guys would be stabbed five, six, ten, twelve times,' he told me, 'and unless it went through their brain or through their heart they could put them back together.' Combine the stabbing rate with the delicate situation of the race wars and the predatory environment of an inmate-controlled prison and you had to tread carefully in San Quentin not to put a target on your back. 'You're in a different reality there,' Abbott told me. 'Cutting in front of a convict in the canteen line, that's grounds to get stabbed. Not paying back five packs of cigarettes, that's a stabbing. Every mistake you make you pay in blood.'

It was just a couple of weeks into his stint at San Quentin that Abbott found out just how easy it was to make such a mistake. His cell was on the fifth tier with a long and fatal drop to the ground. Incredibly, San Quentin had no safety net between the tiers and just a three-bar railing around the edge. On his second week at the maximum-security prison, Abbott left his cell to see two men trying to throw a third guy off the tier.

Unfortunately for the two men, their victim was putting up a good fight, holding on to the railings so desperately that they couldn't get him over. However, the predators caught the man later at lunch and beat him savagely with a pipe before the guards could intervene. Abbott later found out what the man's mistake had been. The two attackers had asked if they could borrow the man's TV to watch a football game and the man had agreed. After the game the men had sold the TV to some Mexicans for $20. And this is where the man had made his mistake – he had gone to their cell to ask for his TV back.

Abbott noted the behaviour of the inmates who witnessed the attempted murder. 'Every convict – black, Chicano, white – we're just gently stepping around these two guys trying to throw this kid off the tier. And of course we can't look at this because that's dry snitching.' (Dry snitching is where, by means of body language, you hint to a guard that something irregular is taking place.) It was another mistake that could cost an inmate his life.

Abbott was learning survival skills quickly. The key, as he saw it, was to keep your head down and maintain a fine balance between appearing ready to fight, without ever having to actually throw down. As he told me, 'If you get into a fight in prison, you've failed. It means you haven't been playing your cards right.' Treading such a fine line meant keeping your wits about you at all times and in Abbott's case, never getting drunk or high, and being out of your bunk in the morning as soon as the cell doors opened. Fitness was paramount. He had managed to bulk up in the gym but he also concentrated on stamina by jogging and speed by playing badminton and handball. He had noticed that in boxing matches between some of the supposedly toughest guys, both men were punched out within a couple of rounds. That taught him another useful rule: never accept a challenge to fight in the ring. It gave the other cons a chance to analyse your weaknesses.

Fitness exhausted you, which meant you slept well at night – one of the most important psychological factors for surviving a prison sentence. Another way to sleep well was to get a trusted friend as a cellmate. Cells were one of the main places where violence took place, so a trusted cellmate was essential: 'If you have some guy who you don't trust, then you can get taken out any day. Those cells are pretty small and if two guys are standing shoulder to shoulder, no one's coming in.'

As well as cellmates, it was good to have trusted friends and even better if those friends were some of the hardest men in the prison. Abbott cultivated such friendships with men like Phil Thompson and Hells Angel Doug 'The Thug' Orr. Thompson may not have been the most impressive-looking man around, according to Abbott, but he was certainly one of the most dangerous and his past was darkly fascinating. He had fought in Vietnam, doing black ops under the CIA. One of these was Operation Phoenix, an American terror tactic which involved sending commandos into Vietnamese villages at night to slit the throats of Vietcong collaborators. Thompson was one of those commandos. As Abbott said, 'When you've had guys, young guys, doing work like that night after night, month after month, and then the tour of duty ends, what kind of person are they going to be?'

Abbott saw just how dangerous Thompson could be when he accepted a challenge to fight in the ring. Thompson was no boxer and at thirty-five years old, he was getting on a bit. But he was a big man and his bag of tricks was enough to put down any enemy. Abbott explained, 'When they came to the first bit of boxing, he just leaned into the guy and he put his thumb into his eye and pushed down on his optic nerve. And the guy just went unconscious, didn't even know what happened to him.'

But even Thompson wasn't the most dangerous prisoner Abbott said he ever met. That title went to another friend he cultivated, Doug Orr. Abbott described Orr as an assassin for the Hells Angels. He was the right-hand man for Sonny Barger, the first president of the Oakland chapter of the Hells Angels. According to Abbott, Barger called Orr the most violent man he had ever met. Abbott himself described Orr as 'about six-four, blond-brown curly hair, big classic like a Viking god' and 'a straight-up berserker' whom he had once seen break a pair of metal handcuffs with his bare hands in a fit of violent strength. He treated Orr as a mentor because, he said, in prison he was interested in running into the 'real deal', not just the storytellers who sat around talking nonsense all day about their criminal and violent exploits. It also can't have hurt to have a man like Orr on your side.

But even with all these precautions in place, sometimes a fight was unavoidable. Abbott described one of his first as also one of his most educational: 'It was about two in the morning and the TV was still blasting in the cell and I couldn't stand it any more so I just suddenly said, "Turn the fucking TV off!"

And I thought to myself, *what have I done? I've just thrown out a challenge to anybody who likes TV. And do I sit, do I stay in my bed, or do I jump up and face whatever happens?* So, I jumped up to try and face what happened, but I wasn't ready at all for what happened.'

What happened next was one of the fattest men in the whole prison stormed into Abbott's cell, a man so big there was no room to manoeuvre around him. 'He had one move and he did it exactly right,' Abbott said. 'I was in the narrow space between the bunks and the bars and he just charged straight down like a hippo and he just threw himself on me, and I went back on the bunk and 300 pounds of fat just enveloped me. And I realised suddenly I couldn't move. The fat just covered every space in between and I'm just, I'm nailed.'

Now the man had Abbott trapped, he tried to strangle him. Abbott's hands were free so he was able to grab the man's wrists. Although he was big, fortunately, the man had been weakened by drug addiction and was unable to break Abbott's grip.

The two were now at an awkward impasse, neither able to move nor get the upper hand. 'So finally, I said to him, "Hey, could you get off me, please?" And he just rolled off and let go. And he went and sat down in the TV room and I went to bed. But I mean, I've never lost a fight so badly.'

The lesson he learned from this embarrassing defeat? If you do ever have to fight, make sure you're the one who acts first. Abbott explained to me the brutal reality of most prison fights: 'All these Hollywood movies, I mean, it's just embarrassing to watch because, you know, a guy gets a tremendous smack on the jaw, jumps up and he's good to fight. The fact is, you hit a guy hard like that in the jaw – one, he's got a broken jaw; two, he's on the ground stunned. And then you just go to work on him; that's what really happens. Prison fights, if you ever get into them, are usually sucker punches and the sucker punch nearly always wins.'

One thing on Abbott's side in San Quentin was the kudos of his crimes. This, combined with having people like Phil Thompson and Doug Orr on his crew, earned him serious 'manna' as he calls it. In his first stint in jail he had been content to keep his head down and not get noticed, but this time he wanted more: he wanted his own racket. The opportunity presented itself with a friendly guard and a colour printer.

Abbott had got a job as an education clerk so he had access to a high-quality printer. The opportunity to make some money out of this machinery presented itself to him one day when he was considering his TV guide. 'In those days everybody had a TV but if you had a subscription to a TV guide, by the time they searched it and you actually got it in the mail, they made sure that it was Thursday so there were only two or three days left on the guide by the time you got it.'

Abbott saw his opportunity. He approached one of the few guards who was friendly with the cons – a Russian citizen who had fled to America – and asked if he could smuggle in a TV guide. He put the guide through the printer and ran off 500 copies. He then needed to sell them and here he made one of the mistakes that could be so costly in San Quentin – he decided to cross the racial line. 'Who you gonna sell them to, just white people? Well, I couldn't see that working so I took the chance. I decided well, I'm just gonna walk across the tribal lines here. So, I went down the tier to every cell and I come to the black guy and he says, "Fuck off, white boy," but a lot of guys just took it.'

Abbott gave away the first copy for free then sold the guides for fifty cents each. Soon he was getting through 200 copies a week. After that, guys from different blocks asked if they could be distributors. Abbott gave them half the profits and took half for himself. Soon he had ten to fifteen guys working for him and was making hundreds of dollars a week. The scam didn't go unnoticed by the guards of course but, as Abbott told me, 'For the guards this was positive because people watching TV is how the guards want you to do your time. You just fall into this endless zone and a decade passes, twenty years pass. If every inmate sat down and said, I'm going to spend the rest of my life in prison, and they internalise that reality, then why not take all the guards hostage? Why not a hundred guys run and try and climb over the fence and maybe twenty get away? Why not? But if you're all watching TV and waiting for your next movie and, you know, when is Kim Kardashian gonna be on the show?'

Abbott soon began widening out his enterprise, moving into the soft drinks market. He started buying bulk cases of soft drinks for twenty-five cents a can and cooling them with ice blocks from the kitchen freezer. He would sell the ice-cold sodas at fifty cents apiece, making 100 per cent mark-up. Thanks to these enterprises, he soon became something of a player in San Quentin and all without being gang affiliated or getting involved in serious violence. But nothing was ever quite that simple at San Quentin and soon the mistake of crossing the racial line came back to bite him.

It happened after some wannabe Aryan Brothers stabbed a Black Guerrilla Family member twenty times on the fish tier. Word soon got around that there would be retaliations. White guys better watch out. 'You have two choices when you hear something like that,' Abbott told me. 'You can stay in your cell or you can just carry on, because San Quentin is so mad and these things happen so often that if you pay attention to that all the time you're never gonna come out of your cell.'

Perhaps he was getting overconfident or sloppy but Abbott decided to go to the library. A friend warned him not to go, but he decided to ignore the advice. He was reading the newspaper with his back to the wall when suddenly he saw the flash of a knife heading straight for his neck. He managed to duck just in time and the blade scraped his shoulder. At the same moment another BGF member struck from the other side. Abbott just managed to avoid that blow as well: 'I went into hyper-speed,' he said, 'and I crashed into him and I crashed into this table. The table went over me and him. I sort of crashed through the bookshelves and we went down. I ended up on top of him. His partner came over to give me one and he scratched me in the ribs here and at that moment the alarm bells went. And this guy, he figured he'd already got me so he just sprang over the counter to run. And as soon as he sprang, I turned to face him and this guy who I was on top of broke and ran.'

Abbott was taken to the infirmary but his wounds were superficial – although he did need drugs to bring his blood pressure down from 200 over 100. Four men were stabbed in the BGF's retaliation, including one old guy who Abbott remembers just lying, staring at the ceiling, not even attempting to fight back as he was stabbed repeatedly in the chest. Abbott was put into segregation for his own protection. The prison authorities tried to get him to go on a protection programme but he refused, even when they brought his mother in to try and persuade him. He was savvy enough to know that signing on to a protection programme was to tar himself with a brush that would never wear off.

Eventually, he got out of seg by the unprecedented means of a petition that was also signed by many black inmates (Abbott's partner was selling their speed). But if he thought he had escaped the consequences of the race war, he was soon proved wrong. Word got to him that a newly arrived white gang, which would later become the Nazi Lowriders, was demanding that Abbott do a retaliation hit on some black inmates. This was one of those fork-in-the-road moments like the one with the ice cream. What Abbott did now could affect the rest of his time in prison. If he refused, he would make himself a target for the Nazis. But if he made the hit, he could add years to his sentence and probably be attacked in retaliation.

Abbott takes up the story: 'I talked to a friend of mine. I said, "Where are they?" And he said, "They're down on the yard near the old garden." And so we went down there, my friend and I, and there were five of them there and the guy's sitting there, the leader of them. And I said to him, "You know who I am, and you know why I'm here. Now I don't hold with that racist bullshit. I don't have any tattoos. I ain't gonna stab somebody I don't know. I'll stab somebody who fucks with me. So, the question is, are you fucking with me? Because if you are fucking with me, we can deal with it right now." And he just looks at me and the other ones just look at me. That's it, that was the end of it.'

One good thing did come out of the attack – Abbott thinks it led to his early release on parole. His mother was a professor at the University of California and his father had an important job at the World Bank, so he thinks the idea of him being killed in a race war panicked the authorities into granting him an early release. He had been in prison just over five years – the minimum duration of his five-to-life sentence. It was 1980 and he was back on the streets.

It soon became apparent that the authorities had made a big mistake. One problem was that due to the new determinate sentence law replacing five to life sentences, half of Abbott's prison gang got parole at around the same time. They quickly formed a criminal gang and, in Abbott's words, 'took it to the next level'. One example of this next level was recovering debts from a Chinese restaurant owner with connections to the Triads. 'People were afraid to do that,' Abbott told me, 'because of the Triad connection. But we were out of San Quentin. We weren't afraid of anything. So, we went over and grabbed him and convinced him to do what he should.'

Probably because of his background, Abbott had always looked straighter than straight, the kind of guy you'd expect to see working in a bank rather than robbing it. This came in handy a couple of times on the outside. One time he and a friend decided to check out their police files at the station. They walked straight in without anyone sparing them a second glance. On another occasion, Abbott's appearance as a good white kid probably saved Phil Thompson's life.

The big man was due to have a meeting with a high-up Nuestra Familia gang member. Abbott decided to go along to provide some backup, with his AR-15 assault rifle concealed in a guitar case. As he watched the meeting between Thompson and the NF guy on a street corner, he noticed two Chicanos hanging around nearby, who were almost broadcasting the fact that they were gang members.

Abbott takes up the story: 'Now I'm wearing a Stanford University T-shirt, right, and Harold, who's with me, is wearing, he loved these Hawaiian shirts with the bright colours. So, we look like a couple of tourists. Anyway, so Phil's walking along with this general, the Nuestra Familia general, and they get into this mobile home, this RV that's parked there. And Phil sits in the front with the guy. And then these two Cholos come and they open the door and sit right behind the two of them. So there's three of them all around him. So I just opened the door, and get in, flip the guitar case so it's open, and just stand there. And all of a sudden, I don't know what they had planned but whatever it was, they decided it was time to go home.'

But again, Abbott's crimes were beginning to draw the attention of the FBI. One day he was stopped on the highway. He had a gun in his bag and he knew that meant a ticket straight back to San Quentin. He managed to escape from the officer but he knew it was time to leave the US. He decided to head for Canada with his friends, Phil Thompson and Michael Hennessey, accompanying him. The trio had a tentative plan to rob a gold refinery in the mountains just over the border, but they never got that far.

The Canadian authorities had been warned about their presence. A trap was sprung and Abbott and Hennessey walked straight into it when they went to pick their car up from a garage. Abbott continues: 'As I was talking to the garage owner he started acting very strange and looking over his shoulder at this door, and I've got bad vibes from him, so I sort of backed up a bit. And suddenly two guys in plain clothes burst out of the room and went to tackle me. And I backed away from them. And my friend was outside and he saw these guys coming for me. And well, as far as he was concerned, I was being attacked. So, he shot one of them through the leg, told the other not to move. And they turned out to be undercover RCMP officers. Anyway, there were two more of them. And another one came from behind and shot him twice.'

Abbott now found himself in the Mounties' firing line: 'I had this RCMP officer that I was sort of punching in the face regularly and by this time he was kind of punch-drunk. And so I held him, I wanted to hold him in place so this other guy couldn't shoot me. And the other guy was sort of angling for his shot, because of course, you know, their blood's up and they've already clipped one guy. And fortunately, the last policeman came out, who hadn't seen all this drama, and he ran over and smashed me in the face with his pistol. And instead of being shot, I just had my nose broken.'

Hennessey was less fortunate. Although his wounds weren't fatal, one of the shots had clipped the back of his tongue and, because he was left lying on his back, he drowned in his own blood before the ambulance could arrive.

Abbott was arrested on an attempted murder charge and placed in a Canadian prison. One of the upsides of Canadian jails, he would soon discover, was that there were none of the racial tensions that dominated Californian prisons. Despite this, however, he managed to stumble into a racial situation within just hours of being put in the Oakalla remand centre. He noticed immediately that the mattress in his cell had a pool of blood beneath it and that some Native Americans from a nearby cell were giving him evil looks. The next thing he knew, a little white kid had run in complaining that the Native Americans had beaten up his friend, breaking his arm, and that he would be next. Apparently, the Native Americans were forcing people to play cards with them, then extorting them heavily if they lost, followed by severe beatings if the victim couldn't pay.

Abbott continues: 'I said, "There's only one way out of this, you gotta show some heart. So you just run into that guy's cell and give him your best shot as hard as you can." But he's looking a bit nervous. I said, "Seriously, if you don't do this, I'm not gonna help you, you're on your own."'

The kid manned up. Despite being only five foot six compared with the bully, who was six foot two, he ran into the man's cell and threw hot coffee into his face. 'The Indian just roars,' said Abbott. 'He comes barrelling out of the cell. I hook him around the neck, kick out his legs. He goes on the ground. I stomp on his jaw a couple of times. He starts screaming. As soon as he starts screaming, the guards come. But the kid suddenly recovers his balls and he comes running in to put the boots on this guy.'

It wasn't to be Abbott's last run-in with the big Native American. At his sentencing four months later, he was sitting in the court waiting room when the big man was brought in and sat next to him. Abbott was panicking because his hands and feet were shackled while the other man's hands and feet were free. He braced himself for an imminent beating but instead the big guy smiled and offered him a cigarette – 'He was friendly as pie,' Abbott told me.

The mystery was soon cleared up. When they entered the court for sentencing it turned out the Native American had been convicted of raping a thirteen-year-old girl. Now Abbott had the goods on him, which was why he was desperately trying to butter him up. 'I go back to the remand centre,' said Abbott, 'and the same kid was there. And I said, "You'll be interested in this." And I told him the tale. And boy, the posse was out after this guy after that.'

It was only a minor sweetener to Abbott's court visit – he came away with a ten-year sentence for attempted murder. He was incarcerated in Kent maximum-security prison on Canada's west coast, near Vancouver. According to him, the jail was mostly populated by desperate addicts, whom he refers to as, 'About the worst prisoners in the world, because they combine being sleazy with being weak, with ratting people out easily, with being selfish and greedy.'

But if he thought these weak sleazy inmates would make for less violence, he was wrong. Amid the general population of dope fiends were hardcore dangerous gangsters from Quebec, who had been moved to the west coast to isolate them from their criminal networks. This caused a certain clash of world views which could prove fatal, as Abbott witnessed first-hand.

An English dope fiend had stiffed one of the Quebecers on a drug deal. The man was as surprised as he was hurt when the gangster walked up to him and stabbed him in the chest in front of everyone. 'This English guy was just standing there – he almost died – and he was just stunned: "He stabbed me, he stabbed me!" And you can understand because, for him, that kind of move in the Vancouver dope world was just run-of-the-mill everyday activity – stiff other addicts and they stiff you, and steal each other's stashes and whatever. But for the Quebecois, they played by San Quentin rules.'

Kent prison may have been less hardcore than San Quentin but it was still a place where mistakes could mean death. Abbott told the story of an American gangster who, like him, had fled across the border and got in a shoot-out with the cops. The man had been shot in the head and lost one of his eyes. His skull was a patchwork mess and another sizeable hit to his head would kill him: 'This guy, he had a disconnect in his head between who he was now and who he had been: a hope-to-die gangster or an escaped convict and all the rest, but now he was essentially a cripple and that disconnect caused what came next.'

Some dope fiends had their eye on the ex-gangster's coke stash and they stole it. Still seeing himself as the alpha male, the former gangster put up a poster on the bulletin board, declaring he knew who had taken his coke, and would soon get revenge. As Abbott pointed out, this was a classic mistake: 'One thing you do in the joint is you never threaten anybody. You either do it or keep away. But what you don't do is broadcast that you're gonna do it.'

The dope fiends decided to act first. They hired the services of a certified psychopath who had beaten an old woman to death for complaining about his loud music: 'He ran in with a weight bar and he broke the guy's arms and broke his legs and then whacked him in his skull, shattered his skull again. So, I wouldn't say that prison was particularly peaceful.'

Despite these incidents there was a more relaxed air in the Canadian maximum-security prison than its American counterparts. Abbott noticed that the vegetarian food from the kitchen was far more appealing and healthier than the carnivore slop, so he converted to Buddhism to gain access to the vegetarian menu on religious grounds. The jail even had social occasions where members of the public could join the inmates for meals and live gigs. The atmosphere was so liberal and indulgent that Abbott even managed to get lucky with a woman inside a giant speaker, of all places, during one of these socials.

Abbott puts the relative liberalness of Canadian prisons down to the 'bone stupidity' of the race wars in the US. Because the Canadian inmates weren't expending their time and energy killing each other in racial violence, they could spend it fighting against the system itself, instigating huge riots that, in one case, burned down an entire prison. The governors weren't stupid and realised they had to keep their prison population happy, rather than in California, where they could just maintain control by playing one race off against another.

Abbott embraced the new system and got a job teaching remedial students within a prison educational programme. He was also able to study for a university degree. This helped set him up for his release after six and a half years in Canadian jails. On his release in 1987, he was deported back to the UK, the land of his birth, and from there he moved on to Japan and New Zealand.

Upon release from Kent prison, Abbott made the decision to quit a life of crime, even though he admits that part of him was still tempted by the excitement of the underworld. But he really had no choice. One more conviction and he would have been looking at life behind bars, or a worse fate. In our interview he counted on his fingers, one by one, the fates of his crime associates, 'Dead, dead, life sentence with another life sentence and natural life.'

Unlike his friends, Abbott went on to lead a successful life outside of crime. He is now in his sixties and has kids who are all pursuing career dreams of their own. Unlike many of my guests, he harbours no regrets about the things he has done. He says he doesn't suffer from nightmares or flashbacks. He hasn't become a born-again Christian to assuage the guilt for his crimes because, he says, he doesn't feel any guilt. He doesn't even regret the time he spent in prison, which he sees as a necessary stage in the journey towards the man he has become: 'That was my rite of passage, going to San Quentin,' he told me. 'I knew who I was after that and I was secure in myself, and that means something.'

Some of my viewers commented that Abbott is a psychopath whose blood pressure wouldn't rise at the most extreme acts of violence. He certainly never seems to get flustered and it is easy to imagine the level-headed way he must have conducted himself during intense confrontations. He is certainly one of the coolest customers I have interviewed. But having sat in a room with the man for many hours, I have to say I don't think he is a psychopath at all, just a measured man who has seen a lot of things in life and who responds to whatever is thrown up at him with equanimity and poise.

Abbott says his main motivation for talking about his past is to pass on some valuable lessons: 'I'm not doing it to try and make myself look the big criminal. Actually, I was in many ways a shit criminal. I set off alarms, got into gunfights where people got killed. But I do feel one of the jobs of older men, who've been through experience, is to pass on their wisdom, their knowledge, their experience to the new generation.'

Indeed, he gives off the energy of a wise tribal elder but most of all, he seems happy and comfortable in his own skin. As he said, 'If you feel comfortable with yourself, you've been successful, because money really doesn't matter that much. The simpler things are the ones that are the most pleasurable, so enjoy the small things. And that's one thing prison teaches you.'

9

Michael Franzese

Colombo Crime Family Caporegime Portrayed in *Goodfellas*

As a caporegime in the Colombo crime family, Michael made $350 million from a petrol tax scam, involving the Russian Mafia

Michael Franzese felt the adrenaline pumping through his veins like cold fire. It was all he could do to sit still and pretend to look casually out of the window. The car ride through Brooklyn was one of the longest and most arduous of his Mafia career. Earlier that day he had received the call that every member of La Cosa Nostra dreads – a summons to a meeting at an undisclosed location. The kind of meeting that you walk into and leave in a box.

Franzese wasn't naïve. He knew this had all the signatures of just such a dreaded call – the lifeless tone of his friend and fellow mobster, Jimmy Angellino, on the phone, the fact that Angellino had picked him up and was driving him to an unknown location, the silence and tense body language of his friend as they drove through the Brooklyn streets – every tell-tale sign was there that this was a meeting Franzese might never leave.

He knew the reasons behind it, too. As a captain in the Colombos, one of New York's five Mafia crime families, Franz-

228

ese was doing a superb job. Too well, some thought. His petrol tax fraud scheme alone was making tens of millions of dollars a month and that was just one of the pies he had his fingers in. Dubbed the 'Yuppie Don', Franzese was touted as one of the biggest Mafia earners since Al Capone. His personal crew numbered in the hundreds – big enough to form his own separate crime family.

And this was the problem. Rumours were circulating that Franzese wanted to be the head of his own family and that perhaps he wasn't paying the family's due share of his profits. Neither rumour was true, but either was enough to cost him his life if the family took it seriously. And, it seemed, they were. Even his own father, legendary Colombo captain, Sonny Franzese, had been snooping around, asking Franzese's soldiers uncomfortable questions about their earnings.

As he sat in tense silence, watching the grey Brooklyn streets slide past his window, Franzese envisioned how the hit would go down. The meeting would be in some nondescript building, probably in a soundproofed basement where the noise of shots would be muffled. He would be marched down the stairs with Angellino behind him. Once he opened the door, he faced two possibilities – either an empty room or one filled with the Colombo family hierarchy. The first possibility meant certain and immediate death, delivered from behind by his old friend-turned-executioner, Angellino; the second would provide the chance of explaining himself to the bosses and, perhaps, talking them out of killing him.

As the car pulled up outside a nondescript house in Brooklyn, Franzese swallowed nervously; it matched exactly the kind of destination he'd been expecting. Angellino got out and escorted him into the house and down a narrow flight of stairs to the basement. Franzese fought with all his willpower

229

to stay calm and not betray any signs of fear. He stood before the door that would seal his fate and waited for it to open. All he could do now was pray that the room behind it would not be empty.

'One of the horrors of that life, really horrors, is that you make a mistake, your best friend walks you into a room, you don't walk out again,' Franzese explained when we sat down for an interview in 2022. Talking to him, he certainly comes across as the archetypal Italian-American mobster, with dark good looks and a softly spoken manner that conceals a steely toughness behind the eyes. Perhaps this is because Franzese comes from a Mafia family. His father, Sonny Franzese, was one of the toughest and most feared gangsters in New York. And Franzese's own career matched that of his father's, single-handedly earning hundreds of millions of dollars for the mob with various tax frauds and other white-collar crimes. By the age of just thirty-six, *Fortune* magazine had listed Franzese as number eighteen on its list of 'Fifty Most Wealthy and Powerful Mafia Bosses'. Yet for much of his life, Franzese had wanted nothing to do with the mob, instead setting his sights on becoming a doctor. It was only when his father, Sonny Franzese, was jailed for fifty years that Michael decided to follow in his footsteps to earn the money to fight for his dad's release.

Much of Franzese's life and career can be traced back to the influence of his father. John 'Sonny' Franzese was born in Naples in 1919. He was one of eighteen children born to Italian immigrant parents, Carmine and Maria Franzese, who ran a bakery in the Greenpoint area of Brooklyn. Sonny was a tough street kid who was soon taken under the wing of Colombo capo, Sebastian 'Buster' Aloi. The Second World War briefly interrupted his criminal career but he was discharged from the US Army in 1944 after being diagnosed as 'psychoneurotic with pronounced homicidal tendencies'. Back in Brooklyn, Sonny quickly rose from made man to capo [a caporegime or capodecina is a rank used in the Mafia, usually shortened to capo and informally referred to as 'captain' or 'skipper'] and then underboss of the Colombo family, leaving in his wake a parade of dead bodies, more than thirty of which, according to Michael, he had personally dispatched.

In his book, *Blood Covenant*, Franzese recounts a story of his father's cold-blooded coolness under pressure. It was the late forties and a typical night at the Orchid Room, a bar owned and run by Sonny in New York's buzzing Jackson Heights area. Sonny was sitting in a back corner, drinking and talking casually with a young man. It was two in the morning but the bar was still packed. Suddenly a shot rang out. The patrons turned to see Sonny Franzese holding a smoking gun, his conversation partner slumped over the table, his own unused weapon clutched in his now-lifeless hand. The young man had been sent to assassinate Sonny, but had been too slow to beat the experienced killer.

But it wasn't the practised professionalism with which he'd dispatched his would-be assassin that impressed everyone that night: it was Sonny's reaction to the incident. Once the corpse had been dragged out and dumped a block away, and the blood-stains cleaned from the floor, Sonny went back to drinking, talking and laughing affably with friends as if nothing had happened. Needless to say, when the police arrived, no one talked.

Yet the mobster who dominated the streets of Brooklyn wasn't the same man that Franzese knew as a child. Sonny was a doting father who always made an effort to spend quality time with his children, not favouring any of his sons or daughters despite them coming from different marriages.

Sonny met Michael's mother, Christina, at the legendary Stork Club in Manhattan, where she worked as a coat check-in girl. The two fell in love and were married one day after Christina's eighteenth birthday in 1951. Sonny already had three children from a previous marriage and Christina had a two-month-old son from her marriage to an Italian-American soldier called Louis Grillo. The baby was Michael. Although he wasn't Sonny's natural son, the mobster took Michael under his wing and treated him with the same love and kindness as he did his biological children, including the three he subsequently had with Christina.

Franzese remembers hours spent with his dad throwing a tennis ball against his grandfather's house, a game that became competitive but always good-natured. The young Michael idolised his father and tried to emulate his characteristics, like the way he always kept his composure no matter how tense the situation.

Growing up in a mob family, Franzese enjoyed all the perks that his father's power and connections offered, such as ringside seats at the legendary Copacabana club. 'We saw everybody from Sinatra to Sammy Davis to Bobby Darin, you name it,' Franzese told me. 'These were regulars, people that we knew.' In fact, Sinatra was rumoured to owe a personal debt of gratitude to Franzese's father, even going so far as kissing Sonny's ring after one performance. Apparently, Sonny had helped Sinatra's son, Frank Sinatra Jr, after a gig at a nightclub on Long Island, where his singing act had bombed. Responding to a request from Sinatra Sr, Sonny began packing Sinatra Jr's show with crowds full of mob associates and their friends, who cheered wildly for every single song and gave standing ovations at the drop of a hat. The music press, swayed by the hammed-up adulation of the crowd, duly posted great reviews and Sinatra Jr's show began to pick up a legitimate crowd of real fans.

The darker side of his father's life was only revealed through the newspapers and the jibes of the other children at school, a private Catholic institution where the majority of the boys were Irish and where the few Italians, like Franzese, were the targets of bullying and harassment. Franzese got an early education in street fighting, defending the honour of his dad from his school-yard detractors.

But unwanted heat increased throughout the sixties until it became almost unbearable. The Feds were following Sonny's every move, almost permanently staking out the family home in Long Island and tailing anyone who left it. One of Franzese's first memorable encounters with law enforcement was as a ten-year-old chasing after a baseball in the street outside his house. He found the ball trapped under the brown leather shoes of a man in a long overcoat. The detective pulled back the coat to reveal a large pistol. 'See this gun,' he said, pointing it at Michael's face. 'This is for your father. Bang! Bang! He's dead!'

A few years later, when Franzese was seventeen, he tried to get his own back on the surveillance teams by taking them on wild goose chases in his car, but one escapade backfired when his father got wind of Michael's antics. 'These two guys ring my doorbell and they tell my father what I was doing,' Franzese told me. 'My dad never really hit me except for that day – "Do you realise what you're messing with? Do you want to go to jail?" He was so upset with me. "Don't you ever do that. You respect these guys, they're dangerous."'

The pressure on Sonny culminated with the arrest of four bank robbers in 1965. Seeking to mitigate their sentences, the four heroin-addicted criminals agreed to finger the mobster as the mastermind behind their crimes. It was a ridiculous charge and the robbers all admitted privately that they had framed Sonny, but it was all the Feds needed to finally arrest the man they had been after so long. Visiting his father in prison in 2012, Franzese asked Sonny why he thought the Feds had pursued him with such a vengeance. The answer he got was unexpected to say the least.

Franzese tells the story: 'He said, "I was in the Stork Club and one day Marilyn Monroe happened to walk into the club." So they met, they had an affair according to my dad. And then he tells me, "Mike, you're not going to believe what happened. She was having relations with Bobby Kennedy and while they were doing their thing, she called out my name. And Bobby Kennedy got very insulted. He jumped on the phone with J. Edgar Hoover and he said, "I don't know who this Sonny Franzese is but put him in jail forever."'

Whether or not the Marilyn Monroe story was true, the heat was real. The four bank robbers testified against Sonny at their trial and Franzese's father was sentenced to fifty years. Franzese and the family were devastated. They began mounting a legal case to challenge the decision. Michael was studying medicine at the time, hoping to become a doctor, as his parents wished. Now, he started taking time out from his studies to picket the FBI's Manhattan office as part of the new Italian-American Civil Rights League, founded by Colombo boss, Joe Colombo, after his son Joe Colombo Jr had been arrested on similar flimsy charges. However, as the protests gained momentum and the League rose in strength, it began to attract too much attention to the Mafia. The bosses of the other four New York families became concerned and ordered Joe Colombo to desist. Colombo responded by organising the biggest rally yet to be held on Columbus Day, 1971 at Columbus Circle in Manhattan.

Franzese was near the front that day as Colombo waited on the podium to make his speech to 50,000 protesters. Spotting Franzese, the Colombo boss called him over and asked him to hand out a pile of programmes advertising the day's events. As Franzese turned away from the stage, the air was rocked by two loud bangs. Franzese turned around just in time to see Colombo fall. In front of him, the gunman was being mobbed by police. Two more gunshots followed and the gunman too was hit, seemingly by a Colombo soldier seeking revenge. The hitman was killed and Colombo taken to hospital. He survived but was paralysed from his wounds and effectively out of the picture.

Meanwhile the young Franzese was becoming frustrated with several stalled legal attempts to free his father. Focusing less and less on his medical studies, he decided to try his hand at business to earn quick money to fund the ongoing legal battle. He opened up a car repair shop, fixing up and selling on insurance write-offs. He added a car rental operation and a used car salesroom to the repair project and was soon making decent money. Then he expanded his small empire with a pizza shop near a busy train station and within a year was making around $5,000 a month in profits. Yet despite the fact that his businesses were legitimate, Franzese's reputation as the son of a mobster hounded him. Firstly, he had a never-ending string of mobster connections visiting his businesses, pestering him for good deals and lines of credit on cars. Secondly, and more worryingly, the police were on his case almost from day one, repeatedly raiding his premises and arresting him on trumped-up charges. He beat all the cases in court but it was an additional headache he didn't need.

With legitimate business proving so frustrating, Franzese finally gave in and decided to try his hand at his father's less salubrious approach. In 1975, he made the life-changing decision to give up his ambitions of being a doctor for good and enter the world of organised crime.

With the support of his father, he was proposed as a Colombo family member by Sonny's long-term friend, Jo Jo Vitacco, and put forward for induction. But first he had to prove himself by 'making his bones' – working as an associate for one of the family members until he proved himself ready. Franzese's boss would be Colombo captain, Andy Russo. His 'pledge' period lasted for nearly a year in which he did various low-level work, such as chauffeuring the acting family boss, Tom DiBella, to his meetings. During his indoctrination, Franzese was invited to tag along on several armed robberies but he always declined. He wanted to stick to being a white-collar criminal. This was acceptable as long as the 'invitation' to do some 'work' didn't come from the higher echelons of the organisation. If that was the case, there was no refusing.

One of these 'jobs' usually involved an initiation murder. Every wannabe Mafia member had to prove that they were willing and able to kill. Fortunately for Franzese, he didn't have to perform an initiation murder. He had entered the organisation at a time when the mob was desperate for fresh blood, so there were more recruits than targets the family wanted killed. Franzese was formally initiated alongside five other recruits on Halloween 1975 in a darkened room containing acting boss Tom DiBella, family consigliere (a trusted advisor to the boss in a Mafia crime family), Alphonse Persico (brother of the imprisoned boss, Carmine Persico Jr) and all the top hierarchy of the Colombo family.

In the ceremony he was ordered to cup his hands and hold a burning piece of paper which symbolised what would happen to his soul in hell if he violated his oath. Then his finger was

236

pricked and his blood spilt to indicate the blood oath that he was bound to. Like his father before him, Franzese was now a member of La Cosa Nostra and, typically, his father was at the forefront of his plans. Franzese had a three-point strategy for his trajectory as a mafioso. Points two and three were to succeed in business and be a good mob soldier, but top of the list was freeing his father.

As a fully-fledged Colombo family member his life didn't change much. He carried on his already burgeoning business pursuits and added a few more profitable enterprises to the balance sheet. One such was a shipping container repair firm servicing Japan Lines, an international marine cargo company. With the help of an insider at Japan Lines, Franzese would bill the company for five containers for every one that he actually repaired. This ratio soared from 5:1 to 20:1 as the scam gathered momentum, earning Franzese big profits for virtually no work, which he could then invest in his street-level money-lending operations.

Just three years after Franzese became a made man, his dream of freeing his father came true. Sonny was released on parole after serving just eleven years of his fifty-year sentence. With his dad free, Franzese immediately renewed his old custom of sharing a coffee with his father first thing in the morning but now their morning chats included family business. Sonny took the opportunity to educate Michael on the lifestyle. He told him which family members he could trust and whom to steer clear of, and instructed him never to say anything incriminating on the phone or in an enclosed room. Every stranger should be treated as if they were an undercover FBI agent – such was the secrecy required to stay out of jail.

Despite his focus on being a white-collar criminal, as a mafioso Michael Franzese couldn't always keep his nose clean.

He experienced the darker side of family life when the newly released family boss, Carmine 'The Snake' Persico Jr, ordered a hit on one of Franzese's crew members. Although the man was a fiercely loyal and valuable member of Franzese's team, it turned out that many years ago he had been part of a group who had kidnapped several mob soldiers and held them for ransom. Finally, the crime had caught up with this man and despite Franzese's pleas, revenge had to be taken. There was nothing more Franzese could do but sit back and wait. Two weeks later, it was confirmed – the man had been killed.

His father free, Franzese transferred to work in Sonny's crew. With his father as his captain, part of his profits would siphon off to Sonny, keeping the money in the family. And the money was growing. Franzese netted $400,000 for keeping the labour unions out of an apartment project. This led to more construction projects amounting to a further £2 million in profits. He became a partner in a project to buy and renovate a Las Vegas casino. He also muscled in on a Long Island security guards union, skimming profits off their health insurance payments. And he became a partner in a profitable flea market in Brooklyn after the co-owner complained that his current partner had become a drug addict and was dealing on market grounds. Franzese chased the addict out and took his place.

It was through the flea market that Franzese first came into contact with John Gotti, later to become the infamous head of the Gambino family. At this time Gotti was just a soldier but something of a rising star. It turned out that the man Franzese had ejected from the flea market was working for Gotti. Now the Gambino man wanted a sitdown with Franzese to discuss the delicate inter-family situation this had caused.

Gotti was cagey at the meeting and feigned surprise that his man was on drugs. He offered to rehabilitate him but insisted the man be kept in his position. Franzese pushed the line that the Mafia oath forbade the families from having anything to do with drugs. Gotti countered that he would replace the man with another of his crew. It was clear to Franzese that Gotti was lying and that he had nothing to do with the man at all, that the drug addict had fled to Gotti for help when Franzese kicked him out of the market, and now Gotti was using him as an excuse to muscle in on Franzese's new-found turf. But none of this could be said out loud. Sitdowns with other made men were subtle games of cat and mouse with strict rules of etiquette that couldn't be broken.

'These could be very important meetings,' Franzese told me. 'Somebody's life could be at stake and when you had two made guys that took the oath sitting down, there were rules. You had to be very respectful. For instance, if Sammy was sitting across from me and he was lying through his teeth and I called him a liar, I lose. Can't do that. Can't be disrespectful. I had to figure out a way to expose him so that people would understand – the guy who was in charge, the boss – this guy's not telling the truth and then things come in my favour.'

Despite his man's link with drugs, Gotti refused to back down and further sitdowns were arranged with captains present. In the end, Franzese agreed to be bought out of his share in the market and walked away with a $70,000 pay-off from Gotti. It was an interesting and educational experience in the art of sitdowns, one which Franzese would repeat many times throughout his Mafia career: 'It was like a way of life for me,' he said. 'When you become as high profile as me, you're sitting down all the time. And I had a big crew and they're always getting in trouble. You got to sit down and bail them out.'

In 1982, Franzese's father was charged with violating his parole for meeting with known mob associates and was sentenced to ten years in prison. At around the same time, Franzese was moving into his most lucrative scam yet, one which would turn the hundreds of thousands of dollars he was making each month into millions.

The scam was tax fraud, the business, petrol. Franzese was approached by a man complaining that his boss, Lawrence Iorizzo, head of a multi-million-dollar petrol company called Vantage Petroleum, was being targeted by gangsters. At first Franzese stalled but after meeting Iorizzo – an impressively overgrown giant who had once reportedly eaten fifty hamburgers at a sitting – he decided he could trust the man. Franzese sent out a gang of his men headed by an intimidating scar-faced soldier called Vincent Aspromonte and the gang of small-time hoodlums who had been taxing Iorizzo were quickly scared away.

Franzese now had a share in 300 petrol stations in and around Long Island. The insane profit margin would come from taking advantage of the government's lax attitude to collecting its 27 per cent share of the company's revenue in taxes. It generally took the authorities a year to claim the tax and in that time Vantage could close the petrol station concerned before reopening it under new management in a different location. Franzese and Iorizzo formed a new company, Galion Holdings, based in Panama, to oversee the joint operation. Twenty per cent of the profits from the new venture would go straight to the Colombo family. Franzese and Iorizzo would split the rest 50:50.

Soon they were making millions of dollars a month from skimmed taxes. Through the company, Franzese purchased a Learjet, a private helicopter, a speedboat and a forty-foot yacht, which he moored at his half-million-dollar home in Delray Beach, Florida. The petroleum operation grew even further when a Russian gang controlling a string of petrol stations on Long Island reached out for help to defend them from other gangs of sharks. Franzese obliged and received a massive 75 per cent stake in their billion-dollar operation. Despite their fearsome reputation, Franzese liked working with the Russian mobsters. 'Best partners I had up until that point,' he told me. 'Got along great. They don't have a structure like we had. They were more family, close-knit that way, and whoever was making the most money became the leader.'

Profits soared so that Franzese and Iorizzo were earning at their peak, by some estimates, $60–100 million a month. This was just from skimmed taxes, not to mention the legitimate profits. And this was only from the petrol business. Franzese had his fingers in dozens of other pies. As he points out in his book, *Blood Covenant*, by contrast John Gotti at his height as head of New York's largest crime family was making between $5 and $10 million a year.

In recognition of his success, Franzese was made a captain in the Colombo family. He now had a crew made up of about forty made men and several hundred associates – enough to start his own crime family. But success bred attention of a different kind. His rise had caught the eye of several government crime agencies, including the FBI, the IRS, the Postal Inspection Service, the Department of Labor, the New York Attorney General's office and the US Attorney's Office. A fourteen-agency taskforce was convened with a single goal in mind: 'It was a Michael Franzese task force,' Franzese told me, 'where their sole job, they would meet in a house at Uniondale, Long Island, and their sole job was to take me down and put me away forever.'

Concerned by the growing police pressure and fed up with the traditional mob associations in Brooklyn, Franzese began focusing his operations on Florida and California. He began moving into the movie industry, funding the production of several B movies and handling film distribution. At the same time he bad-mouthed both Miami and LA to his mob associates back home because he didn't want them muscling in on his new-found freedom.

It was through one of his film productions that Franzese met the love of his life. He was producing a breakdance-themed action movie in Miami called *Knights of the City* with a cast filled with local street kids from impoverished areas. Franzese had managed to open up Florida's usually prohibitive attitude to the movie industry in typical mob style. The problem was the truck drivers' union, the Teamsters, which demanded its drivers be used exclusively on all film productions in Florida. The prohibitive cost of using Teamsters' drivers scuttled the budgets of most small productions. But when the Teamsters representative came to Franzese with the usual ultimatum, he received one of his own – never come back or he would find himself freefalling out of the second-storey window of Franzese's Fort Lauderdale office.

In spite of his strong-arm tactics, Franzese became a local hero in Florida for providing opportunities for kids from impoverished and minority neighbourhoods. He received the key to the city from the mayor of Miami Beach and the Broward County Sheriff's Department made him an honorary police commissioner. Given his Mafia ties and the massive inter-agency taskforce that was pursuing him in New York, the irony of the situation wasn't lost on him.

Camille Garcia was one of the dancers in the movie. From the moment Franzese spotted her emerging from a swimming pool at the performers' hotel, he was smitten. He was soon dating the nineteen-year-old Mexican-American girl from

LA. But Cammy was from a strict Catholic family so things went slowly, especially as her co-performers kept telling her Franzese was a typical movie producer, looking for an on-set affair which would end quickly once the filming stopped.

In a sense they were right. Franzese was already married. He and his wife, Maria, had three children, but the marriage was over in everything but name. Franzese had had flings before but there was something different about Cammy. He soon realised he was in love and determined to leave Maria.

The dancer was a welcome distraction from the pressure coming out of New York. The joint taskforce was bearing down on Franzese's operations. Matters peaked in 1984 when his petrol partner, Iorizzo, was arrested for grand larceny, tax evasion and mail and wire fraud. Iorizzo wasn't keen on going to jail so he fled to Panama, where he intended to continue running his end of the business. But Iorizzo didn't keep his head down in Panama, instead flying lavishly around the world in his private jet and attempting to set up a similar tax evasion scheme in Europe. The Feds were soon on to him and set up a deal with Panama president, Manuel Noriega, to arrest Iorizzo and deport him to the US.

Imprisoned in a fetid Miami prison filled with Latin American gangsters, Iorizzo was soon ready to squeal. He made a plea to Franzese to bust him out by killing his police guard en route to the Brooklyn courthouse. Franzese was trying everything he could to release Iorizzo by legal means but he rejected the big man's crazy rescue plot out of hand. With Franzese having, in his mind, betrayed him, Iorizzo was now free to rat on his one-time business partner and friend. The rumour was that Iorizzo had a file of evidence on Franzese that was six inches thick, which he had stored away for just such an occasion.

Things culminated when Franzese was arrested at JFK airport on a trip back from LA. Oddly, it wasn't the joint taskforce that orchestrated the arrest but the Southern District of New York and its ambitious anti-Mafia State Attorney, Rudy Giuliani. Giuliani was in the midst of taking on the New York Mafia with his Mob Commission case, using racketeering charges to bundle up crimes and secure devastatingly long sentences. So successful was Giuliani's war on the mob that, according to Franzese, his life was in danger: 'Different than the Mafia in Italy, we didn't go after law enforcement,' he told me. 'Families in law enforcement we don't touch. Giuliani was an exception. They were really talking about it.'

In Franzese's case, it seemed the ambitious Giuliani had decided to steal a march on his taskforce rivals by including Franzese in a separate prosecution. The other group of criminals in the case were led by a rabbi and ran a loan-sharking operation on Long Island. Despite the low-level charges compared to his multi-million-dollar tax fraud (and the fact that he was innocent of these particular crimes), Franzese faced a 140-year prison sentence if convicted of all charges. In the subsequent trial, Iorizzo testified against Franzese, including allegations that his old friend and business partner had forced Iorizzo to flee to Panama and that he had threatened the life of Iorizzo's son, Lawrence Jr, neither of which were true.

Suddenly, everything seemed to be happening at once. During the trial, Cammy announced that she was pregnant with their first child. Then Franzese got the call that every family member dreads – the 'invitation' to an anonymous location to meet with the family heads.

Franzese resisted the desire to skip the meeting or – even more serious – turn up with a gun and go down fighting. Instead, following the advice of his father, he went along peacefully, sitting out the uncomfortable car ride to Brooklyn with his old mob friend Jimmy Angellino behind the wheel.

When they arrived at the nondescript house and Franzese was escorted down the narrow staircase to the basement, he knew his life depended on what he saw on the other side of the door. If the room was empty, he would be dead, shot in the back of the head by Angellino before he even had time to react. If it was full of the top hierarchy of the Colombo family, he wouldn't die – immediately, at least – but would be given a chance to explain himself before judgement was passed.

He took a deep breath and opened the door.

The room was occupied.

Inside was acting boss Andy Russo (Carmine Persico was back in prison) and a group of other high-ranking family members. Only one of the men present was a low-ranking soldier, a young man sitting at the end of the table near Franzese. Michael knew that if things went badly for him, this man would be his executioner. At a subtle gesture from Russo, the young soldier would pull a gun and shoot Franzese in the head before he had time to react.

For the next two hours, Franzese faced a grilling about his financial operations with Iorizzo. It turned out that Iorizzo had been exaggerating his earnings at Franzese's trial to increase his importance as a government witness, hoping this would keep him out of prison. This, combined with various wild press reports, had raised suspicions that Franzese wasn't paying his due share of profits to the family.

Using the skills learned from hours of painstaking negotiations in dozens of sitdowns, Franzese fielded all the questions, pointing out politely that all the allegations against him were based on rumour and hearsay and that there was zero hard evidence. Then Russo played his trump card: Franzese's father had been called in a couple of hours earlier to testify. Now Russo mentioned something Sonny had said that contradicted Franzese's story. Franzese batted the trick question away, saying he wouldn't play that game with his father. Sonny knew nothing of his operation because Franzese had insulated his father from his businesses for his own protection. Any questions about the operations should be directed to him and his dad should be left out of it.

The tension in the room seemed to escalate for a moment. Russo made a gesture. Fortunately for Franzese it was not directed towards the assassin, but for someone to pour the wine.

Franzese was safe, for now, but he would never forget the two hours in which he had to fight not to be killed by the people who were supposed to be his family. Escaping death marked an upturn in his fortunes. Not long after, he was found not guilty on all seven counts of racketeering and loan sharking. But although the result was good, he knew he couldn't beat the rap forever. Between the massive inter-agency taskforce and Giuliani's Southern District team, sooner or later they would come for him again and next time the charges would be much stronger.

Quietly, Franzese began preparing for his next battle with the authorities. At the same time, he divorced Maria and married Cammy in Las Vegas, followed by a more formal Christian ceremony in LA. Under Cammy's influence and that of her ultra-religious mother, Franzese was beginning to take an interest in the Bible and the religion of his birth. Combined with his new-found family happiness and his growing disaffection with the mob life, he began to consider the unthinkable: quitting the Mafia.

In December 1985, the inevitable happened. While in LA, Franzese got a call from New York – the Feds were looking for him; the taskforce had finally made its move. Franzese was resigned to his fate but determined to do it his own way. He told his associates to tell the FBI he would hand himself in on 2 January after the holidays. But the Feds weren't so keen; they sent agents to his and Cammy's house in LA. Anticipating the move, Franzese had moved to the Bel Air Sands Hotel. He slipped out of LA on a flight to Florida under Cammy's brother's name. In Fort Lauderdale, he handed himself in, as he had arranged, to a Broward County detective. The detective led him out of the airport, dodging the waiting FBI agents and directly to the courthouse. It was a small gesture but a satisfying way of thumbing his nose at the Feds.

Inside the courthouse, Franzese was faced with a massive 177-count tax evasion indictment from the state of Florida. He posted bail and went outside to face the waiting FBI agents, who flew him to New York to face the taskforce's 28-count racketeering indictment. In New York, he was held in Manhattan's Metropolitan Correction Center, where he joined a select crew of other top mobsters who had fallen foul of Giuliani's Mob Commission Trial. Among them were Carmine Persico Jr, the Colombo family boss, Jerry Langella, the family underboss and Anthony 'Fat Tony' Salerno, the Genovese family boss.

Unlike in Florida, Franzese didn't get bail. This time he knew the authorities would throw everything at him. He knew too that Cammy, as an innocent twenty-one-year-old, wouldn't be able to handle him being imprisoned for a long stretch. All things combined, he decided on a plan both to shorten his sentence and find a way to do the impossible – walk away from the Mafia: 'After I beat the Giuliani case I had leverage,' Franzese told me. 'I said, OK, they lost five times with me. They really wanted a conviction. Giuliani thought he had me and, boom, I'm acquitted. So now the next case comes up. I said, OK, I got leverage. I met this woman, I want to marry her, I'm in love, I want to get out of this life because eventually I'm going to jail forever. How can I use this leverage? That's when I told my lawyer, let's take a plea.'

Franzese and his legal team hammered hard at the prosecution for several weeks to get the deal he wanted. Eventually they settled on something acceptable – Franzese would plead guilty to two of the federal charges and sixty-five of the Florida counts. He would serve ten years in prison in LA so he could be near Cammy and he would pay restitution of $15 million. Franzese knew that with good behaviour he would be free in five years. There would be a further ten years' probation in which he was not allowed to associate with mob contacts on pain of reimprisonment. That meant a total of fifteen years in which he could legitimately avoid the mob. After that, he reckoned, living in LA and keeping his head down, he could surreptitiously slip away from the life for good.

After the agreement was signed, Franzese was flown to LA with Cammy and his new baby, Miquelle. In LA, he was allowed to spend the weekend at home with Cammy before moving into a halfway house for three months prior to his sentencing. At the centre for transitioning prisoners, he was allowed to spend from 6 a.m. to 11 p.m. each day outside, effectively only having to sleep in the jail. Franzese hoped to extend his stay at the halfway house indefinitely by arguing that in order to pay his $15 million restitution, he needed to be free to work. However, his dreams came to an end when a TV news crew filmed him in LA cruising down Wilshire Boulevard in an open-top convertible. Cut in with scenes of other prisoners doing hard time in grim-looking institutions, the news piece, unsurprisingly, didn't make a good impression on viewers whose tax dollars were paying for Franzese's 'incarceration'.

Not surprisingly, not long after the news report was televised, Franzese's term at the halfway house ended. He was flown back to New York and jailed in a correctional facility near Middletown. After New York, he was transferred to Lewisburg, Pennsylvania, where he was held in an underground basement level that had previously been condemned but reopened after a riot in Washington DC had led to an overspill of prisoners. At Lewisburg, Franzese met Jimmy 'the Gent' Burke, played by Robert De Niro in the film *Goodfellas*. Burke was friendly and would stash cigarettes, candy bars and other treats in a bag tied to a string, and lower it to a window in the shower room for Franzese to collect.

After Lewisburg, Franzese was moved to El Reno, Oklahoma, followed by Scottsdale, Arizona, in quick succession. 'They put me on what they called "diesel therapy",' he told me, 'where they ship you to all different prisons. You're in lockdown the whole time. They're changing it and they just keep moving you around just to break you. It's very, very tough. It's the toughest part.'

Finally, he made it back to LA and the prison he had been promised as part of his plea deal – Terminal Island, a federal facility near LA's San Pedro district. Here, Cammy, who was pregnant with their second child, could visit him regularly. And, because it was his permanent facility, Franzese could get a job. He was trained as a psychiatric aide and worked in the psychiatric ward of the prison which, he said, was like *One Flew Over the Cuckoo's Nest*, only worse.

At Terminal Island he met another *Goodfellas* character, although this one was decidedly less pleased to see him. Henry Hill had been played by Ray Liotta in the movie. When he spotted Franzese in the prison yard, he freaked out and went running to the governor, demanding to be placed in solitary.

After ratting out all his friends, it turned out that Hill was convinced Franzese was there to murder him. Franzese told the governor he had no intention of killing Hill but nevertheless the paranoid ex-mob associate was shipped out within the week.

Hill had nothing to fear. Franzese's only concern was being as good a prisoner as possible. He was taking his new-found Christian faith more seriously than ever, reading the Bible constantly in his cell. Besides, he wanted to get out and back to Cammy as soon as possible. In fact, Franzese was such a well-behaved inmate that one time, when he was given an eight-hour pass mistakenly written down as a full twenty-four-hour pass, he spent hours convincing reluctant guards to let him back into the prison after the eight hours had elapsed. Franzese wasn't as crazy as the guards figured – he knew that if someone spotted the mistake in the paperwork overnight he could be arrested and re-charged for attempting to escape.

Franzese got an easy time in prison – from other inmates because of his name and reputation, and from the guards because he was unwaveringly polite and friendly. This wasn't just an act, but following the advice of his father, who had taught him how to do time well. 'My dad, he was a very wise guy,' Franzese told me, 'and he told me, he says, "Michael, I'm going to give you three things that are going to help you tremendously when you go to prison," because he knew one day I was gonna go. He said, "Know how to say please, thank you and excuse me." He says, "If you're bumping into somebody, excuse me." He said, "Somebody hands you something, thank you. Do you mind if I cut in line, please?" And you know what, he was so right because I saw things happen in there when guys tried to push their weight around, people don't take it kindly in there. I remember one guy getting hit over the head with a mop ringer, one of those thirty-pound mop ringers, all steel, Just, boom, smashed his head open.'

The only grief Franzese ever caught in prison was a case of mistaken identity. He tells the story: 'One of the hot points in prison are the telephones, because everybody has a limited time on the phone and there's a line at times. And if somebody's behind you and you're cutting into their time, that's bad. They're trying to talk to their family, their lawyer, whatever. So, I'm on the phone and I was very respectful of that because I don't want anybody taking my time. I hang up the phone, I walk through the dorm and somebody comes from somewhere and, boom, sideswipes me. And I was stunned for a minute. I look at him and the guy goes, "I hit the wrong guy!" He hit me by mistake. And he goes, "Oh, Michael, I'm so sorry!" And I said, "All right, don't worry about it, I understand."'

In 1989, Franzese was released. On winning his freedom, one of the first things he did was to receive a proper religious baptism. His faith had strengthened in prison and he now wanted to live his life as a committed Christian. But living in LA, cut off from the mob way of life that had been his modus operandi for fifteen years, not to mention the ever-present threat of a Mafia bullet through the head, proved more difficult than Franzese had expected. After two years he was rearrested for violating his probation and sentenced to four more years in jail.

Most of the three years Franzese served were spent in solitary confinement in prisons in California, Oregon and Colorado. The authorities saw him as an assassination risk and kept him locked down. He spent much of his time reading the Bible and when released in 1994, he felt his faith was even stronger. Looking back on his second period of incarceration, Franzese saw it as an act of God – at the time the mob were getting extremely agitated about his public denunciation of the life, which had been reported nationwide in an article in *Life* magazine. The likelihood was, if he'd stayed out of jail, he would have been the victim of a mob hit. The three years' incarceration provided a cooling-down period which probably saved his life.

In 1997, Franzese was released from his parole and was finally free to live a normal life, if such a thing is possible for a top-ranking mafioso who has walked away from the mob. He quickly channelled his energy into living a life based on his new-found Christian faith, helping others to avoid the mistakes he had made. He became a public speaker, advising professional athletes about the dangers of gambling. He then created his own charity called Breaking Out, which steers street kids away from crime by educating them about career opportunities in the sports and entertainment industries.

With his high-level mob experience, Franzese was approached by the producers of an upcoming drama series about the personal life of a mob boss. The series' creators wanted him to advise on the accuracy of the Mafia content, but he turned the offer down. The show turned out to be *The Sopranos*, one of the most successful and best-loved TV drama series of all time. But not to miss out, a new series is in the works, which will dramatise Franzese's own life story.

To add to the TV success, Franzese has recently become something of a YouTube sensation after his interview with Patrick Bet-David went viral on the Valuetainment channel. In particular, his heated discussion with Sammy 'The Bull' Gravano, the ex-Gambino family underboss, has become a massive YouTube hit. He now has his own YouTube channel, where he hosts 'sitdowns' with various characters from the organised crime world and critiques crime movies in his playlist, Mob Movie Monday & Movie Reviews.

Today, Franzese radiates a calm, peaceful energy that fills the room. Having not known him as a gangster, it is hard to tell how much of this comes from the iron self-control which he learned from his father and exercised as a Mafia capo and how much it emanates from his strong Christian faith. I sense it is a mixture of both. It probably also comes from the loving grounding that his family life provides. He is still married to Cammy after more than thirty years and from the light in his eyes when he speaks about her, you can tell they are still very much in love.

And what about the ever-present threat to his life that comes from having walked away from the mob? 'I always look over my shoulder,' Franzese told me. 'It's instinct. I'm walking down the street, I hear a footstep, I'm looking back . . . I'm always looking around to see who's around me, that's instinctual. It's never changed, even when I was on the street right up until now, so just part of who I am. But I don't worry about it. I'm not hurting anybody, I don't want to hurt anybody. I don't talk bad about anybody. Why, you know? It don't make sense. So, I don't live in fear.'

10

Wild Man

English Enforcer in Arizona Prison

**Banned from America for being a menace to society,
Wild Man went on the rampage in Arizona and Mexico**

'Who wants to break my arm?' said Wild Man, still a teenager, to a gang of hooligans guzzling pints of beer in a pub.

'Why do you want your arm broken, Peter?'

'I've got a cunning plan. I need my arm breaking as part of the cunning plan.'

After they agreed to do it, a few of them fetched a cricket bat, a baseball bat and a lump hammer.

In an interview with Wild Man's cousin, Hammy – 'Wild Man & Purple Aki Stories: Podcast 223' – he told me: 'It was just a normal humdrum day. I hadn't slept in twenty-seven hours. [The hooligans] all ran excitedly over to the church-yard, which was yards away. Anyway, it's a historical church, been there for over a thousand years. So, there's Wild Man with his arm in between graves, saying "Go on, give it your best shot." It took about four or five shots because they tried different things. It was obviously the last shot; everyone heard a sickening thud. Wild Man goes and has a few minutes with himself and all that, then comes back and says, "Nice one, lads!" That's when the cunning plan came in.

'He walks three quarters of a mile to an old railway bridge that everyone in the area knows as Iron Bridge. It's 300 yards from Widnes station, where the song "Homeward Bound" was written by Paul Simon. So, he's looking at that. It's a Victorian iron bridge with big planks of wood. It's a poetic bridge full of needles, empty bottles and wraps. So, he goes down there and goes to work. So, when he was walking up there, he [had previously] noticed there was a plank slightly loose.

'He should have [dislodged it] before he broke his arm. But that's Peter. He didn't want anyone else to claim the money. That's the best thing about it. There's no common sense there: breaking your own arm. Then he's struggling to [dislodge] the bloody thing. So, he's doing this and he manages it. Fair play, he pulls it off. He needs to be on his own. He didn't want anyone else jumping in on his scheme. So, he walks up to a beat copper. So, Peter throws himself on the floor. Imagine the acting, the ham acting, "Oh, oh, oh!" He's going on like this.

'This copper said, "What's up with you, Peter?"

'"I fell over."

'"You fell over the hole? Peter, you'd better get up. You'd better get to hospital, that arm looks broke."

'So, the copper was his witness. Seriously, so about so many months later, Peter gets sent to the big house. He spends about a year in there. A third up in Morpeth in the North East with the Newcastle lads. He comes out and I've been on a session. He wasn't due out then, they let him out early. They probably had enough of him, so they said, "Just go. Just behave yourself. Just go."

'So, I'm lying in bed. I've been out with my mates the night before. So, this had all happened. Peter, he'd broken his arm, he's put in a compensation claim and won it hands down. And

255

I'm lying in bed with a whisky hangover and he's throwing stones up at my bedroom window. What the hell is this?

'"Oi, Big Nose!" I'm like, no, it can't be? It can't be. "Baldy, Big Nose!" I go down and look out the window. He's there, he's like all right. He's got thousands in his hands, like, and a bottle of whisky. The doors open, he comes in. We gave each other a hug and all that shit.

'So, he then phones a taxi. I'm like, "Let me get showered first." "I want to go tenpin bowling." So, we get a taxi. He had been dreaming about bowling. So, we goes up, he gets bored. The pair of us are rubbish, you know what I mean? So, he says, "Do you remember when I was a shot-putting champion at school?" People are playing the bowls. He says, "Can I borrow this?" So, he decides to shot-put the ball down the lane. And I'm thinking, *No! He's just got out of the nick! We have them crap shoes on.* So, he has three or four goes. I said, "Let's do one," then we left – that was his first day out. Then we got leathered.'

The compensation money was soon squandered on slot-machine gambling and buying drinks for everyone – a trait that meant Wild Man would always immediately spend any amount of money entrusted to him, just as he would consume any amount of alcohol or drugs in his care.

A few years before the broken arm, Wild Man's temper had ignited at his high school. He had grown to be the biggest student in his year group with a dislike of authority figures, including his teachers. He said he had red dots in his head telling him to hurt people. His unruly behaviour had earned him the nickname 'Wild Man' from his Uncle Bob, a whisky-nosed old-timer.

On the *True Geordie* podcast, Wild Man described an incident with a teacher: 'One of them was threatening me and all that, called Mr Hayes. So, I threatened to put him in – right near where the canteen is, there's these big bins where they put all the slop – I said I was going to throw him in the slop. So, I had to go to the headmaster and the headmaster was like, he had this traffic thing on his door: red do not enter, amber please wait and green go in. I'm waiting to go in. By this time my mum and him were just best friends. First name terms every Friday. She was down there, having a cup of tea. "What are we going to do with your Peter?" "Oh, just give him one more chance, will you?" "We're going to have to do something with him, he's running rampant," blah, blah, blah, blah and in the end I kicked his door down. He kept me on red. So, I booted his door and it come off the hinges. But what I didn't know was he was having a staff meeting and all the teachers were there. So, I got suspended indefinitely for that. What they did is [they] got me a private tutor from 9 a.m. to 11 a.m. doing English and maths and then I could go back home. After six months, they let me go back to school and I got into a fight with a couple of guys. Then that was it. "If you want to stay and do your exams, you can help the caretaker out." That's what I did – when all the kids were going to the chippy, getting their chips, I was going to the pub, having a half of Low C. I didn't get no qualifications. I could have, I knew most of the questions. But I wasn't motivated. I was the class clown. There wasn't really much stuff I really liked. Nothing actually motivated me. I would rather disrupt the class. Just being an arsehole really.'

By my late teens, my two best friends were Wild Man and his cousin, Hammy. In an area called Pex Hill at the top of Widnes, we would squeeze through the perimeter fence that prevented people from falling over the cliff face into the quarry and sit on a tree overlooking the quarry that we called the Thinking Tree.

'What're you two gonna do when you finish school?' I asked, while perched on the Thinking Tree.

'I'm going to prison,' Wild Man said.

'Why's that?' I asked.

'I see these red and white dots.'

'Red and white dots! Why'd you see them?' I asked.

'White dots are fine. They're normal everyman's anger. Red dots are slaughter.'

'How often do you see the red ones?' Hammy asked.

'More than enough.'

Hammy laughed.

'What about when you finish school, Hammy?' I asked.

'I don't know. What about you?'

'I'm going to be a millionaire in America,' I said.

'You probably will, with all that stock market stuff,' Hammy said.

'Will you take us with you?' Wild Man asked.

'Yes. When I make enough money, I'll fly you two over.'

'If you bring Wild Man over,' Hammy said, 'you'd better build a cage for him first. We'll give him grub but won't let him out. When he misbehaves, we'll poke him with sticks.'

Wild Man snapped a branch off the Thinking Tree. 'What's it like in America?' He threw the branch at hikers in the quarry, but it missed them. As they scowled and pointed at us, Wild Man waved and smiled.

'The people talk funny, but they're really friendly,' I said. 'The women buzz off our accents. Everything's massive. Roads. Houses. Cars. And they've got swimming pools in their back-yards.'

'In their backyards!?' Wild Man said.

'Like on *The Beverly Hillbillies*?' Hammy asked.

'Yes, exactly,' I said.

'How come they have swimming pools in their backyards?' Wild Man asked.

'When the plane comes in to land, you see all the swimming pools. America's the richest country in the world. That's why it's easy to be a millionaire there. Even you can get a job as a wrestler or something, and you won't end up in prison. There's no hope for you in Widnes.'

'There's no hope for any of us in Widnes, Atty,' Wild Man said. 'That's why you're going to America.'

It wasn't long before the pub owners banned Wild Man. In a podcast, he told me why: 'Being an arsehole, fighting. I was getting kicked out of the nightclubs and the bouncers would, like, always chicken wing me. Throw me on the floor and then throw me out. In the end I thought, *Fuck it, I'm going to start fighting back with you bastards.* When I started to get into fights with the doorman and all that, I just used to have not so much red dots but all this anger. I'd glaze over. Like some people have a stop mechanism, but no, I just glaze over and punch harder and harder. Until I'm getting dragged off. Then I started to go to magistrates' court for ABH [Actual Bodily Harm] and stuff like that. In the end when I got to sixteen, seventeen – 'cause I was going to clubs at sixteen – as I started getting older, the charges started getting worse and worse. So, I started to go to raves, take a pill and chill out. It did work and I stopped fighting. I mean, later on, it did get moody. You'd get wannabe gangsters trying to rob pills and all that, but at the very beginning it was very fresh and nice. There was no one in your face. There was no one trying to pick a fight. No one had to prove anything. You just took a pill and had a laugh.'

But the early rave years in the late eighties only chilled Wild Man temporarily as he ended up in prison for a botched robbery. Misinformed about a large quantity of Ecstasy, he knocked out the wrong person. While he served his sentence, I rose through the ranks of the stockbroking world and flew Wild Man to Arizona in 1996.

Within months of his visit to America, I received an urgent call from my aunt in Arizona: 'Have you seen this morning's headline news?'

'No. What's happened?' I said, alarmed that she had called my office so early in the morning.

'It's Peter's place,' she said. 'There's yellow tape all around it. Someone's been shot dead. It might be Peter. You need to go up there!'

I slammed down the phone, snatched my keys, raced to the elevator and through the car park to my twin-turbo Mazda RX-7 and sped to Wild Man's in record time. The crowd at the yellow tape, TV crews, cops and what appeared to be a corpse on the doorstep caused me to panic and drive away because I had drugs in my car. Back at my desk, I replayed the scene in my mind, concerned my best friend was dead.

When Wild Man first arrived at Phoenix Sky Harbor Airport, our conversation had synced naturally as if there hadn't been a five-year absence.

Walking back to the car, I said, 'Peter, do you still see the red dots?'

'They don't just go away, do they? It's not like chickenpox. They're still randomly here and there.'

I housed him a mile or so north of my office in Central Phoenix, in an area behind the George & Dragon British pub, where we celebrated his arrival. While I worked long hours as a stockbroker, I hoped he would spend his days in the pub with the ex-pats and not go looking for trouble in the wrong places. Within days, Wild Man expressed concerns about sharing his bathroom with a heroin user. He said he was going to have a friendly word with his roommate about putting away the needles.

Later that day after work, I knocked on his front door but no one answered. Hearing his voice inside, I let myself in and walked through the bathroom to the roommate's living room. Shocked, I found the roommate and his friend moaning and wriggling around on the floor, with Wild Man alternatively picking up a TV and dropping it on their heads.

'What're you doing?' I yelled. 'Come on, stop that!'

'These junkies keep leaving their needles all over the house, for fuck's sake! I almost got pricked by one. They'll pick them up from now on. But look, I missed one of them with the TV.' Wild Man gazed down at his grossly swollen ankle.

'How'd you do that?'

'It started with three of them asleep. I kicked two in the face, dropped the TV on one's head and dropped the TV on another, but one corner hit his head and the other corner hit my ankle.'

'You've gotta go to the hospital,' I said, trying to get him out of there.

'I don't like hospitals, la'.'

'Why don't you like hospitals?'

He rested the TV on the floor. 'Hospitals are annoying 'cause they smell of a) death and b) way too strong disinfectant.'

'Look at your leg, you might get gangrene.'

'Hospitals do my head in. I'm self-healing.'

'Can we at least go to the George & Dragon for fish 'n' chips and a game of pool?'

'The red dots are telling me these need more TV treatment.'

'Looks like they've had enough to me. Come on, let's get out of here.'

'Take me to the George & Dragon then.'

Two weeks later, my girlfriend and I visited Wild Man's house at night. I knocked and four Mexicans appeared, none of them smiling.

'Where's Peter at?' I said.

They looked us up and down, suspiciously.

'Where's Peter at?' I asked louder, hoping to attract his attention.

They conferred in Spanish.

'Pizza?' one asked.

'Not pizza – Peter!'

'We no order pizza.'

'Not pizza! Where's Peter? He lives here. Peter! Peter!' I yelled, convinced that he was being held hostage.

Handguns emerged.

Praying not to get shot, I stammered to my girlfriend, 'Let's walk slowly back to the car.'

While I back-pedalled, my heartbeat roared in my ears, a noise interrupted by Wild Man greeting us as he swaggered over the street.

'What the fuck's going on in your house, la'? We almost got shot!'

'Who the hell are these guys?' my girlfriend asked.

'Oh, don't worry about them,' he said nonchalantly. 'Come and meet them.'

My girlfriend and I exchanged reluctant glances.

'Come on. They aren't gonna shoot you if you're with me.'

We followed Wild Man.

'This one's Luis,' Wild Man said. 'He's a coke dealer from Colombia and these are his workers from Mexico.'

Smiling thinly, Luis nodded. The Mexicans disappeared inside.

'They like to move around a lot, so I've rented my place to them. They're letting me stay in their old place across the street. I'll move back in when they're done here in a few weeks.'

'Rented it out!' I said.

'They're paying me in crack. They can't believe how big a rock I can do in one hit. It's amazing. It goes sizzle-sizzle, and thirty seconds later, heart attack, heart attack. It calms down my red dots.'

'Peter, I do drugs, but smoking crack with armed dealers! And you've only been here two weeks! Jesus Christ!' I feared police trouble and losing my friend again, especially as he had ridiculed my plan to launch him as a wrestler. 'How're you ever going to get a job if you're doing all these drugs? And why didn't you tell us you were moving them in? They could have shot us!'

'No need to trip out, Shaun. They're good people. Luis even wants to invest in the stock market with you. He's a drug lord with a lot of money.'

Fortunately for the crack dealers, they had moved out by the time Peter's place made headline news for the fatal shooting. Hours after my aunt had called my office urging me to go and check whether Wild Man was still alive, I returned to his place.

Fortunately, the crowd of people and the corpse were gone. Apprehensively, I stepped over the bloodstained doorstep and went inside and found a homicide detective questioning Wild Man. After the cop had left, I said, 'Good to see you're alive, la'.'

'Speak up, la'. I can't hear properly. Them guns are totally loud.'

'What the hell happened?'

'The guy killed himself. I was up for days on crack and tweak, and he came over in the middle of the night with his bird looking for the Mexicans. I sent his bird over the street so she could get drugs. He stayed here. I see he's got a gun. I told him there's no guns in England and would he mind showing it me. He lets me hold it and I ask him to show me how to shoot it. He takes it back, says, "The safety's on. This is how we do it in America." He pulls the trigger, and it goes off – *bam!* It hits him in the head and he falls out of the doorway. So, he's on my step with a chunk of his head blown off. Totally fucking dead.'

Having nightmares about the shooting, Wild Man asked to be moved to an apartment in Northwest Phoenix, with two females and a big bouncer with curly blond hair. Immediately, he put the bouncer's head through the plasterboard walls and was evicted.

Wild Man got into my car. 'All of us are getting evicted because of the fight. This Madison I live with is pretty cool. She's moving in with her boyfriend in Tempe in some apartment complex and it's got three bedrooms. She said her boyfriend's behind on the rent, so, if you can fix the rent situation, I'll be able to live there.'

Figuring that an apartment would work out cheaper than a hotel and that there would be less crack there because Tempe was a college town, I said, 'I can stop the cheque I used to pay for this apartment and use that money to set you up in Tempe, so I won't be out of pocket on this mess. But you've got to stop causing chaos. I've not got endless money for this, Peter.'

After Wild Man moved in, he invited everyone he met on the streets to party at his place, ranging from street-walking Native American trans sex workers and homeless crackheads to gangbangers and Mexican Mafia members. With drug consumption and property damage rife, he was yet again evicted, only this time with Tempe police investigating and asking questions about the overgrown unruly Englishman.

So many properties were destroyed during his first visit that he ended up living in Tempe Beach Park, sleeping under a tree next to a Rambo knife and a baseball bat. His homeless neighbours were getting bullied by two thugs, so Wild Man demolished them with his baseball bat and the homeless people hailed him as their king.

In court after a crime spree that included walking out of restaurants without paying, he was banned from America for life by a judge who announced that Peter was a menace to society. He was deported back to England, to live once again with his partner, Wild Woman, who had been furious over his disappearance – before stepping on a plane to America, Peter had told her that he was simply going to the shop.

In 1998, I sent teams of people around the world to smuggle Wild Man and Wild Woman into America. I employed the Wild Ones as senior members of my Ecstasy enterprise. Their collective skill set – with Wild Woman in distribution and Wild Man threatening to move into the home of anyone that owed money – helped the business flourish.

When Sammy 'The Bull' Gravano's crew moved into the Ecstasy scene, one of my workers, Handsome Mark, started to source pills from both sides. He took money from one of our customers for 1000 pills, and purchased them from the Gravanos, who were under surveillance. Driving away from the deal, he was pulled over and the pills were confiscated by the cops. Before I knew what had happened, our customer contacted Wild Man and he described what happened next in an interview we did in 2019: English Enforcer In Arizona Prison, Part 1.

'Basically, she said, "Look, I'm upset and I don't know what to do about it. I give Mark the money for the pills and he's gone to get them off of someone else and he's not even gonna give me them either. So, he has basically ripped me off."

'So, I thought, *Right, leave it with me*. I found out where Mark's flat was. Give him a day or two to come correct. I thought it might take him a couple of days to get a thousand pills and get decent ones. So, he might still come good. Either way, he is using our money. But I didn't want to just spark him out if he hasn't got the money or the pills. That would just be pointless really. So, a friend of ours comes and picks me up and he takes me over to Mark's. I confront him and ask him what the fucking hell is going on. He said he just thought at the time it was a good idea and blah, blah, blah.

'I said, "It's never a good idea, is it? To use Shaun's money for fucking Sammy. How do you think that's going to go down? We are not gonna touch you ever, fucking again." So, he went to answer me back. So, I just fucking launched him. He was, like, over the counter there near the breakfast bar and I just sparked him and he literally went over the breakfast bar. In doing so, one of his handsome teeth got stuck in my fucking hand. There. Don't know if you can see the scar there.' He pointed at his knuckles.

'So, I've launched him, he's on the floor. We go to search the house. We searched up and down. Can't find the pills or we can't find anything. But what we did do is take his passport off of him. We just thought he can't fucking go anywhere without a fucking passport. Do you know what I mean? So right, so we get in the fucking car.

'[The driver] said, "Dude, we're gonna have to take you to fucking hospital."

'I said, "Nah, I'll be fucking all right."

'He said, "You've got a fucking tooth stuck in your hand!"

So, I goes to this fucking hospital. The nurse pulls it out and she goes, "What happened here?"

'Well, I'm not gonna lie. "I got into an altercation and smacked someone in the mouth. Really, how else do you think I got a tooth in my hand?"

'She said, "There's no need to be sarcastic, is there?"

'I thought, *Oh me and my stupid mouth!* So, she gets this hydro-peroxide and she poured it and it's stinging like fuck. This stuff bubbles. It bubbles, but she cleans it all out. And I thought, *That's good enough*. I should never have given this nurse jip. She got like a rag then and like a Tipp-Ex. Then she starts digging in and digging in – "Well, I've just got to clean it, haven't I?"

'"The mouth is very infectious. You get lots of diseases from the mouth."

'I went, "All right, all right." I thought, Never again will I give nurses any shit!

'So, she's cleaned it all up and she goes, "We are going to have to put stitches in it. You are going to have to come back tomorrow for the stitches. We are going to have to let it clean and we will bandage it up and come back.'

'I thought, *Fuck off. There is no way I'm coming back to you for anything after you done that*. I nearly fucking passed out with the pain! You know what I mean!

'So, what I basically did is I got a needle and thread 'cause I could sew. I got a needle and thread and put a few stitches in myself. And I thought I roughly know what I'm doing. So, I got one of those hook threads, like the needles, and I stuck it in, then hooked it round. Then after doing a couple, I thought, *Yeah that's all right, that. Sound that*. But the thread I used was more like fishing fucking wire, so it was like that forever.

'So, eventually, I had to go to the hospital to get it cut off. They asked, "Who done this?" 'Cause they knew it was not professional.

'I said, "Oh, I done it!"

'He said, "What did you use fishing wire for?"

'I went, "It was the only thing I had in the house at the fucking time, do you know what I mean?"'

Then some of Sammy Bull's crew start taunting Wild Man, who explained in the podcast: 'And this one guy – we met him in prison a bit later on, we caught up with him – he was on the phone to me and he was like, "We know what you done with Mark and we don't approach things like that. Me and you meet for a [fight].'

'And Shaun was telling me, "Take no notice of him, he's trying to fucking set you up. He wants you to get to a certain fucking car park and as soon as you fucking get there, he's gonna have you fucking nicked."

'So, he is phoning me up, saying, "I know where you live. I'm gonna come get you. I'm gonna come do this, do that."

'So, in the end, I'm just laughing about it. After a while I thought, *Fuck you! You ain't gonna do fucking shit.* So, I fucking remember going to this nightclub where he hangs around. He wasn't there though, that night, but he kept on pestering, pestering, pestering. In the end I caught up with him many years ago in Towers [jail]. I said, "Fucking hell! Let's go sort that little deal out."

'He said, "Oh no, no! Listen, listen. I'm sorry about all that. I've been told by fucking some of the heads that we had got to get you out of the equation. We've got to get rid of you somehow. So, we were literally gonna dry snitch." He actually told me he was gonna get me to the fucking car park. Watch me blow his car up and then have me fucking arrested. Yeah, so that's what happens when you work with rats!'

But such illegal operations are always ill-fated. Wild Man's meth intake increased his paranoid and unpredictable behaviour. In a podcast in 2021 – 'UK Wild Woman, Sammy the Bull Gravano, Arizona, Mexico: Kerry Osborne' | *True Crime Podcast 214* – I asked Wild Woman about Wild Man's paranoid delusions.

'There was no conversation with him,' she said, 'He just sat there sweating, with that one eyebrow up. Waiting for like Mexicans or whatever to come charging in and get him. Or waiting for anybody to kill. He was just off his barnet.'

'Wild Man,' I said, 'would just go off walking for days on end. When he wouldn't even know where he was.'

'[We'd] send out search parties to go out and look for him,' she said.

'He'd come back with his shoes all falling apart, his feet all blistered and everything,' I said.

'Burnt to a crisp,' she said.

'He would get so dehydrated walking around on crystal meth for days on end under the sun,' I said, 'he ended up being hospitalised a few times as well. But he got really paranoid, didn't he, about the Mexicans because when he was walking around, they would appear in the morning. They do all the manual labour in the mornings.'

'They were just going about their daily business,' she said. 'He's like rambling, hiding in bushes and stuff like that.'

'He had these crazy ideas,' I said. 'On one occasion, while making love to Wild Woman.'

'Oh my God!' she said.

'He just grabs a huge Rambo knife,' I said, 'and starts stabbing the mattress in between Wild Woman's legs.'

'The bed was on the floor, there wasn't even legs. There was no gap under the bed for anybody to get under the bed. There was no common sense, it was crazy.'

'Thinking that Mexicans are under the mattress messing with Wild Woman's bum.'

'Yeah, tickling my bum. He was nuts.'

Having fallen out with Wild Man, my top Ecstasy salesperson, Skinner, organised a firebomb attack on Wild Woman's place, while Wild Man was in a federal deportation prison. After Wild Man was deported, I smuggled him back a third time, but he only had one thing on his mind: to murder Skinner.

Wild Woman explained the story: 'He wasn't interested that he hadn't seen me or anybody else in nine months. He was just on a mission to go and get that sorted because he nearly killed me with that bomb. More than anything, it was because besides being loyal to you, it was because of what he'd done to me. In Peter's eyes, it was a piss-take, taking advantage of me being on my own. Thinking I was a little weak woman.'

'And what was his drug intake at that moment?' I said, referring to crystal meth and crack.

'Ridiculous,' she said. 'I couldn't say how much. I had to hide it and keep the stuff away from him and hide money.'

Wild Man was staying awake for endless days and hunting Skinner. Wild Woman told me that he was 'hiding in bushes and acting like a lunatic. Remember we had to go and find him at one point. He got lost.'

Eventually, Wild Man figured out where Skinner lived. A guy called Joey Crack showed up at Skinner's, expecting to find Skinner, but Wild Man was inside with assorted weapons. Coated in sweat thinking Skinner had arrived, Wild Man grabbed Joey Crack, who witnessed the weapons: a hammer, pincers, golf clubs, a screwdriver, a baseball bat and every kind of knife you could think of.

Wild Woman added, 'A plank of wood with nails in it. He put the nails in it. He'd do that on a regular basis. They were in the house like normal. He'd sit in this big armchair with all these weapons. He'd make me a nervous wreck half the time. I'd have to go out for a walk.'

Wild Man told *True Geordie* about Skinner: 'No, I didn't trust him from day one. Just the stories he would tell. He was fucking off his head. When you've been off your head enough times, you know when you're off your fucking head – you know what I mean? And his stories and the way he was going on and on. I thought, *I don't trust this bastard*. I said, "Look, let me have him. Either throw him off the balcony or take him to the desert and have him." And [Shaun] said, "No."'

In fear of his life, Skinner went to the police and gave them the inside scoop on our organisation. In May 2002, we were all SWAT team raided.

A van with armed guards took us to a subterranean lot at the Maricopa County jail in Phoenix. A guard allowed our female co-defendants out first. The thirty or so male arrestees waiting to go inside the jail stopped heckling the sex workers in the line and focused on our female friends:

'Ooh, babies!'

'Nice ass!'

'Show us your titties!'

'Come and play with the bad boys!'

'This way, honey!'

'With those boobs, I'm surprised you ain't got two black eyes!'

Shuffling towards the men, the women cowered. The last woman out of the van was Wild Woman.

From inside the van, Wild Man watched his fiancée. Other than an eyebrow reacting – one shot up and stayed up, while the other didn't budge – he seemed unperturbed. But I knew that particular eyebrow formation meant that he was about to do something in character with his name.

In a Liverpudlian accent that sounded as if she were hawking phlegm, Wild Woman scolded the men, who responded by turning up the volume of their chant, 'Show us your boobs!'

'Get out of the van!' a burly redneck guard yelled at Wild Man.

Wild Man stooped out, stopped on the top step and unfurled the physique of a bear. He cocked his head back, targeting the men over his Viking's beard: 'If you don't pack it in and leave my woman alone, I'll have any of you when we get inside those cells.' He nodded at the jail and grinned. 'If you think I won't, just keep it up and see what happens.' Wild Man's maniacal laughter signalled that he really knew how to hurt someone. The hecklers shut up.

A year later, sentenced to eight years for a dangerous drug violation, Wild Man arrived at the Arizona Department of Corrections. It didn't take long before he clashed with the neo-Nazi Aryan Brotherhood prison gang.

'So, basically, so we are on the bus,' Wild Man said on the *True Geordie* podcast. 'We arrive at lots of different prisons beforehand and the first of all, we went to Buckeye, which is a level four. And like, you see people and they are all looking at you and like, you know staring you down and me thinking, *I'm not gonna be intimidated*, but you can't be cocky either, you can't go in there like, thinking, *Oh yeah, whatever*, because you get filled in real quick. There's always a lot of people bigger than you and if they're not, they'll just shank you. So, the one tip is: check your attitude. Doesn't matter how hard you think you are, there's always one or two people who can do you in!

'So, walking through, I went and had a shower and all that. It had been kind of a long day of travelling so I was happy just to finally sit on the bunk and it was different from Towers jail – we had sort of like a cell and it was dead tiny. There was a bit more room. So, I'm thinking, *I like this, it's all right.* So, I put my stuff down on my bed and I have a lie-down and then, within five minutes, one of the head representatives of the whites [neo-Nazis] comes to me and he said, "I'm Booney." I said, "All right," and he said to me, "What you in for?" He was a chunky guy. He was probably about seventeen stone. He had a bald head and lots of tats.

'OK, so I sit down and he's like, "What you in for?" and I automatically get an attitude. I'm like, "What the fuck has it got to do with you?" and he went, "Hey, I'm asking you a question." You know I'm such and such. I said, "I don't give a fuck who you are! I've had a long day, so fuck off!" So, he said, "Look, I won't tell you again!" So, I just turned around and punched him and then grabbed him by the neck, threw him on the bed and started pummelling him. Then two of the white boys come grab me. They didn't touch me because one of them had been in Towers jail with me – he's like chill out and he'll explain. So, the guy goes off to his bed and he said like he's probably going to call you out in a bit to go in the shower room. So, I said, "Fuck the shower room! Let's do it here now."'

'So, basically, the Aryan Brotherhood decide who lives and dies in the white race in the prison,' I said in the *True Geordie* podcast. 'Wild Man has just shown up at this prison where there's an established hierarchy. The low-level dude who was sent to check your charges out, Wild Man's just knocked him out and now they're saying, "He's gonna call you out," which means he's going to try and earn his respect back by having a fight with Wild Man and trying to win Wild Man in the fight so he can get his respect back on the yard as Wild Man has totally took his respect. In the meantime, these Aryan Brotherhood guys are thinking, *Who the fuck is this guy? Just showing up on his own, knocked one of our guys out.'*

'Yeah,' Wild Man said. 'Well, there's a guy called Adam who was in Towers jail with me. This happened about say, like, five o'clock. Well, we had to go to chow. Then at chow, we were sitting at the table and this guy went over to the whites table, everyone's segregated and the white heads are always in the far corner. I'm sat around and at the torpedoes [foot soldiers] so basically to get to them, you got to get through the torpedoes.

'So, Adam's talking to this lad. He come over to the table and he said that such and such wants to see you, forgot his name at the time, it was one of the white heads [Aryan Brotherhood shot-caller]. So, I go over and I sat down. He made some guy move and I sat down and he said, "What's your deal? Where you from? What you doing?" I said, "I'm from England. I'm not used to American prisons, I've had a hard day. I just sat down for the first time I've been in a prison and I've got this fucking gobshite asking what I'm doing." He said, "That's the routine. You know you can get smashed." I said, "Well, I don't really care. Look, I'm just telling you what happened." He said, "You know what? I like your attitude, I really do like your attitude. You're going to have to apologise to him. And if you want, he'll fight you." I said, "I'll have the straightener with him, I don't care." He said, "For some reason, I don't think he wants the straightener, but you need to say sorry to him and explain you didn't understand the situation."

'As it happens, later on, I actually got to know the lad and got to like him. We were in the same dorm for three years.

We become really good friends and had a laugh and a joke about it. But at the time, I thought, *Shit, my first day here and I'm gonna get smashed. I know I can handle myself, but I also know two or three can get on me and that's it. Put batteries in a sock and that's my head cabbaged*. That was my first day in prison.'

'Did you apologise to him?' I asked.

'Yes, I did! He just shrugged it off: "Good job you got me on my blind side." He said something stupid. I felt like saying – boof! – "This ain't the blind side! I'll get you right in the face, you little tit." But I just left it. He sort of ignored me for a while and eventually got to know me. Eventually, I took his job over because after a while of being there, after six months, the Aryan Brotherhood confronted me and they said we want you too: "There's a lot of young lads going into your pod. They're not getting enough exercise and they're disrespecting our race. He's getting out soon. Will you take over? Will you help us out?" They ask you as if like you've got a choice. You don't have a choice. You just say yeah and make the best of it. Which happened for a good reason. I could make hooch. I got to gamble, I had a big fat store [bags]. My life was getting better. All I had to do was to put people in check. I just got seven and a half years. I didn't give a flying fuck, to be quite honest with you. You know what I mean? I couldn't see the end, so I thought, *This is me and I'm going to make a statement. I'm not going to get cocky. I'm not going to let anyone disrespect me and if I'm going to fill them in I'm going to fill them in properly, so I don't get no repercussions.*

'I started making the hooch, started off really good. I had young lads go to the canteen who brought me oranges and I had a baker, who was in the dorm next to me, he brought me the dried yeast. Made the hooch, and out of every twenty-four bottles, the Aryan Brotherhood would get twelve.

They were meant to get twelve. Very first one they got eight as I said a couple didn't work. I thought to myself, *I'm taking all the risk here. I'm taking all the shit. If they catch me, it's me going in the hole.'*

Wild Man excelled in his leadership role. The feral young prisoners looked up to him as a role model and any that got out of line, he punched, but not too hard. When it came to real violence, he was always happy to demonstrate his skill set. But the outcome of one fight would change the shape of his nose forever.

'I've lost a couple of fights in prison,' Wild Man said in a YouTube video titled 'What Happens If You Lose a Fight In Prison?' 'The main one I can think of was my fault. I thought, *I can handle it, I can do this, I can do that*. I'd been in there for about two years. I was still fresh, thinking I've got seven and a half years! Fuck it, throw shit to the wall. I don't give a fuck! If anyone says anything about me, I'll do this, I'll do that. I was a bit of a hothead, a bit of a prick.

'Anyway, this guy comes up. We are playing cards and I fucked up. I threw the wrong card down. Playing spades and threw the wrong card down and the guy I was playing cards with was a black guy. And he turned around and said, "You cheating motherfucker!" I came out with and I don't know why I said, "Fuck you, punk!" And as I said it, I thought, *Why did I say that?* This guy was nineteen stone, worked out, young fucking muscles. As he was dealing the cards, you could see his muscles popping out.

'So, I thought before he calls me out, I'll call him out. So, I said, "Let's get to the shower and have it out." He goes to put his boots on. I go and put my boots on. He goes in the shower. You've got that feeling in your stomach where it's like butterflies. You're nervous, your palms are sweating. You can't just go swinging, you've got to wait. There's him there and you there. Not too many people can go and watch. If you're at a bunk where you can watch, you can't really have an audience, especially in a pod. You wait for the guards, to say it's all clear. Meaning you have to make sure the guards in your tower are not looking in your direction. Wait for the guards not to be walking. So, he comes up to me and I thought, *Fuck it! I thought I could step back and do him in.* As I stepped back, I slipped on the fucking ground. He comes down on me and he fucking launches two. He hit me and elbowed me right in my nose. My nose just instantly fucking broke. I managed to get back up. I managed to get one in. But then it was game over. He got two or three more on me and I said, "All right, enough," because I couldn't see a fucking thing. My nose was fucking broke. My jaw was fucking broke. My two teeth here were fucking blackened and he helped me up and said, "Fair play. You had a go." It was left at that.

'My pride was a bit hurt and I washed up. I thought, *Fuck it I might go again.* And then I thought, *Nah, that would be fucking stupid.* I was thinking after I washed up, sat on my bunk, my nose absolutely throbbing, tissue up my nose, my eyes instantly blackened, and I thought, *I'm going to call him back out.* Luckily, I changed my mind, because the guy was quite tough. And to be quite fair even if I hadn't slipped, his punch was so fucking hard, it knocked me fucking senseless. I was a big lad at the time. I can fucking handle myself, but I was completely out of my depth.

'To be frank, I was lucky just to get a few in. They have a thing in prison where you don't kick them in the head and all that, but everyone knows there ain't no rules in fighting. He could have bit the fuck out of my nose. He could have done anything he wanted. I couldn't fucking see. My nose was busted in two places – I had to say I slipped in the shower. Went to medical. They gave me painkillers. Paracetamol for me nose. They said, "Do you need to stay here?" I said, "No, I'm fine." Went back on the wing. The main guy asked me, "What's going on? Why did this happen?" I explained it was my fault, came out with the punk word and there's no repercussions. He said, "Fair enough," and left it at that.

'You don't always have to win your fight, it's the taking part that counts. If you sit there and get twatted and don't do nothing about it, your own race is going to twat you if you don't stand up for yourself – you can get the shit kicked out of you. As long as you get one in and look like you're trying to do something, then you're all right. I would recommend when you're playing cards and things like that, in the heat of the moment, watch what you say. It's so easy to say you fucking tit. It's just two words you know for a fact you shouldn't say. Don't ever call anyone a punk or a punk-ass bitch. For me to say it, I was asking for fucking trouble. So, I deserved what I got really.

'That's a lifetime experience for me and I'm giving you youngsters a warning not to do that because it's not fucking worth it. We were fine, a week later we were playing cards again. I'll tell you what, I never called anyone a punk again – not in that prison anyway!'

Throughout various prisons, Wild Man maintained his leadership role for the Aryan Brotherhood prison gang. As well as brewing hooch and running gambling tables, he hustled by making clothes for prisoners, including gloves and beanies – with skills he had cultivated by sewing up his own injuries over the years. He was offered the Aryan Brotherhood membership tattoos, but declined on the basis that England had fought Hitler and that he wasn't a Nazi.

By far his favourite job in prison was as a dog handler training dogs destined to help blind people. He always said he would happily murder anyone who hurt a dog. It was perhaps a passion born of his dog walking as a teenager. With a Doberman Pinscher called Max, he used to frighten local people and cats (including my mum's) and generally terrorise our neighbourhood, which ultimately got him banned from dog walking.

Caring for a dog that lived in his cell combined with reading and ruminating on the stress that he had caused his family triggered changes in Wild Man that led to him resolving to amend his ways so as not to spend the rest of his life in prison.

In a YouTube video, Wild Man described his release from prison in 2008: 'The first time I got deported, no armed guards. The second time, armed guards and cuffed. The third time deported, no armed guards, but escorted in cuffs to the plane. [My final time], I had butterflies. I was really excited. I got out of prison and that felt good. I kinda knew I was not going straight home from there. I knew I had to go to Immigration [prison] and I'll be there for a while. I went from Kingman, Arizona, to Florence. I was in Florence for two or three days and I was sleeping on the floor. Then I was on a coach again to LA, Los Angeles, Immigration at Los Angeles and I was actually kept there for five and a half months before all my paperwork and that came through.

'Now when I finally got to come home – they told me the night before – I felt really fucking good about it. I lost a bit of weight, felt really good. My hair was long and as I was going through the process, the Immigration came up to me and said, "You've been deported three times," and they could charge me with it. Thank God for the British Embassy, they are a godsend! They can't actually do anything for you, as in send you money, but they can step in, they can put words in or whatever. But they got me through it. I could have been charged and done more time for coming into the country three times in a row. I had to sign a declaration saying, "Look, you're out of the country. You're banned for life. Do not attempt to come into this country and if you do, you can get up to twenty-five years in prison." So, I signed away.

'Finally, the guards take me to LAX. On the way to LAX, it was quite a long journey. They stopped off at McDonald's and got me a burger. I'm like, *This is fucking cool this*. First time I'd had a street burger in ages, you know what I mean? They said, "What do you want?" I said, "A cheeseburger, please." They were like, "What?! Are you taking the piss?" They got a big meal with chips and a drink. If I'd have known, I would have got one of them. But the burger was nice, it was fit!

'So, we were at the airport. I'm sat down and the guards said, "Are you going to behave?" I said, "What do you mean?" "We will take the cuffs off you and not embarrass you, if you behave." So, they actually uncuffed me. The guards were next to me, two armed guards! What was I going to do? But I didn't have the embarrassment of putting my jumper over my hands because I'm cuffed. Another really cool thing they did, which I respect them for is before I went into the airport, I said, "Listen, is there any chance I can have a cigarette?" They actually stopped while I was cuffed up and let me have a fag, which is good 'cause the journey is eight and a half hours. So, I'm buzzing at this point. Now I didn't exactly phone home and tell them I was coming home, I thought I would surprise them. They walked me to the gate. I thought they were coming home with me. They uncuffed me and thanked me for being a good prisoner and said, "Don't bother coming back!"

'They let me go on my way. At that point I'm just like a normal traveller. The lady come round, it was about eight o'clock at night this time. I got a meal at 10 o'clock. It was steak, mash and peas and there was a little apple crumble.

'So, I come on and they sat me. You know as you get on that first seat there, you've got legroom. It was eight hours. The plane I was on, you know the planes you go on to Spain, the journey with two aisles, it was a four-aisle plane, a big fucking thing. So, I sat there and I'm buzzing now. They asked me what I wanted, like a meal, drink and free drinks. Through the flight I probably had three whiskies and three Heinekens – I was quite merry, me.

'I land at Gatwick or Heathrow, can't remember which one. My name clearly over the speakers: "Peter Mahoney, a person will be meeting you as you get off the plane. Thank you and have a good day." I thought, *Oh for fuck's sake!* But there is nothing I can do. So, I put my hair in a ponytail. Had a quick wash in the little toilet thing. People were getting off the plane. I didn't wait till last. I got half off. I'm mingled in the crowd and as I'm walking, I see two people stood there and they look like authority. Don't know who they was. But I just blended in, carried on walking a bit more. I thought, *No, I'm not going to wait around.* So, I went to one of the phones – I think it was credit card only at the airport. So, I just walked out the exit and I thought, *Let's just get away from here for a little bit.* So, I walked fifty yards up the road. I thought then, *I'm gone, I'm free.* Then I saw [Shaun Attwood]. You picked me up, didn't you?'

As requested by Wild Man, I had been wandering around the airport with two litres of Strongbow cider. He guzzled them down, barely pausing to breathe, and then we heard a voice over the speaker system asking for Peter Mahoney to come to a certain desk, so we decided to abandon the airport in a hurry.

Wild Man continued: 'Giving each other hugs and that it felt brilliant. I wanted to make a call 'cause my brothers were meant to be meeting me. They were going to meet me in a hotel. The best feeling ever, but scary as fuck. I don't know who the people were [calling my name], but we never followed through on it.'

True to his word, Wild Man was never arrested again. He changed his moniker to Mild Man, got married and settled down with his wife and his beloved massive dog Sadie, an Alaskan Malamute. Preferring to stay home, he lived a quiet life until he started to appear on my YouTube channel in January 2018, with a video titled 'Wild Man Enters Arizona Prison'. The viewers quickly fell in love with his humour and authenticity. As a natural on camera who always spoke his mind, Peter became my co-host for dozens of podcasts. In total, he appeared on almost 170 videos on my YouTube channel. I received endless messages from people saying how Wild Man's videos had inspired them, including from people who were on the verge of committing suicide and had decided against it because watching Wild Man had lifted their spirits.

Peter was enjoying his online stardom until his health started to deteriorate after the death of his dog, Sadie in 2018. He began to get short of breath and became exhausted after walking short distances. During podcasts, I noticed his swollen ankles and fluid leaking through his trousers. He joked that he was going to bottle it under the brand Wild Man water and bless people with it. During the pandemic, I urged him to go to hospital, but he said he didn't want to take up bed spaces that were needed by old people with Covid.

In late 2020 – at six foot two and weighing 29.5 stone – Peter was rushed to hospital with breathing problems, where he died of multiple organ failure. Taking us all by surprise,

WILD MAN

#RIPWildMan trended on Twitter for several hours as his followers expressed their love, support and condolences.

My Tweet read: 'RIP my best friend since childhood Wild Man Peter Mahoney the bravest biggest baddest realest person I ever met'.

On the day of the funeral, Hammy (Peter's cousin) and I waited outside Wild Man's house for the hearse to arrive. When we saw the size of the coffin, we sobbed on the pavement. When the cortège drove by Pex Hill, our tears streamed again as we remembered setting our life goals as kids up the Thinking Tree.

RIP, Wild Man.

Acknowledgements

A huge thanks to our podcast team: James Esposito of Underground Films, Joe Adams of Audio Avalanche, Jen Hopkins of Gadfly Media, David James Wood and James Power at Material Studios in Liverpool, Liam Galvin of Liam Galvin Film and Freddie of Spiral Studios in Guildford.

Thanks to Lee Williams for the extra research and editing and to Derick Attwood for proofreading.

Credits

Seven Dials would like to thank everyone at Orion who worked on the publication of *Sitdowns with Gangsters*.

Agent
Robert Kirby

Editor
Vicky Eribo

Copy-editor
Jane Donovan

Proofreader
Ian Greensill

Editorial Management
Sarah Fortune
Tierney Witty
Jane Hughes
Charlie Panayiotou
Tamara Morriss
Claire Boyle

Audio
Paul Stark
Jake Alderson
Georgina Cutler

Contracts
Dan Herron
Ellie Bowker
Alyx Hurst

Design
Nick Shah
Jessica Hart
Joanna Ridley
Helen Ewing

Finance
Nick Gibson
Jasdip Nandra
Sue Baker
Tom Costello

Inventory
Jo Jacobs
Dan Stevens

Production
Katie Horrocks

Marketing
Katie Moss

Publicity
Ellen Turner

Sales
Jen Wilson
Victoria Laws
Esther Waters
Group Sales teams across
  Digital, Field, International
  and Non-Trade

Operations
Group Sales Operations team

Rights
Rebecca Folland
Alice Cottrell
Ruth Blakemore
Ayesha Kinley
Marie Henckel